"IN THE LIGHT OF LIKENESS— TRANSFORMED"

"IN THE LIGHT OF LIKENESS— TRANSFORMED":
The Literary Art of Leon Forrest

Dana A. Williams

The Ohio State University Press
Columbus

Copyright © 2005 by The Ohio State University.
All rights reserved.

Library of Congress Cataloging-in-Publication Data

Williams, Dana A., 1972–
  In the light of likeness—transformed : the literary art of Leon Forrest / Dana A. Williams.
      p. cm.
  Includes bibliographical references and index.
  ISBN 0-8142-0994-7 (cloth : alk. paper)—ISBN 0-8142-9072-8 (cd-rom)
  1. Forrest, Leon—Criticism and interpretation. 2. African Americans in literature. I. Title.
  PS3556.O738Z97 2005
  813'.54—dc22
                                            2004024142
Paper (ISBN: 978-0-8142-5762-3)

Cover design by Dan O'Dair
Type set in Adobe Garamond

contents

Preface and Acknowledgments — vii

Introduction:
"Let there be Light, baby, let there be light!":
Black Cultural Traditions and Leon Forrest's Healing Narratives — ix

Chapter One:
The Meteor in the Man—The Artistic Light of Leon Forrest — 1

Chapter Two:
To Survival and Beyond: The Journey Motif and Transcendence in *There Is a Tree More Ancient Than Eden* — 35

Chapter Three:
"Salvation Is the Issue": Black Music as Metaphor in *The Bloodworth Orphans* — 57

Chapter Four:
"Learn it to the Younguns":
Bearing Witness to the Blues in *Two Wings to Veil My Face* — 79

Chapter Five:
Though I Am Many, I Am Yet Still One: Reinvention in *Divine Days* — 93

Chapter Six:
"The Transformation of Grief":
Self-Invention and Survival in *Meteor in the Madhouse* — 116

Epilogue — 136

Notes — 139

Bibliography — 147

Index — 153

Preface and Acknowledgments

I remember the first time I heard the name *Leon Forrest*. It was in a graduate seminar titled Studies in the African American Novel taught by Eleanor W. Traylor at Howard University, and select novels Toni Morrison edited as senior editor at Random House focused our study. Forrest, of course, was one of only a few such novelists whose books were edited by Toni Morrison. While I was familiar with the works of two of these authors—Gayl Jones and Toni Cade Bambara—I had never read any of Leon Forrest's fiction. On the day we were scheduled to discuss his first novel, *There Is a Tree More Ancient Than Eden*, I remember gathering a stack of notes that resembled a jigsaw puzzle. Despite having read the novel twice in less than seven days and having started over a number of times, I was convinced I had somehow missed some pages or skimmed over some crucial information that would help bring logic to this experimental text. I was also convinced that I would be forced to sit quietly through this particular session, since I knew I would be unable to articulate the text's meaning to myself or to anyone else. Quite simply, I was hopeful that after that class period, this man, Leon Forrest, and his novel would regress peacefully into the recesses of my mind, never to return with their difficulty again. But through Nathaniel-like self-discovery, disguised as guidance from a professor (who is a scholar by trade but an artist in spirit and in truth), by the end of the class period, the artistry of Leon Forrest had taken over my imagination. I did not know it then, but I now know that I was drawn to him because he wrote beautiful fiction that contributed to the sustenance and the growth of black culture and black life. The pages that follow grew out of that course and out of my appreciation for meaningful African American literature. The artistry Leon Forrest's novels exhibit is among this literature's greatest sustaining forces.

I am grateful for financial support for this project from the Ford Foundation and from the Council on Research in the College of Arts and Sciences at Louisiana State University. For their morale, encouragement, and support, I thank John Lowe, John Cawelti, Merle Drown, Sandra Richards, and Marianne Duncan Forrest. For the many conversations about spiritual agony, religion, and black spirituality which so heavily inform my reading of *There Is a Tree More Ancient Than Eden,* I must thank the true Spirit people I am glad to call friends: Eric Walters, D. Stephen Lewis, Carl Lashley, and Joan McCarley, and D. Mitchell Ford, who introduced me to James Cone and black theology.

For offering fruits of the black sisterhood in the academy, I thank Saundra McGuire, Tara T. Green, Angelyn Mitchell, Cherron Barnwell, Tracey Walters, Tiwanna Simpson, and Katrice Albert. For his most astute critiques of black ideologies in this book and elsewhere and for his incredible selflessness with his ideas and his time, I am grateful for my friendship with John V. White, who is a literary and cultural critic in the disguise of a law professor. I also thank Lawrence P. Jackson for sharing with me his intellectual curiosity and for constantly raising the bar of expectation and excellence.

A number of people willingly read any number of drafts of this book. For ultimately making this a better book, I gladly thank Merle Drown, John Cawelti, Angelyn Mitchell, and James A. Miller. I owe a huge debt of gratitude to my 1998 dissertation committee at Howard University for guiding me so graciously, so I thank two of the sharpest African Americanists I know, Jennifer Jordan and Eleanor W. Traylor, and Thorell Tsomondo and the late John M. Reilly, who helped shape my thought process about ways to approach great literature.

Finally and most importantly, I thank my family—my parents, Thomas and Zola Williams; my sisters, Gia, Jann, and Tommi—and my friends, especially Marc McKayle, Sonya Sims, Adeyinka Smith, and Kim Walk for their constant love and support.

Introduction:

"Let there be Light, baby, Let there be light!": Black Cultural Traditions and Leon Forrest's Healing Narratives

Leon Forrest is easily among the best of hidden treasures in contemporary African American literature. He takes the predicament of the contemporary African American as the principle in his fictional investigations and reveals in the form of narratives what he finds worthy as responses to this predicament. Emerging as a writer in the first decade to follow the civil rights and black arts movements, Forrest investigates the contemporary African American's quest for an identity independent of his slave past and his struggles to combat the fragmentation created by being orphaned in America. In their exploration of ways to negotiate this highly racialized existence, the novels, then, offer his characters and, likewise, his readers viable means of surviving in a world that devalues (at the very least) and denies (at the very worst) African American humanity. Thus what Forrest sought to do with his Forest County Sagas was to use black cultural traditions[1] to explore the possibilities for African American identity in the contemporary moment and to suggest ways that his characters and the reader alike might be healed of race-related fragmentation.

Significantly, Forrest does not assume that his protagonists can speak for all African Americans or that all black cultural traditions are sustaining or healing. In fact, to combat these assumptions, each novel in the Forrest canon avoids creating a traditional protagonist and, instead, develops a central consciousness focalized primarily through recurring characters—Nathaniel Witherspoon and Joubert Jones. At times, this central consciousness also conflates a variety of characters' perspectives through experimental, modernist narrative situations to express variations of African American consciousness more generally. Additionally, each novel avoids romanticizing black cultural institutions, particularly those that are ideologically flawed and limited or those that fail to facilitate a character's healing or quest for expressive wholeness. Avoiding these pitfalls is of particular significance when considering the tenuous nature of African American identity in the early 1970s.

Despite having survived Jim Crow and having made significant, though limited, strides during the civil rights movement, African Americans in the 1970s were still largely uncertain about their futures. A leading cause of this uncertainty was the question of personal and, to some degree, communal identity. Previously, African American cultural institutions, including literature, had failed to address this subject adequately.[2] This void became especially pronounced in the post–Jim Crow world, where options for new black identities should have abounded. Yet, in the absence of an abiding binary construct against which the African American was forced to argue that he was not, African American identity was perhaps less clear than ever. To a large degree, the African American was still an Invisible Man, both in terms of his own ambiguous self-definition and in terms of others' (mis)perception of him.

Oftentimes, Forrest's characters are no clearer about the meaning of African American identity or the Invisible Man's grandfather's deathbed confession than Ralph Ellison's Invisible Man is. Forrest's characters are, however, more inclined to find refuge within the community and, subsequently, in black cultural traditions than is Ellison's protagonist, who is tragically obsessed with individuality. Arguably, it is this privileging of individuality over community that prompted Ellison to limit his portrayal of black ethnic culture as a fulfilling institution in the novel, despite his obvious appreciation of the artistic and survivalist capabilities of certain black cultural traditions. In Forrest's affinity with black ethnic culture, he most aggressively departs from his literary mentor and one of the African American authors with whom he is most frequently associated. Ultimately, this departure leads to a characterization of Forrest as a significant African American novelist, one who is perhaps best assessed in terms of his ever-questioning investigations into the contemporary African American self and his aggressive use of black cultural traditions and experimental narrative techniques to conduct these investigations. Thus, I use black cultural traditions as a pathway into the novels.

Without such a practical entrance, the texts are largely inaccessible because of the complexity of the narratives, which is created by, among other things, nonlinear narrative times, the modernist techniques Forrest employs, the attempt to have characters represent a central consciousness rather than their individual experiences, and the absence of a traditional plot in the first two novels. My focus on black cultural traditions is also one of the most viable means of access to the texts because black cultural traditions are the starting point—the springboards—for Forrest's fiction. Besides using these traditions to explore the predicament of the contemporary African American, he adds levels of complexity to the novels by adapting traditions from other cultures and reinterpreting them in terms of blackness, by utilizing innovative narrative techniques, and by complicating traditional African American vernacular culture. He reconciles these divergent approaches with his contention that integration and adaptation are at the heart of black survivalist culture. He simply draws upon traditions from other cultures, relates them to African American experiences, and then presents them in a distinct manner, one which melds the experimental modernist with the vernacular. But even here, he seeks to expand traditional vernacular approaches to literature and to create a niche of his own.

His novels, for example, are not easily characterized simply as jazz or blues narratives, though they do borrow from music's philosophies. Instead, they often integrate such vernacular approaches to narrative with modernist techniques and other more traditional narrative styles. If we take *There Is a Tree More Ancient Than Eden* as our case in point, we see the modernist influence of stream of consciousness (among other things) throughout the novel. Through this technique, we are privy to the random, unedited (in the figurative sense), and often dissonant thoughts of Forrest's characters as they travel through the history of the African American. In this same novel, at different points, the narrative adopts a jazz and then a gospel impulse in its attempt to bring order to the chaos that plagues its characters' consciousness. Yet in the novel's final section, the narrative assumes the form of an epistle and is offered in a relatively straightforward manner. As a unified text, however, *There Is a Tree* is anything but straightforward. Its experimental style, perhaps best characterized as a modern jazz narrative, is alienating to the average reader. Unable to penetrate the narrative, readers have difficulty appreciating the novel's attempt to use Nathaniel's feelings of motherlessness to express, more generally, the contemporary African American's feelings of motherlessness, fragmentation, and displacement as a figuratively orphaned American without a clear-cut identity. The difficulty of the narrative similarly denies readers access to the various approaches to survival Nathaniel encounters as he attempts to come to terms with his orphaned status and, subsequently, to find a way to move beyond his fragmentation and toward healing. One of the ways to decrease this inaccessibility is to focus on the novels' most consistent and most available technique—the use of black cultural traditions to explore Nathaniel's dilemma as a representation of the condition of the contemporary African American.

Like the Invisible Man, Nathaniel opts for isolation after his mother's premature death, hiding underneath the bed because he has no sense of self that is independent of his family structure, now disturbed by the death of a matriarch. But unlike the Invisible Man, who, at the end of the novel, refuses to return to Mary, the novel's most obvious representation of black culture, Nathaniel accepts the support of Forrest's black culture representative, Hattie Breedlove. Nathaniel borrows from her strength and wisdom to regain enough hope in the future to stand naked (literally and metaphorically) before a full-length body mirror to examine his *self*. Significantly, it is Aunt Hattie's kinship with black cultural traditions—she incorporates lyrics from spirituals and borrows inspiration from the folk preacher to coax Nathaniel to emerge from his hibernation—that allows her to *breed love* and hope within Nathaniel. Equally important is his willingness to use the cultural resources available to him. From Breedlove's faith, he gathers enough confidence in the traditions that have sustained her to know that he can indeed achieve personal freedom and identity in the midst of the cultural community. Again, it is here that he departs from the Invisible Man and that Forrest departs from Ellison.[3] And as the Forest County Sagas progress, they seem to suggest that Nathaniel is not only able to achieve individuality in and through the community, but his individualized quest for wholeness and freedom is actually a pilot for the community, which seeks to achieve its own healing and meaningful group identity.

Here, we see not only Forrest's departure from Ellison but also more generally from the protest tradition's tendency to discount the community and black cultural traditions as a sanctuary of sorts for black Americans. This shift away from the protest tradition is inevitably a move toward the black arts movement and the general 1960s return to a focus on the collective community. But unlike the more essentialist tendencies of the black arts movement, Forrest's community was more accepting of diverse traditions and rejected the movement's claims of racial authenticity. Displaying his refusal to use black cultural traditions in ways that feed desires for authenticity or claims of cultural purity, Forrest tells Madhu Dubey:

> I resist anything in this [African American] culture that has to do with purity. That's so anti-American in the first place. And yet at the same time it's a crucible on which much of race relations and white supremacy is based—the idea of purity. But there certainly aren't any pure Americans culturally, not at this time, [*sic*] that's one thing for

sure. And obviously the heritage, the background of blacks is very complex, not just on color lines but lines of culture. Think about the blacks that are most admired—whether it be Ellington, or Lightnin Hopkins, or Mahalia, or Leontyne Price—these are people who are consequences of so many different cultural forms that influenced them[. . . .] (Forrest and Dubey, 590)

He goes on to suggest that it is the nationalists' obsession with defining authentic blackness that limits the black arts movement and falsifies any singular conception of a black aesthetic. This limitation, along with the movement's lack of complexity, made Forrest and the black aesthetic mutually unreceptive of each other. And while he had begun to experiment with writing during the black arts movement, Forrest was more attracted to the artistry of Ellison, whose lectures he sat in on while Ellison was at the University of Chicago,[4] than he was to the black arts movement, which he sought to vault over in content and in style. Even so, he shares with black arts movement writers an admiration of black cultural forms and their usefulness as springboards for artistic expression. But as there were few novels to emerge during the period, he clearly moves beyond the movement's limitations, in part because his idea of black ethnic culture and, correspondingly, African American literature included both distinctly black cultural creations and black Americans' reinterpretations or reinventions of other ethnic and American cultural and narrative forms.

Thus, by the early 1970s, Forrest had constructed for himself a literary identity that drew from the literary traditions that preceded him, in general, and from black cultural traditions in particular. And, as an African American author, he would soon find a home in African American literature that escaped the confines of nationalist literature. The 1970 appearance of Toni Morrison's *The Bluest Eye* at Holt, Rinehart confirmed that white publishing houses were eager to rival nationalists' literary efforts and to create a space for themselves among an emerging black readership. Morrison was, in fact, hired as an editor at Random House to capture what they thought would be a fleeting surge of black literature initiated by the creation of black studies departments at American colleges and universities.[5] The consistent production of black literature turned out to be anything but fleeting, and the black arts movement laid the groundwork for a new tradition in African American literature. And the tradition that emerged, the tradition that Morrison helped to initiate, along with Forrest, Toni Cade Bambara, Gayl Jones, John McCluskey, and James Alan McPherson—five of the contemporary authors whose fiction she edited while at Random House—was one that took the horrors and the beauty alike of black cultural traditions, one that explored the vastness of African American experiences and the varied meanings of an African American self, and one that ushered in the contemporary era of the novel as an agent of healing.

Surely, not all of these authors' characters experience healing. Nor are all black institutions always helpful to the people who populate Forest County. *The Bloodworth Orphans'* Rachel Flowers' obsession with religion precludes any chance she might have had of creating a meaningful existence for herself. Saltport's affiliation with the Black Muslims in the same novel eventually drives him mad and back to drugs when he realizes that he has been ousted unfairly from the group, because of jealousy, in Malcolm X–like fashion. Imani commits suicide in *Divine Days* after she fails to gain acceptance from black nationalists who reject her because of her middle/upper-class upbringing, her white conservative education, and her white patron. The failures of the civil rights movement in *Meteor in the Madhouse* drive Marvella insane after she learns that fellow activists did nothing to prevent the death of her lover. And the movement's many shortcomings cause Leonard Foster so much despair that he ultimately turns to drugs and is left dead in an alley after being robbed in an incident that mirrors the murder of Huey Newton. Hence, we see that Forrest does indeed avoid romanticizing black institutions, cultural and otherwise, and, instead, uses them as a medium through which to investigate contemporary black experiences and to offer his racially and psychologically oppressed characters options for surviving and transcending their oppression.

Thus in the chapters that focus specifically on Forrest's fiction, I examine Forrest's use of culture and the narrative techniques he uses to present cultural experiences in each of the four novels—*There Is a Tree More Ancient Than Eden* (1973), *The Bloodworth Orphans* (1977), *Two Wings to Veil My Face* (1984), and *Divine Days* (1992)—and in the final collection of novellas, *Meteor in the Madhouse* (2001). Though the black cultural traditions that inform these texts are my primary focus, I attempt to complement my cultural readings of the texts with relevant critical analyses of the narrative style Forrest embraces in his respective novels. This, of course, is not to argue that discussions of Forrest's use of black cultural traditions in the novels hold more significance than his narrative or literary experiments. This approach does, however, acknowledge that it is more often than not the limited accessibility to the narratives, which is due largely to Forrest's highly experimental style, that accounts for their difficulty and, subsequently, their critical neglect. Ideally, this dual approach to the novels will, first and more practically, offer readers entrée into the narratives through examinations of the author's use of black cultural traditions as sustaining forces for the contemporary African American and will, secondarily, observe and analyze the narrative techniques he uses to present these traditions.

Preceding these chapters is chapter 1, which gives a bio-critical introduction to Forrest and offers relevant commentary on Forrest's characterization as a modernist writer. His narrative style finds stylistic affinity with authors like James Joyce and William Faulkner and traditional modernism, particularly its tendencies toward stream of consciousness, mythic representations of the ordinary, non-linear narratives, and the like. But if we accept that traditional European and American modernism emerged in response to World War I and cultural self-doubt in the early twentieth century,[6] then we must also concede that, for African Americans, an earlier form of modernism that emerged as a consequence of and in response to slavery exists. Thus Forrest, along with a number of other African American authors such as Jean Toomer, Zora Neale Hurston, Ralph Ellison, and Toni Morrison—all of whom recognize black cultural responses as techniques that mirror and precede modernist technique and critique—makes significant modifications in his representation of modernism as an ideology and as an aesthetic through which to portray African American experiences.

Remarkably, the progression of the novels suggests an evolution in Forrest's ability to articulate that which Euro-American modernism characterizes as unpresentable—(black) experience as reality. *There Is a Tree More Ancient Than Eden* seems to accept Nathaniel's experiences and confusion as ineffable. He can only experience them, always without expression; hence the novel's use of the journey motif (which allows for investigation and representation without articulation). He knows that he should be able to express himself (that he cannot is part of his frustration), and Hattie Breedlove leads him in the direction of articulation (though he never fully achieves it in this novel). *The Bloodworth Orphans* moves the narratives and Nathaniel one step closer to articulation and to a belief that experience can indeed be rendered artistically. Though Nathaniel never postures himself an as effective narrator or as one who can communicate the Bloodworths' chaos, close examination of the novel reveals articulation through musical impulses—blues, jazz, and gospel music. By *Two Wings to Veil My Face*, Forrest seems convinced that the African American experience can be presented in words, and he anoints Sweetie Reed for this task. She becomes the "articulate kinsman" who presents more than two hundred years of African American history to her grandson to ensure his and subsequent generations' survival and to suggest that storytelling (as well as the written word) is an effective means through which to express black modernist chaos. She knows that teaching Nathaniel to accept his fate and to negotiate this chaos is key to his survival. And she symbolically bestows upon the next generation the gift of authorship, as she insists that Nathaniel write their family's history both on his heart and on paper. It is not Nathaniel, however, who fully accepts the call as author in the novel that follows Sweetie's directive. It is, instead, Joubert, whose journal entries (which express his desires and frustrations as a playwright) shape *Divine Days*. That Nathaniel is not this author is far less important than Forrest's clear conviction that race-based chaos (in its many variations) can be and must be articulated and accepted as presentable by the African American artist. Thus, the novel spends a great deal of time investigating African American experiences and suggesting that these experiences are so varied that any attempt to render them as prescriptive, monolithic, or definitive is false. By the final collection of novellas, *Meteor in the Madhouse,* Joubert has come to articulate the fullness of an essential element of black experience—black intellectual history. Joubert's success notwithstanding, Forrest's fiction acknowledges that much in African American life resists articulation; thus much is left unsaid, though not unacknowledged.

In chapter 2, "To Survival and Beyond: Journeys Down Under and *There Is a Tree More Ancient Than Eden,*" I argue that the journey motif that shapes the novel allows Forrest to address the historical and cultural politics that inform contemporary African American identity. This motif subsequently allows Forrest to reveal how black cultural traditions—which, in this novel, include distinctly African traditions, diasporic African traditions, and African American ethnic traditions—help Nathaniel to move beyond psychological fragmentation (created both by racism and by his mother's death, the latter of which heightens his awareness about his lack of an individual identity) to possible and probable transcendence and on to an emerging sense of *self*.

Though Forrest still uses black traditions to present the racially inspired Bloodworth curse and to render his characters' varied responses to it in his second novel, *The Bloodworth Orphans* presents a more ambiguous portrayal of cultural institutions than does *There Is a Tree More Ancient Than Eden*. Through its extensive use of characters and its aggressive approach to character development, *The Bloodworth Orphans* accesses a variety of black cultural traditions and institutions to explore their usefulness in combating orphanhood and the fragmentation these characters suffer because of their alienation from their families and from broader American traditions. One tradition that proves to be most effective is black music, particularly its ability to posit African American experiences of oppression, fragmentation, and alienation in a more universal context. By exposing the orphans' flawed responses (irrelevant folk rituals and corrupt black institutions, among others) to their fragmentation, the novel suggests a cultural integrationist approach to healing these disconnected characters. The lone surviving Bloodworth, for instance, realizes that he has a better chance at survival if he adopts jazz culture's survivalist tendencies than if he remains culturally detached or naively embraces traditional and alternative black religions. Thus, in chapter 3, I highlight Forrest's use of black music as one of the few metaphors capable of telling the story of the African American as a cultural orphan (of America) and as a tradition that places the African American experience at the center of American experience.

Chapter 4, "'Learn it to the Younguns': Bearing Witness to the Blues in *Two Wings to Veil My* Face" highlights Forrest's creation of Sweetie Reed in the tradition of blues-women Bessie Smith and Ma Rainey, both of whom used the blues as a discursive site of resistance to patriarchy. Because Sweetie's blues involves her attempt to assert her self and, subsequently, to show Nathaniel how to achieve selfhood, I argue that the novel's adaptation of traditions of the slave narrative to tell Sweetie's tale follows the contemporary tradition Angelyn Mitchell calls the *liberatory narrative*. By combining two African American traditional expressive forms of resistance and expression—the blues and the slave narrative—*Two Wings* allows Sweetie to negotiate the tension between orality and literacy and between oppression and reconstructed notions of freedom and, subsequently, to achieve a sense of self and to ensure that Nathaniel can eventually do the same.

In chapter 5, I examine how *Divine Days* uses the technique Forrest terms *reinvention*—a responsive black cultural tradition of survival reminiscent of jazz culture—to highlight the complexity of blackness. Accordingly, this chapter notes the novel's attempt to resist prescriptive and stereotyped images and essentialist ideological notions ranging from W. E. B. DuBois's idea of double-consciousness to that of the black aesthetic. Through its survey of these black ideological and literary traditions, *Divine Days* highlights the variability of blackness and uses black cultural traditions to support this notion and to offer alternative aesthetics of blackness. Ultimately, the novel uses Joubert's desire to become a playwright capable of capturing the voices of his black heritage, a desire which mirrors Forrest's self-proclaimed quest to dramatize black life, to explore the complexity of the lives of black characters ranging from preachers to writers to hipsters and tricksters. What Joubert finds as he explores this complexity is that reinvention, as survival technique, is at the heart of many of the characters' success. Conversely, those characters who are unable to reinvent themselves or who choose to adopt essentialist ideologies are denied the healing to which they might otherwise have access.

Chapter 6 examines self-invention as a coping mechanism that allows the characters who populate Forest County in *Meteor in the Madhouse* to transcend the grief they experience because of their highly racialized existences. As a black cultural tradition, self-invention encourages the characters to make internal transformations in order to live successfully within the context of a world that denies them the fullness of their humanity largely because of race. While self-invention is not an exclusively black cultural tradition, the forms of the technique the characters adopt in *Meteor*—language, memory, artistry, and myth—engage black cultural traditions of creativity and resistance that mirror reinvention but which depart from it in reinvention's concentration on external rather than internal transformations. Rather than be consumed by the agony she experiences at the hand of a racist existence, Lucasta Jones, for instance, engaging creativity as a form of self-invention, elevates ironing from its basic domestic purpose to the point of artistry. Ultimately, what this chapter reveals is that, more often than not, self-invention works when it is used mainly as a coping mechanism, but it inevitably fails when characters use it to displace reality. Thus the characters in *Meteor* must learn to distinguish its power from its limitations if they are to transcend their grief successfully.

As a whole, this examination takes a culturalist approach to Forrest's novels, which, to me, are best understood when read as his attempts to transform the expressive modes of presentation of African American life and history from everyday occurrences to life-explaining and life-sustaining events and achievements. His success as a major novelist, however, rests in the magic of his language, in his ability to reinvent narrative strategy, and in his tendency to highlight the continuities that do and must exist between the African American past and present. Despite their occasional weaknesses, the novels teach us to embrace and to celebrate those cultural traditions that have the power to sustain and to heal, if only temporarily, the character in agony. In the tradition of the gospel and spiritual singer and of the Negro folk preacher, Leon Forrest becomes not only a singer of language, as was his desire, but also a singer of African American culture—with his novels leading the way, screaming, "Let there be Light, baby, Let there be light!"[7]

chapter one

The Meteor in the Man—
The Artistic Light of Leon Forrest

Leon Forrest was born January 8, 1937, in Chicago's Cook County Hospital to Leon and Adeline (Green) Forrest. Both his formative and adult years as a writer were heavily influenced by his parents, who were talented amateur artists in their own rights. Though he was primarily a bartender for the Santa Fe Railroad, the elder Leon was also a musician/songwriter who had a number of his songs recorded, while Forrest's mother wrote short stories, though she never had any of them published. Their greatest influence on Forrest in terms of his writing, however, has more to do with their religious and ancestral backgrounds than their creative desires.

A Mississippi-born mulatto who never knew his white father, the elder Leon seemed to the younger constantly in search of something to fill the void left in his life by the absence of his father. And while most of Forrest's characters suffer from motherlessness, not fatherlessness, the issue of familial connections or the lack thereof nonetheless dominates his works. His father's family was Protestant, as was typical of the Mississippi Negro. And the influence of the Protestant faith, particularly the folk preacher and gospel music, is evidenced throughout Forrest's fiction. As a choir member at Chicago's Pilgrim Baptist Church and director of its youth choir, the elder Leon was a part of black church history—quite probably without being aware of it. The church's pastor, C. J. Austin, went on to become one of the most renowned preachers in the black Baptist tradition, and Thomas Dorsey, who served as the church's musical director, is easily recognizable as one of the premier gospel songwriters and composers of his time. As gospel music was not widely accepted in black Baptist traditions upon its inception, particularly in churches with a large middle-class population, the fact that Dorsey was welcomed in Pilgrim Baptist speaks to the church's willingness to accept change, transformation, and growth. Undoubtedly, its liberalism and its awareness of the need to find ways to blend the sacred and the secular for the purpose of salvation had some impact on both father and son, since much of the younger Forrest's fiction makes a similarly liberal attempt.

Forrest's mother, Adeline Green Forrest, was a New Orleans Creole whose family was Catholic and whose Creole background exposed Forrest to the interracial tension that existed between darker- and lighter-skinned blacks. He explores this tension briefly in *There Is a Tree More Ancient Than Eden,* in his depiction of the character Uncle Dupont, who passes for white on occasion and who refuses to allow darker-skinned Negroes such as Jamestown Fishbond to attend what Nathaniel mockingly refers to as a *mulatto-purity party.* Unlike most of his maternal relatives, Forrest did not attend Catholic school. However, he did attend weekly catechism classes in order to receive his confirmation. And as much as the preaching and music of his father's Baptist faith later influenced his writing, the ritualism of his mother's Catholic faith had a similar effect. Thus, from two different denominations, Forrest garnered religious influence and utilized it throughout his writing.

Forrest's "aunt," Lenora Bell, also lived with the family during his early years, and her "magical" ability to transform ordinary pieces of cloth into extraordinary garments influenced Forrest as well. Recognizing transformation and reinvention as an African American cultural attribute, Forrest adopted from his seamstress aunt the ability to add creative imagination to an object and, subsequently, to transform it into something more spectacular than the original. Forrest also recognized Lenora Bell's love of reading and her storytelling abilities as an influence on him as a writer, and he recreated her character in the form of Bella-Lenore Boltwood in *The Bloodworth Orphans.* Notably, Lenora Bell was not actually a blood relative of the family, But she had raised Adeline Green and helped to raise Forrest. So Nathaniel's discovery that he is not actually a blood relative of Sweetie Reed in *Two Wings to Veil My Face* and the pattern of orphans that recurs throughout the sagas was also at least partially influenced by Forrest's relationship with Lenora Bell.

Similarly, Forrest's maternal aunt, Maude White, took in orphans from time to time through the Catholic Home Bureau, and he cites this familial compassion as one that forced him to think about the crisis of the American family. Forrest's paternal great-aunt, Maude Richardson, was influential in Forrest's life and in his writing as well. He frequently spent weekends with Maude Richardson, who taught Bible classes and who reinforced in him his father's Protestant faith. Though she and her husband migrated from Greenville, Mississippi, to Chicago during the Great

Migration, they took with them a southern ethos with which they combined urban Chicago life. She also blended with this her Baptist and Methodist faith to create for herself an ideology that ensured her survival. Many of Forrest's characters privilege this idea of integration, and he recreates Maude and her husband in *Meteor in the Madhouse* as Forrester and Gussie Mae Jones, the couple who had migrated to Chicago from Mississippi many years earlier but who still keep their southern patch of vegetables in the backyard and beds of flowers in the front yard in spite of the fact that they are surrounded by Forest County slums. Though they are uneducated, they know how to tap into a number of different sources to maintain their sanity, and they know how to reinvent themselves to make a way out of no way.

As a child, Forrest attended the all-black Wendell Phillips Elementary School, where he gained a sense of pride for his culture from teachers who exposed him to black history and black writers such as Langston Hughes, Countee Cullen, Richard Wright, and W. E. B. DuBois. In an interview with Kenneth Warren, Forrest acknowledges the significance of attending an all-black public school—not just because he learned to be proud of his heritage but also because it kept him from being limited to and by an indoctrinated Catholic-school perspective. From 1951 to 1955, Forrest attended the newly integrated Hyde Park High School near the University of Chicago. This transition—from an all-black grade school experience to one where he was one of only a few black students in a predominantly white high school in his freshman year—was one he seemed to make fairly well. During this time, a number of his teachers at Hyde Park High, along with members of his family, encouraged him to write. And his ability to function well and competitively in an interracial environment undoubtedly enhanced both his view of the world and his confidence.

Following high school, Forrest attended Wilson Junior College from 1955 to 1956, and from 1956 to 1957 he attended Roosevelt University. In 1960, he enrolled in the University of Chicago, but he was drafted into the U.S. Army later that year. After completing basic training, he became a public information specialist while touring in Germany, where he served for two years. He returned to Chicago in 1962 and reenrolled at the University of Chicago, where he began taking creative writing courses and occasionally sat in on Ralph Ellison's lectures. At the University of Chicago, Forrest met Perrin Lowrey, a liberal white southerner who was an authority on Faulkner. It is Lowrey, in fact, whom Forrest credits with exposing him to the limitless possibilities of the folk preacher. And it was also around this time and under Lowrey's influence that Forrest moved away from his desire to be a poet and a playwright and moved toward focusing on being a novelist.

While taking classes at the University of Chicago, Forrest also worked at 408 Liquors, his mother's bar and liquor store. He re-created and transformed many of the voices, people, and stories from this experience in *Divine Days*. Like Forrest, Joubert, the novel's focalizer, has just returned home after a two-year military tour of duty, and he works in a bar while pursuing a career as a journalist to please his family, but he also pursues his dream of becoming a writer to fulfill his passion. But Forrest's world—like Nathaniel's in *There Is a Tree*—was shaken completely when his mother died of cancer in August 1964. She was only forty-five years old. One month after her death, Forrest moved to the Avon, a rooming house occupied by different kinds of artists, and began to pursue his writing career much more seriously. Months later, Forrest experienced another devastating loss when Lowrey, now his friend and mentor, was killed in an automobile accident. And though Forrest did not meet Ellison, who was a friend of Lowrey's, until some years later, a eulogy Forrest published upon Lowrey's death caught Ellison's attention.

From 1964 to 1968, Forrest wrote for local community weekly newspapers including the *Woodlawn Booster*, the *Englewood Bulletin*, and the *Woodlawn Observer*. The last was the voice of the Woodlawn Organization, which was one of Saul Alinsky's community action groups headed by Leon Finney Jr. This experience kept him aware of the racial tension that plagued the city but allowed him to release himself from it through newspaper articles rather than in his fiction. Similarly, his experience as a contributor to and editor of *Muhammad Speaks*, the official news organ of the Nation of Islam, allowed him to write about racial injustices as nonfiction by day while he explored the spiritual agony of man through fiction by night.

In 1966 Forrest's first short story, "That's Your Little Red Wagon," was published in *Blackbird*, a literary magazine that published only a few issues. Ultimately, the piece became a part of *There Is a Tree*, which was not published in its first form until some years later in 1973. It was also in 1966 that Forrest met noted University of Chicago anthropologist Allison Davis, whose work on black youth and on class disparities between races was seminal in sociology circles. Davis's awareness of the nuances of race and culture certainly had an impact on Forrest as an observer of culture and as a writer. This is evidenced in his eulogy to Davis, where Forrest writes of his friend's "epiphanies of eloquent insight," and of how, even when he disagreed with Davis, he "often found [him]self, months, or years later, hearing the echo of

Allison's voice, and seeing the truth of his wisdom; reflecting an especially clear-eyed focus, an oracle-like rendering of a dreaded truth, or a delicately renewing perception" (Forrest, *Furious Voice,* 255).

In November 1967 Forrest's three-act play *Theatre of the Soul* was performed at Parkway Community House in Chicago, but it was never published or reviewed. Because he began to focus on fiction in the years that followed, it was not until he wrote *Re-Creation,* a one-act verse play, which T. J. Anderson set to music, that playwriting resurfaced publicly in Forrest's career. *Re-Creation* was presented at Richard Hunt's studio in Chicago in June 1978. In 1982 Forrest again collaborated with Anderson, writing the libretto for *Soldier Boy, Soldier,* an opera composed by Anderson. *Soldier Boy, Soldier* was produced at the University of Indiana at Bloomington from October to November, receiving unfavorable reviews, though most criticism of the libretto commended its underlying focus on the forgotten black Vietnam veteran while condemning its subplot of the love triangle, which allegedly overshadowed the former and more important theme.

As he worked to hone his talents as a creative writer, Forrest continued to contribute articles to *Muhammad Speaks,* where he was an associate editor under Richard Durham, a non-Muslim Marxist thinker who expanded Forrest's ideological base, if only marginally, from 1969 to 1972, when Forrest became managing editor of the weekly after Durham's retirement. It was, in fact, through *Muhammad Speaks* that Forrest met Ellison in 1972, when he interviewed the author for the paper, and it was also through a contact at *Muhammad Speaks* that he was introduced to an editor at Holt, Rinehart, which had just published Toni Morrison's *The Bluest Eye* in 1970. Ultimately, the editor at Holt, Rinehart referred Forrest to Morrison, who was then an editor at Random House.

Just weeks after he married the former Marianne Duncan on September 25, 1971, Forrest met with Morrison in New York while reviewing a play by Mario van Peebles for *Muhammad Speaks.* Under Morrison's editorship and through her recommendation to the other editors at Random House, Forrest's first novel was published in May 1973. Endorsed by Saul Bellow and introduced by Ralph Ellison, *There Is a Tree* gave Forrest the confidence he needed to finally pursue creative writing full time, so he resigned as managing editor of *Muhammad Speaks* on the eve of the novel's publication. In June of the same year, after his friend Jan Carew introduced him to the dean of the College of Arts and Sciences at Northwestern University in Evanston, Forrest accepted an associate professorship at the university. In 1985 he became chair of the Department of African American Studies there, a post he held until 1994.

During his tenure at Northwestern, Forrest, of course, continued to publish novels that examined contemporary African American life and to teach courses that examined themes ranging from families in American literature to spiritual agony in world literature and which, inevitably, influenced his writing. But even as he "read the broadest library" to master and reshape the techniques he found useful, his ultimate desire, he tells Charles Rowell, was to take them "back to the story" of his people (Forrest and Rowell, 353). Thus, even as Forrest acknowledges the influence of other traditions on his fiction, he often reinvented them in terms of black culture. This attraction to other cultures and traditions as sources he could reinterpret in terms of black experiences is perhaps why Forrest found little about the black aesthetic useful. To Forrest, the black arts movement, which argued for the black aesthetic, seemed segregationist. And because his writing escaped the bounds of the aesthetic in the broadest kinds of ways, "[s]elling Random House on Forrest's novels," according to Morrison, "was very hard at a time when the 'dumbing down' of novels was taking hold" (quoted in Dodge, 17).

Even so, Forrest was careful not to downgrade the black arts movement, despite its obvious limitations, because it created the need for a middle ground between a black aesthetic and a white aesthetic, which is where his works rests. And he also greatly admired the work of Sterling Plumpp, who came out of the Chicago black aesthetic. Yet Forrest was very clear that he was ideologically opposed to the black aesthetic and that he would never have gained acceptance into the movement even if he had tried. Instead, he attempted to do that which the aesthetic too often avoided—to use black cultural traditions to connect the racial, ideological, and political reality of African American life with other traditions of soul-searching fiction both as a reflection of the African American tendency to make things anew and as an attempt to infuse African American experiences into American and broader literary traditions.

Interestingly, during much of the period that constituted the black arts movement, Forrest was writing politically oriented articles for community weeklies and for *Muhammad Speaks*. Under Durham's editorship, *Muhammad Speaks* catered to a largely non-Muslim readership and gave priority to "the crisis of black America, the economic tragedies facing the Third World, and [. . .] the ways of dealing with the vestiges of colonialism around the globe" (Forrest, *Furious Voice*, 88) rather than to exclusively Muslim or Nation of Islam issues. Thus, Forrest's awareness of the racial implications of the period's politics—both locally and globally—was keen, and as a journalist, he had the freedom to talk about the hard issues in a way that was, perhaps, unavailable to other fiction writers. He tells Rowell of the relevance of his experience as a journalist to his career as an author:

> I had the advantage of working at papers where I could get out a certain type of heat and protest and anger, and I could come home to write at night and think more in terms as a fiction writer [. . . .] Then there was a benefit of just learning how to write a good sentence or a good paragraph at a paper. One of my chores at *Muhammad Speaks* was to put the whole paper together each week, and organize it [. . . .] I found that organizing principle also helps with my own writing and fiction. How am I going to put this story together? How am I going to put this paper to bed? All these things were a benefit to me that I've used over the years. Also to be around Muslims, and yet not be a Muslim. I've written about Muslims in my novels as well. (Forrest and Rowell, 355)

Notably, his depictions of Muslims in the novels range from straightforward, like Saltport X in *The Bloodworth Orphans*, to allusive like W. W. W. Ford, who appears more or less as a trickster in the Bloodworth trilogy but who is clearly a mocking spoof of W. D. Fard of the black Muslim tradition in *Divine Days*. In an interview with Keith Byerman, he confesses why he blatantly mocked and used Fard as a base on which to build his own comic and demonic trickster figure Ford:

> There's the actual closeness in both stories, both the story that we know of Fard and my Ford, to manipulation and mystery—the intrigue and perhaps even a sense of the closeness that so many religious figures have to the magician and to the trickster. . . . So then I take Ford (and the tradition) a step further and have him a hermaphrodite who keeps coming back again and again. Of course, we only see manifestations of his maleness. He's a stud. He's wearing all these different masks, and actually what we have left of Fard is a series of masks of interpretations. (Forrest and Byerman, 444)

In the essay "Elijah" in *The Furious Voice for Freedom* (a reprint of *Relocations of the Spirit*), it also becomes clear that at least part of Ford's character is also inspired by Elijah Muhammad, who referred to himself as the Messenger of Allah and who was, for years, the leader of the black Muslims in the Nation of Islam. Clearly, the idea of the "lost-founds," which Forrest re-created in the form of literal and figurative orphans in the Forest County sagas, was inspired by Muhammad's concept of the "spiritually famished flock of lost/found" Africans who lived in America. A masterful storyteller and myth creator, Muhammad, according to Forrest, was always aware of his target audience's beliefs, limitations, possibilities, vulnerabilities, and tendencies; thus, he manipulated this sharp sense of awareness to make his re-creation as plausible as possible. Muhammad knew that "the way to create the new was really through a cunning transformation of the old" (Forrest, *Furious Voice,* 67), a technique Forrest and his characters adopt. Like Ford in *Divine Days,* Elijah, according to Forrest,

> played all roles in the creation of [his] nation. He was a trickster both in the sense of the magician, and in the spirit of the trickster as demon. He took on the role of playwright of his own play, "The Recreation of the Blackman," raiding the Bible and the Koran, like Shakespeare raiding Ovid, and Joyce soaking up the *Odyssey.* (96)

Subsequently, Forrest raided Muhammad's myths and re-created both character and concept as Ford.

In spite of his apparent mockery of Elijah Muhammad and his disdain for Muhammad's shameless manipulation of his followers, especially Malcolm X, Forrest frequently commended Muhammad for the discipline he instilled in his flock, particularly as it related to the group's abstinence from drugs and violence, and for Muhammad's ability, however misplaced, to create a mythology that validated black humanity. This mythology, however, had its shortcomings in Forrest's opinion, especially its denial of all things *Negro*. Although the African American had been stripped of his African culture during the early years of slavery, Muhammad advocated that he be stripped again, but this time of his newly adopted Western cultural tendencies. Thus, all forms of *Negro* culture, including those the African American had created himself, were repudiated. This narrowness was as unappealing to Forrest as the narrowness of the black aesthetic, and he makes this clear throughout his culturally integrative fiction but especially in *Divine Days,* where a character repeatedly proclaims that "it is the *Negro* that saves us." And it is the *Negro* that saves Forrest as a writer, for as he notes, it is African American culture that serves as the springboard for his imagination and for his fiction.

Easily one of the most profound *Negro* influences on Forrest's writing is black music. From the spiritual to the blues and from jazz to gospel music, black music provided Forrest with inspiration, form, and style. Two vocalists who were perhaps the greatest inspiration to him were Mahalia Jackson and Billie Holiday. Because he believed that part of what was missing in African American literature during the time he was struggling to become a writer was the spiritual agony the African American faced, Mahalia Jackson's incantations were artistically inspiring to him. Writing on the cusp of the black arts movement, where blackness was celebrated and glorified, Forrest found himself struggling with ways to articulate the less celebration-worthy and glorious aspects of African American life until he heard Mahalia singing "Didn't It Rain?" He confesses:

> Mahalia was saying that I was lucky to have a spiritual embattlement to write about . . . to sing about. But how did she know that I wanted to be a singer of the language—in the tradition of her majestic self and the Negro Preacher. Had she read a draft of one of my ranting revisions—in a language not even a mother could love. (29)

He goes on to write that Mahalia's singing told him that "the world would hate him if Jesus changed his name." In essence, he had to be who he was and who he wanted to be, even if that meant departing from the more popular, more dominant, and more commercially successful black aesthetic. What he was interested in more than anything was expressing the spiritual agony of the soul. It was the same personal agony he experienced upon his mother's death at a young age and the same communal agony that destroyed so many artistic geniuses, such as Charlie Parker and Billie Holiday. It is through Mahalia's art, then, that he realized and accepted that "the only way to get to heaven is to die." He, too, would have to pay his dues:

> She showed me one meaning of a mountain I'm still trying to climb. Told me I would have to stand all alone by myself; for in the end the artist is constantly transforming himself again and again out of the chaos of his soul. . . . My one problem was—to find a brand new way of singing. (30)

On the stage appears Billie Holiday, singing "Strange Fruit."

Forrest's love for Billie Holiday's art is best exemplified in his "Solo Long-Song: For Lady Day," where he expresses not only admiration for her work but a very clear understanding of what it is she does with her voice, her band, and her audience. *There Is a Tree*, in fact, takes as one of its epigraphs lyrics from Lady Day's "Strange Fruit." Forrest frequently acknowledged that he was "artistically bred more on music than books" and that he was "weaned on Billie Holiday's music" (344). So it is not surprising, then, that his first novel was his own "attempt to play out Lady Day's most haunting and memorable long-song [. . .] in narrative form" (345). The lynching/dismemberment ritual in the section "The Vision" is obviously inspired by the song. But, as Forrest notes,

> the character of Jamestown reveals a keening, haunting, engagement with Holiday's song, in the early days of his own evolvement. And Jamestown's sister, Madge Ann Fishbond renders up a monologue about her life, which seems, upon reflection, pitched out of the muted memory of Holiday's remembering art. (395)

Holiday's influence on Forrest as writer is not, however, limited to that of inspiration; it transcends to the point of artistry. The eloquence she achieved on stage, the mesmerizing effect she had on her audience, he desired to achieve on paper. And one of the ways to accomplish this was to borrow from Lady Day the art form that shaped her vocalization—jazz and its tendency to transform and to revise all with which it comes in contact. When referring to Lady Day, Forrest calls her transformative powers her "reading of a lyric," which she acknowledges in *Lady Sings the Blues* as her sustaining life force. The freedom—the demand—to reinterpret a song from night to night, from year to year was, to her, the difference between an exercise or a drill and music. From Lady Day and from black music generally, Forrest adopts this tendency toward reinvention or transformation.

As Forrest was acutely aware, all black music, not just jazz, embraced some level of reinvention or reinterpretation, and he drew upon all of these traditions to enhance his writing. In his unpublished lecture notes he writes that the spiritual or the sorrow song is perhaps the New World African's first artistic attempt at reinvention. Displaced from their homeland, these Africans in America recast biblical events to place themselves within a new tradition that acknowledged their humanity and their worth. Even in its simplest form, the spiritual is reinventive in that it is a retelling of a biblical story in the vernacular so that it gains social and religious—literal and figurative—significance. To enhance its dramatic form, Forrest notes, creators of the spirituals drew from whatever sources they found useful, both the Old and the New Testament. Consequently, "Job and Joshua and Jesus and Ezekiel may be found in the same song, along with a twentieth-century train that carries the sanctified home" (Forrest, unpublished notes). In this same tradition, Forrest retells stories, draws from whatever sources are available (to increase his dramatic form), and uses vernacular experiences and expressions to lead his reader to the point where he or she can offer a response to his literary call.

Eventually, even reinvention of the spiritual takes place, and gospel music emerges. Gospel shares the tradition of religion with spirituals, but it gains distinction through what Forrest acknowledges as *style improvisation*. Ironically, many traditionalists objected to gospel music's tendency toward improvisation, though it shares this tendency, even if only at a basic level, with the spiritual. In gospel music, the traditional spiritual is the mere skeleton of a song that may be improvised on. What was probably most attractive about this impulse to Forrest is its sometimes indefinable blend of the sacred and the secular. Forrest's exposure (even if only vicariously through his father) to gospel great Thomas Dorsey likely had some impact on him as an artist. Throughout his lecture notes and even in *The Furious Voice,* Forrest speaks of Dorsey's genius with reverence and admiration with Dorsey. As the piano player at Forrest's father's church, Forrest almost certainly saw traditional spirituals being transformed into gospel music, and he heard the influence of the blues in this emerging tradition.

In fact, Forrest notes that gospel music emerges out of the constant reengagement of men like Dorsey with the secular or blues world and their use of this influence on their music when they returned to the church:

> Rev. Dorsey [. . .] was a blues pianist and a composer for a long time; and this base enriched and deepened the kind of music he composed, and he transformed the refinements of the spiritual into a music that fitted the more angular needs of an awakening people, hungry-hearted for a dialogue in song which captured both their secular and their spiritual sense of life, as agony and wonder. (Forrest, *Furious Voice,* 13)

Gospel music's greatest influence on Forrest as a writer, then, has to do with this very integration, since, as he tells John Cawelti, it was the only music that could express the "growing complexity of black American life in the North" after the Great Migration (Forrest and Cawelti, 307). And for a writer interested in expressing the experiences of his Chicago/Forest County–based characters—particularly their racial experiences, which are heavily informed by southern traditions and a southern past and in finding a way to articulate the tension between the sacred and the secular, the sexual and the spiritual, the past and the present—gospel music offers an adequate impulse to do so. It did the very thing Forrest was attempting to do with his fiction: It found a way to bring together, in peaceful harmony, the secular and the spiritual African American experience.

A number of Forrest's characters, however, find little, if any, affinity with religious traditions. For them, the blues carries the impulse that best sustains them. As Forrest notes, in the blues, there is no faith in Jesus to get you through; instead, you get through by your "wit and your wiles," through bravery and humor, and with your sexual skills. Recognizing the blues as a metaphor for "a condition of the heart, of pain visited upon body and soul," Forrest taps into this art form to create a blues voice in *Two Wings to Veil My Face;* he uses its humor to create the comedic and satirical aspects of *Divine Days;* and he confesses that a number of blues songs and artists inform both plot and characters in *The Bloodworth Orphans.*

> The very first scene that I wrote for the novel *The Bloodworth Orphans* evolved [*sic*] a blues man—Carl Rae. I was quite swept up with the lines from Lightnin' Hopkins's blues song "I've Had My Fun." I found particularly haunting the lines "On the next train sound/You can look for my clothes home. . . . But if you don't see my body, Mama, all you can do is mourn." These lines unleashed within me the saga of an aimless drifter who gains a species of honor on his deathbed, wailing his monologue as odyssey home: this becomes his attempt at transformation of the self, as it were, even as it is rendered up from a garbage heap. (Forrest, *Furious Voice,* 26–27)

Like Carl-Rae in *The Bloodworth Orphans,* Hopkins Golightly, who appears in *Meteor in the Madhouse,* pays homage to Lightnin' Hopkins and his transforming powers. Joubert's fascination with Golightly, in fact, is that he expresses his agony and the racial discrimination against him through his music by reinterpreting "The Battle Hymn of the Republic," which, ironically, celebrates the very American freedom he is denied because of race. Like the blues singer, Forrest searches for "words to express the condition of life and perhaps to change the landscape of it" (Forrest, unpublished notes).

While it is the blues singer whose "eternal search . . . is quite similar to that of the working novelist: to try to find true words to capture the ever-changing condition of life upon the highly vulnerable heart . . . a life which is essentially tied to rupture, chaos, celebration, agony, humor, and always trouble" (Forrest, *Furious Voice,* 25), it is the ordering power of jazz that has the most influence on the way Forrest structures his novels. Because so many of his characters are orphaned and fragmented, the tendency of jazz to give order to otherwise unorderable chaos is a particularly appealing impulse. Presumably, Forrest lectured as effectively on black music as he did on creative writing; more than half of the lecture notes included in his papers archived at Northwestern are on black music. Granted, he drew his information from other sources, but he was no less personally knowledgeable of the historical, stylistic, and technical aspects of black music, particularly jazz. After detailing the evolution of jazz as it is known today, he notes its "certain salient elements":

> There is the element of melody. . . . In Western tradition there is the major scale and the minor scale. . . . Jazz is based on a version of the major scale. . . . But in jazz the variation goes this way, in the seven note scale—the third, fifth, and seven notes are lowered; then the scale becomes a jazz scale . . . and these notes are called Blue notes . . . (Modified three different times). . . .
>
> Underneath the harmony of the song remains the same [. . .] The effect of the sound created when the modified melody of Blues Notes in combination with the harmony which is not changed, all of this goes to create this dissonant sound . . . which is the sound of jazz [. . .] They are searching for a sound in between which is a quarter-tone . . . the quarter sound appears to fall somewhere between the flatted-note, the blue-note and the traditional note underneath . . . this appears to be a hold-over from Africa. . . . (Forrest, unpublished notes)

He then notes, parenthetically, to read a passage from Ellison's then unpublished *juneteenth*. Clearly, Forrest was aware of the possibility of transforming a musical impulse and its oral eloquence to fiction. Achieving that transformation is certainly among the most admirable features of his writing.

At least two factors are at play in this regard—his use of poetic language to recreate musical impulses on paper and the style with which he presents this language. The "magic of [his] writing," Forrest tells Rowell, has to do with the poetry of language: "[. . .] I suppose that in the subterranean regions of my own psyche [. . .] I've wanted to create a poem on each page of my prose, and if I can do that then I'm close to this magic" (Forrest and Rowell, 342). As an author who literally read his prose aloud as he composed it,[1] Forrest was overtly concerned with creating lyrical and musical phrasings. Thus, he borrows from a variety of oral traditions to achieve such effects. As Bruce A. Rosenberg notes in "Forrest Spirits: Oral Echoes in Leon Forrest's Prose,"

> Forrest's prose is multigeneric, more thoroughly so than that of most of his novelist contemporaries; it incorporates several generically stylistic levels of social and intellectual modes simultaneously. The novels are a salad of conventional narrative, black folk sermon, popular song and Spiritual, street slang, and idiom. [. . .] By this technique, he manages to tap into the varied strengths of several forms, extracting from each of those components what will reinforce the whole. His novels are thus more than novels. Part song, part spiritual, part record of oral performances, part sermon, part street speech—they exceed all of these constituents. (317)

This combination of "oral echoes" is then presented as the experiences of characters who speak everyday language and through a narrative style that is equally attracted to oral styles. The narrative style of *There Is a Tree,* for example, adopts the nonlinear and improvisational style of jazz, while *Two Wings* is structured in terms of Sweetie Reed's blueslike storytelling of her family's history. Forrest's experiment with musical impulses to structure his narrative reaches its climax, however, with *Divine Days*. When Madhu Dubey questions whether *Divine Days* is modeled on "a jazz method of composition [. . .] to give shape to chaos without imposing a kind of reductive order on it," he responds:

> It is. Chaos is a great driving force in all life [. . . .] I guess though that for me the first connection with jazz is that I will take just a fragment of a story, or a fragment of a character, or a confrontation, and then build on it, [. . .] riff on it like a jazz musician or a solo performer. So in fact a lot of scenes just start off with me working a little riff, and then that develops into a scene. As far as the larger thing goes, I always try to orchestrate a scene so that it starts off in one way, gets involved with some other things, and then comes back to that—a little fugue-like method. But I'm always trying both to orchestrate a scene and orchestrate the novel really, as well as do those individual solos. (Forrest and Dubey, 589)

Forrest also uses the jazz method of composition in a more specialized way in a number of scenes where he adopts Ellison's idea of *antagonistic cooperation.* He likens the concept to multiple musicians participating in simultaneous improvisation where they "celebrate as they battle, cooperate as they harmonize, signify as they quarrel" (unpublished notes). He calls attention to two such scenes from *Divine Days* in the interview with Dubey:

> One is the scene between Joubert and Reverend Roper [. . .] they go back and forth like two jazz musicians trying to outblow each other or duel each other. Ultimately it would appear that this is what Ellison was talking about—there's a lot of fun between the two men as they try to outdo each other in storytelling and these storytelling riffs are really like aspects of jazz. And the other scene that comes to mind is in the barbershop between Williemain and Joubert [. . .] ultimately the reader will want to decide how these two set pieces, between Joubert and Roper, and between Joubert and Williemain, are similar and yet different. Those are two different jazz sets, you see. (599)

He acknowledges that this antagonistic cooperation occurs between texts as well, admitting that his quest is to outplay the masters he riffs on, quarrels with, and celebrates as he invokes their work and their artistry.

In addition to using jazz to structure his narrative (a technique I will examine later in this chapter, particularly as the idea of a jazz narrative relates to Forrest's adaptation of Ellisonian modernism), Forrest uses two of its most basic concepts—improvisation and syncopation—to reflect the cultural attributes of his characters and to bring their experiences to the center of the American literary experience. Like jazz musicians, Forrest's improvising characters are searching for a voice to articulate their experience and to promote their survival. Their use of syncopation—the absence of an expected beat or the stress upon a beat that is usually unaccented—created openings for new voices (unpublished notes). Similarly, Forrest's voicing of Nathaniel's agony in *There Is a Tree,* his return to a slave past and its articulation in a female voice in *Two Wings,* his investigation into the lives of orphans and "lost-founds" in *The Bloodworth Orphans,* and his inquiry into the complexity of the African American hustler in *Divine Days* all express elements of syncopation as Forrest gives voice to unexpected sources, placing stress upon lives and experiences that typically go unaccented. Ultimately, he captures these characters' tendencies to improvise, to make a way out of no way, and then to find a voice that can articulate their experiences. Easily one of the figures in African American culture who best utilizes this technique is the folk preacher, a character who influences Forrest's writing almost as much as black music does.

Notably, there need not be a large degree of distinction between these two influences. To re-create the oral eloquence of the preacher in the written word, Forrest frequently highlights how the folk preacher uses musical techniques, especially call and response, when rendering his sermon. As Forrest suggests, the "role of the congregation during a sermon is similar to that of a good audience at a jazz set—driving, responding, adding to the ever-rising level of emotion and intelligence. Ultimately, the preacher and the congregation reach one purifying moment, and a furious catharsis is fulfilled" (Forrest, *Furious Voice*, 36). In the same way, Forrest's narratives, as recontextualized sermons, demand participatory responses from the reader, who must bring to the texts recollections of group memory and knowledge of Negro folklore, of biblical episodes, and of spirituals if he or she is to experience the narratives fully. Without this knowledge, one can still encounter the novels successfully, but ultimate appreciation of Forrest's artistry requires that one be willing to participate in the texts and capable of connecting the masterful allusions and the numerous puns that he subtly deposits in the texts.

Aesthetically, one of the most attractive features of the sermon is its oratorical strength. But appealing as it may be, that strength is also the most challenging to replicate in the written word. No formatting specifications, regardless of detail and precision, can reveal the rhythms, the intonation, or the vibrancy of an oral performance. Yet Forrest openly accepts the challenge. He tells Cawelti:

> Throughout my work I've been fascinated with the eloquence of the preacher and with the idea of working my way from oral eloquence to written eloquence, linking that to the problems of identity, of religion, of politics, and culture in society and making it a springboard within my own culture. (Forrest and Cawelti, 302)

Without this springboard, Forrest tells Warren, his artistic life may not have survived since it was the folk preacher, the "bard of the race," who "gave [him] voice into the conscience of the race" (Forrest and Warren, 77). Invocations of the folk preacher also provided for Forrest the opportunity to integrate religion into his fiction, which was central to his contention that "true literature is often profoundly religious" and to his artistic vision to add an essential though absent element to contemporary black fiction. Here again, Forrest's mixed Catholic and Protestant background played a crucial role in his intellectual development. As a child, he grew up hearing the sermons of Rev. C. J. Austin, who was heralded by President Franklin

Delano Roosevelt as having "the greatest speaking voice of any public man in America" (Forrest and Cawelti, 310). So, Forrest's ear for the nuances of the folk sermon had been trained since early boyhood. Add to this his frequent listening to tapes of the legendary Rev. C. L. Franklin (father of Aretha Franklin), and Forrest needed only to access his memory of those preacherly voices to transform them into the written word.

Forrest admits that just before he began to pursue his writing seriously, he was overwhelmed by so many art forms of performance and celebration within the black community that he questioned his ability to articulate in an innovative way the voices that plagued his imagination. It was not until Lowrey, who was fascinated by the art of the folk sermon, called his attention to the folk preacher that he realized that the Negro sermon was an ideal medium through which he could simultaneously investigate culture and distinguish himself as a writer. He replays to Rowell a hypothetical conversation about the significance of preachers to his writing:

> "Look, I can't be a preacher. I have no desire to be a preacher, but I know if I'm going to be a writer, an African American writer, I've got to deal with that black preacher; and to some degree, no one has dealt with it the way I want to." So I've got to say, "I love Ellison because I knew him personally and loved his book, and was very much influenced by Faulkner; but I've got to beat those guys. I've got to go beyond them. And here's an avenue to do it." No one has really done very much, when you think about it, with the art of the folk preacher in our novels or on the stage. So I said, "ah, here's a chance to make my way," and of course it fit wonderfully well for me because I wanted to find avenues into the culture that had not been explored very much by other black writers. (Forrest and Rowell, 349)

Much in the same manner that he uses reinventive and improvisational techniques akin to black music, Forrest celebrates the preacher and his sermon for their ability to liberate a text from time-bound and authoritative restrictions and to transform the sermon from its limitations as oral biblical text to the lived contemporary African American experience. Both his narrators and his preachers appropriate larger historical truths as group memory to show their relevance to the contemporary moment. And when his ancestor-guided characters encounter values, beliefs, or experiences that threaten their survival, they act in the same manner as the musician or the folk preacher—they improvise. Joubert, for instance, in *Divine Days,* adopts from the folk preacher his rhetorical eloquence, the freedom of narrative development, and a license to teach via reflection. Like the sermon, each of Joubert's journal entries, which make up the structure of the novel, is open-ended. And like the preacher, who abandons ideas mid-sermon if they prove ineffective, Joubert abates many stories he deems irrelevant. Because they are presented as thoughts written spontaneously and in real time, the entries assume the position of speech acts; hence Joubert's preacherly freedom to ramble throughout the novel's 1,135 pages.

For Forrest, the preacher's voice is an instrument of power that restores value to a people struggling to create and to structure the meaning of blackness. The sermon liberates the *text* of life that devalues blackness and recovers the vision and the voice of the ancestor to resist and to survive. The sermon, as a speech act, shapes history and restructures cultural memory. "The challenge before the black prose fiction writer"—a challenge Forrest accepts—"is to transform historical consciousness into art, to use it as a strategy for representation, and to merge it with the political as he or she presents the emergence of a self" (Hubbard, 19). The preacher and his sermon allow Forrest to achieve this end, and his characters who are in search of self are liberated from the despotism of everyday life through the language and the transforming power of religion. But the supreme achievement the preacher and the sermon afford Forrest is the provision of a vehicle to render the kind of thing he wanted so much for his own work—transformation from oral eloquence into literary eloquence.

Notably, Forrest's invocation of both black music and the sermon contribute to an accurate characterization of the author as a modernist writer. As Cynthia Dobbs notes in her reading of Morrison's *Beloved* as modernism revisited, the folk sermon—in this case, Baby Suggs's—"displays central constitutive elements of [. . .] modernist poetics: a lyricism both constituted and disrupted by an attention to the historical 'brokenness' of human psyches, bodies, and stories" (565). Because of this "brokenness," traditional language has limitations that can be compensated for only through unspoken utterances and, in some cases, through music.

More important than Dobbs's analysis of the role of music and the sermon in modernism, however, is her articulation and application of what Paul Gilroy calls *black modernism,* which "can be defined precisely through its imaginative proximity to forms of terror that surpass understanding and lead back from contemporary racial violence, through lynching, towards the temporal and ontological rupture of the middle passage" (222). In short, for the diasporic African, slavery, not World War I, initiates modernism and its demand for a new ideology. Forrest makes a similar observation when he writes of slavery as the African American's "Genesis Saga" (unpublished notes). Thus his characters, who are interested in reconstructing postslavery stability for themselves and their communities, must create strategies of survival that are inherently both modern and postmodern. And as Dobbs notes,

> The radical new epistemologies of psychology and sociology necessitated by the nearly unthinkable atrocities of slavery [. . .] gave birth in African American culture to a radical suspicion of the normative modes of bourgeois realism, to a corresponding subversion of and play with aesthetic form, and to a thematic preoccupation with personal and cultural madness—the very stuff of what we call modernism. (563–64)

Craig Werner makes a similar assertion in *Playing the Changes: From Afro-Modernism to the Jazz Impulse,* where he seeks to extend the vocabulary of (post)modernism to better accommodate African American cultural traditions. Recalling W. E. B. Du Bois's *The Souls of Black Folk* (1903) and its commentary on double-consciousness, Werner, like Gilroy, notes that African American culture explicitly addressed the concerns of modernism even before the advent of modernism as a theoretical tradition. As early as Charles Chestnut, Werner argues, the African American created

> expressive practices as intricate adjustments to a world fragmented by the communal experience of slavery and racial oppression. Understood from a DuBoisean perspective, then, the central problem confronted by Afro-American culture closely resembles that confronted by mainstream modernism. (186–87)

Forrest, following authors such as Jean Toomer, Zora Neale Hurston, and Ralph Ellison, continues in that tradition of African American authors who utilize traditional modernism's stylistic techniques but who modify its ideology to fit their artistic agendas and to accommodate their affinity with African American history and culture, both of which reflect the "expressive practices" and "intricate adjustments" African Americans made to a world fragmented by slavery and oppression.

To posit Forrest in the dual traditions of the African American modernists (Toomer, Hurston, Ellison, and Morrison) and the more traditional modernists (Joyce and Faulkner) whom he frequently acknowledged as either having influenced his writing or as attempting to achieve in their fiction similar goals as he attempted to achieve in his, a review of these authors' interpretations of and attraction to modernism is in order, particularly as they relate to Forrest's representation of and affinity to modernism.[2] As recent reexaminations of the literary movement suggest, modernism is today perhaps more indefinable than it has ever been. In terms of its approach to narrative, it is equally varied, though a number of techniques have come to be associated largely if not exclusively with modernism. Among them, nonexhaustively, are: the use of stream of consciousness in narratives; the abandonment of chronological or linear time and a subsequent adoption of spatialized and/or psychological time; a frequently corresponding abandonment of realist meaning and subsequent adoption of spatialized meaning, which is best articulated through juxtaposition, collage, or montage; a focus on language and an affinity with lofty language and difficult syntax; and the use of a central consciousness in lieu of an omniscient narrator. Modernism's (nonnarrative-specific) tendencies include (though are not limited to): an emphasis on archetypal characters (oftentimes as artists); a desire for its archetypal character/artist to fulfill himself as a moral being; an attraction to myth, often as an escape from history; a privileging of the primitive or natural over the cultivated or cultured; a view of the world as fragmented and devastated and of man as alienated by modernity; a desire for a heightened sense of consciousness or awareness; and a focus on expression rather than on unity, order, or coherence. At different points, each of the aforementioned authors characterized here as modernist adopts select combinations of the techniques and tendencies of modernism listed above.

As the most traditional modernist of these authors, Joyce has perhaps the greatest influence on Forrest's narrative style, particularly Forrest's first two novels. Influenced by the shift in narrative conception in Dickens's and Zola's novels, Joyce's modernism emerges in part as an attempt to move the novel beyond a naturalistic context to one that viewed sensibility as more important than sentiment (Lehan, 87). Joyce thus adopts the modernist commitment to aestheticism and seeks new ways to present modernist tendencies in narrative terms. Two of the techniques he uses to achieve this end are the superimposition of symbolism onto modernism and the spatialization of time.[3] Believing that objects in nature unfold their meaning and that man achieves higher consciousness by experiencing epiphanies, Joyce preferred the use of symbols over literal objects to express his view of human nature and, conceivably, to encourage his reading audience to have similar experiences of self-discovery. He then complicates this symbolism by allowing the cyclical and/or simultaneous to preempt the sequential or chronological. Add to this Joyce's use of myth to layer his narrative, his highly stylized structure and difficult syntax, and the created form of consciousness that shapes *A Portrait of the Artist as a Young Man* and *Ulysses,* and we have high modernism at its best. Both of these texts especially influence *There Is a Tree* and *The Bloodworth Orphans.*

From modernism in general but Joyce's *Portrait* especially, for example, Forrest adopts a central consciousness as protagonist or archetypal character. Nathaniel Witherspoon is the central consciousness who serves as the would-be protagonist of *There Is a Tree*. Much of what the reader experiences as events in the novel concerns Nathaniel's attempt to come to grips with his mother's death and is focalized through his consciousness. In a manner similar to the flow that characterizes *Ulysses, There Is a Tree* intertwines myth, folklore, and biblical stories[4] and assumes a distinctly Joycean modernist posture. As Richard Lehan notes in "James Joyce: The Limits of Modernism and the Realms of the Literary Text," "[t]he turn toward symbolic myth, cyclical history, primitive awareness, organic reality, and an aesthetic sensibility," which Joyce helps initiate as modernist literature, "resulted in a shared belief of what a literary text should include" (99). Inseparable from modernism, especially as Joyce renders it, "were the twin beliefs in the power of human consciousness [. . .] to illuminate reality and to find in nature and natural process the meaning, symbolic and literal, that explains the nature of human existence" (99). *There Is a Tree* embraces both the literary technique of Joyce's modernism—its difficult syntax, its obsession with language, and its use of psychological time and dreams to suggest the cyclical nature of life—and its ideology—a belief in human consciousness' ability to illuminate reality and in man's ability to find meaning in human existence through natural processes. The latter is perhaps why it is death, a most natural occurrence, that is the catalyst for Nathaniel's journey toward self-discovery and why he is privy to others' consciousness as sources of illumination of reality.

The Bloodworth Orphans is similarly influenced by Joycean modernism. As Lehan notes, in *Ulysses,* "a realistic plane of reference is symbolically held in place once a mythic structure has been superimposed upon it" (90). Like *Ulysses, Bloodworth Orphans* is shaped by myth, then layered with reality and governed by the supposition that the past and the present and different historical layers are superimposed on each other. As Cawelti points out in his introduction to the novel,

> Forrest's fictional world, like that of James Joyce, is a highly allusive one. Words and action continually allude to the legends and myths

> of the Bible, to ancient Greeks, as well as to many other mythical sources [. . . .] Forrest's novels not only frequently allude to legend and myth; their structures echo the archetypal patterns of ancient myth [. . . .] In *The Bloodworth Orphans* we find a recurrent use of the classical myths of Oedipus and Orpheus as well as the biblical legends of the flood and the crucifixion. (xii)

Even as this use of myth to structure the novel is especially influenced by Forrest's study of Joyce, it has its own function and attraction to Forrest, and, notably, he moves beyond Joyce's use of myth. First, by connecting contemporary African American experiences with ancient myths, Forrest highlights the relationship between the past and the present and returns to the theme of origins, which he invokes not only in the title of his first novel—*There Is a Tree More Ancient Than Eden*—but with its fictional interrogation of origins and beginnings. He then moves beyond Joyce's use of myth as a structuring device by combining myth with folk culture and using jazz as the structuring device at the end of the novel to investigate survival techniques for his now mythic and archetypal characters.[5] Ultimately, the result of organizing the novel structurally is the same for *Bloodworth Orphans* as it was for *Finnegans Wake*, which Joyce also organized structurally; as readers, "we lose our sense of foreground and are left with almost only background [. . .] and what is abstractable from the events becomes more important than the events themselves" (Lehan, 98).[6] Thus, even as *Bloodworth Orphans* is chock full of characters, we are not meant to identify as much with the characters as with what we learn from their experiences.

Like Joyce, Faulkner offered modernist inspiration to Forrest. In the sense that his fiction embraces many of the narrative techniques of modernism (including using difficult syntax, multiple perspectives, nonlinear narrative time, and principles of montage) and in the sense that it is critical of the social contexts out of which it emerges and about which it comments, Faulkner can be considered, among other things, a modernist writer.[7] The cultural self-doubts characteristic of modernism become especially attractive to Faulkner as a white southerner, Richard Moreland argues, because of the South's "history of defeat, poverty, and disillusionment" (21).

Like Forrest, Faulkner was deeply interested in the quest for origins, the relationship between family and personal identity, and the role of history in the contemporary moment. But the two authors differ in their approach to history as a meaningful way of negotiating the present. As Patrick

O'Donnell argues in "Faulkner and Postmodernism," high-modernism tendencies reflect authors' attempts to construct a world that will replace the lost world. Faulkner's and Joyce's modernism, O'Donnell contends, "partially resides in the negotiation of an essential contradiction between a rejection of the past and the inevitable repetition of the past in that very rejection" (33–34). Forrest's characters, however, like most characters in African American modernist situations, are not at liberty to reject their pasts. The past too heavily influences their being for them to reject it successfully or for them to achieve transcendence of their agony, which, ironically, is caused largely by their personal and communal experiences with historical (and ongoing) oppression and discrimination. Instead of rejecting history and the past, they must move beyond it.

Because of this accepting approach to history, Forrest, as writer, moves beyond the critical limits modernism imposed on Faulkner's fiction. Inevitably, Faulkner's attempt to replace the lost world with a fictional or linguistic world reproduces the very world it attempts to abandon. Moreland articulates this thusly:

> In performing [its] profoundly *critical* function [. . .] Faulkner's work also inhabits and *represents* much of the force, extent, and subtlety of the very same cultural and psychological currents it criticizes. It thereby represents the difficulties and limitations of its critique [. . . . The] realist dimension of Faulkner's work also represents the limitations of critique by registering the power of dominant cultural currents to circumscribe, to shape, and even to motivate such cultural criticisms. Such critique, then, cannot simply replace, outflank, undercut, or frame representation [. . . . The] past may well be dead to belief, but it retains its haunting power. (22; italics in original)

This realization that the past retains its "haunting power" even when history is suppressed is one a number of African American modernist writers make and use to move traditional modernism beyond its limits of critique. I will return to this argument later in my discussion of the African American modernist writers (especially Morrison) who reinterpret modernism in ways similar to Forrest. But let us first take a closer look at the elements of Faulkner's fiction Forrest adopts with much less modification.

As is characteristic of modernist writers, Faulkner uses biblical titles like *Absalom, Absalom!* and *Go Down, Moses* to suggest the mythical status of his narratives. Similarly, Forrest adopts biblical and cosmic titles for each of his narratives except one—*The Bloodworth Orphans. There Is a Tree More*

Ancient Than Eden, Two Wings to Veil My Face (referential also of a black spiritual), *Divine Days,* and *Meteor in the Madhouse* all, through their titles, illuminate the narratives' tendencies to position African American experiences amongst broader biblical and mythical traditions. Faulkner makes a similar attempt to mythologize southern traditions as he combines southern folklore and myth. In doing so, he "retrieves the residual value of realism—its folklore, myth, and oral narrative epistemology" (Mellard, 475) and creates an innovative modernism of his own, one which "yoke[s] a traditional folk content to modernist technique" (477). Forrest's selective use of realist and naturalist conventional devices—especially mimetic representation, which he uses to capture oral eloquence on the written page—similarly combines folk culture and modernist technique.

In an interview at the University of Kentucky with Cawelti's students, Forrest speaks of Faulkner's influence on his writing in terms of both style and content. A student comments: "I was very impressed by the sentence structure of your prose. I have noticed that it is more or less similar to Faulkner. Did you find yourself consciously using Faulkner's style as a model?" (Forrest and Cawelti, 305). Forrest responds:

> [. . .] Faulkner was certainly a strong influence, in general. [He] showed me a way of breaking open the sentence structure and opening it up so you could go for broke in it [. . .] Also, Faulkner's sensitivity to black life in a general way and his understanding of some aspects of the complexity of these relationships [. . . .] I think the best of Faulkner is involved with black life [. . . .] Faulkner also is very helpful in terms of clues. You can mention what he did with Rev. Shegog's sermon, for example. I have to go beyond that. There's certainly this competition as Faulkner himself said, "The young writer if he is worth his salt, he wants to be the old guy." (305–6)

In addition to all Forrest cites above, Faulkner's use of the principles of montage also informs Forrest's ability to "break open" a sentence and to create his jazz narratives.

In "The Montage Element in Faulkner's Fiction," Bruce Kawin willingly concedes that Faulkner probably used the principles of montage unknowingly. I similarly concede that Forrest was probably unaware of how film's principles informed his narratives.[8] But as Kawin notes, elements of montage were inevitably attractive to modernist writers not only because of film's relationship to modernity but because montage represents the central anxiety of modernism—the belief "that the old, harmonious world lay busted into fragments" (106). And while modernism did not search for tangible connections to restore these fragments to wholeness, it did search for a "conceptual space in which the fragments might cohere" (106). Faulkner was especially attracted to montage and its principles of juxtaposition, Kawin argues, because, among other things, it allowed for oxymorons, dynamic unresolution, rapid shifts in time and space, a continuous present, a dominant visual sense and photographic imagery, multiple narration, and a means of dealing with the ineffable (109, 124). Montage is especially useful for the latter, since "[w]hen description A fails, and description B fails, one can hope that their juxtaposition will point toward C, the thing itself" (124).

In all of Forrest's fiction, but especially in *There Is a Tree* and *Two Wings,* the ineffable plays a crucial thematic role. That he cannot find the words to express his agony and his confusion is a large part of what frustrates Nathaniel in *There Is a Tree.* Thus, his narrating consciousness adopts a visual sensibility and uses principles of juxtaposition to attempt to point to that which he cannot find words to express. The result is the jumbled syntax that informs the narrative and alienates the reader, but which is necessary to achieve the linguistic equivalent of experiences and emotions that are equally inconceivable and ineffable. Take the following passage from *There Is a Tree,* for example:

> Lady day's echo entering, revealing, telling, an instrument working out the burden of hypodermic death . . . strange . . . strange fruit and a long-denied ways from home. . . . or was it a caesarean creation in the furnace? or rebirth and why me/us . . . ? lady: you are my rock . . . prophetess . . . celebrant on ash-faced street ain't no such thing as a shelter unshaken, or a crib untouched by raping death potent only its capacity to crumble, as we are thrown out of the world into the garbage can of the world, after the best is taken, sold, branded, taking our names along with our eyes, tongue, eyeteeth; hair; music; mothers; sisters; and sold for blood merchandise . . . brooding down billie's strange fruit back back back, before it there in the basement/bar, as the needle resurrected her searching, tormented echo— echoing the blood upon the ocean of constant middle passage. . . . (19)

This excerpted passage is one of the best examples of montage as used in Forrest's fiction. The relationship between the similar and dissimilar juxtaposed shots, which fade in and out of the narration, is linked only through the allusions Forrest seeks to present as representations of that which he is otherwise unable to articulate. But these connections are logically visible only after the source of the allusion is established. Just before the passage opens, Jamestown, Nathaniel's mentor of sorts, recalls the time he was accused of raping a woman (a crime that almost always resulted in lynching) when he was "potent only in [his] capacity to crumble." Ironically, he is impotent because he has not yet recovered from a previous racist incident in which he was held under water until he nearly drowned. As this racial prejudice on an individual level fades out, racial prejudice, which invokes the Middle Passage, on a grander scale, fades in.

The narrating consciousness is listening to or contemplating Billie Holiday's "Strange Fruit," which is a song about the lynching of black men in the South. The song and the experience puts Jamestown in the mind of struggles, first his own and, eventually, those of the race. The idea of lynched black bodies hanging from trees in full bloom causes Jamestown to shiver and to wonder why the African American, a cesarean creation "birthed in the furnace of slavery," is denied the natural process of blooming. He thinks first of the cruelty of the slave trade, where the best slaves are taken first, and all others are parceled out into the "garbage can of the world." This discarding of innocent souls again leads him to the Middle Passage, where humans were thrown out to sea because they were viewed simply as excess cargo. Without the benefit of montage and symbolism, Forrest would be unable to express the fullness of the feelings of oppression and discrimination Jamestown experiences both as an individual and as an African American. He cannot articulate description C, so he juxtaposes images and emotions as descriptions A and B in hopes of making C more expressive.

As one of the best examples of how Forrest's narrative structure enacts the act it is narrating, the structure of this passage adopts the intensity of violence it describes. Sentences end abruptly; the punctuation respects no rules of traditional mechanics; the subjects of sentences change with rapid violence. In other words, the sentence structure lacks the fluidity that Jamestown lacks. The passage also reflects the tension Jamestown must feel and shows how Forrest turns words into clashes of sensory images. We feel, we imagine, we experience the acts that cannot be narrated through realist description and must thus be expressed through images and symbols. Sweetie Reed in *Two Wings* and Joubert Jones in *Divine Days* encounter similar problems of linguistic limitation, though to a degree far less stifling than Nathaniel and Jamestown experience in *There Is a Tree*. But like Nathaniel and Jamestown, Sweetie and Joubert adopt principles of montage to accommodate their storytelling and to express symbolically that which they struggle to articulate verbally.

This use of montage and other modernist literary techniques, however, creates a distance between the reader and the text that is sometimes insurmountable for the less ardent reader. Even as he claims that his ideal audience consists of any reader who enjoys serious literature, Forrest must have known how alienating his approach to narrative would be to readers and critics alike. He repeatedly referred to and seriously considered himself as "race man." Thus, his alienation from more popular literary movements and his isolation as an African American writer had to be all the more poignant. In his choice to embrace a Faulknerian style, Forrest also embraced an accompanying degree of alienation and critical neglect.[9] I contend, however, that assessments of Forrest's fiction that cannot move beyond his literary style to appreciate both his skillful use of African American culture and folk traditions to investigate African American life and his invocation of other traditions to posit African American experiences in the context of world traditions miss the very essence of his literary art—which is to celebrate and to explore African American life and culture. At least part of what I hope to achieve in the chapters that follow is, thus, to make clear the cultural connections that (re)establish Forrest's affinity with African American life and its literary tradition.

In addition to taking a culturalist approach to readings of the novels, one of the ways to achieve this is to show Forrest's relationship to other select African American modernist writers with whom he is frequently associated and who make significant modifications to traditional modernism. Among these authors is Jean Toomer, whose *Cane* Forrest describes as the "finest novel to come out of the Harlem Renaissance" (*Furious Voice*, 24). In his attempt to filter "through cycles of baseness and refinement within Negro culture" (24), Toomer adopts modernism's form for a number of reasons. First, he needed a form that could accommodate his mixture of prose and poems and would allow him to place the varied sketches in one collection. Second, modernism encouraged acknowledgment of the complexity of African American life. Thus, it complicated racial categories, which was most important to Toomer, who saw himself as belonging only to the American race and not to any specific ethnic category.[10] Finally, he was attracted to modernism because it helped to facilitate his new vision of life, which would acknowledge the past but which sought to move forward in a fragmented world because of the inevitability of change. More important here, however, than his adoption of modernism as form is his critique of it.[11]

By invoking African American life and rural folk culture, Toomer is able both to show the devastating effects of slavery and modernity on the contemporary African American and to highlight the richness of black culture modernists were so attracted to, in part because of its alleged "primitivism." By using modernism as the form through which to critique modernity and to present this folk culture that modernity was allegedly destroying, Toomer also shows how modernism ultimately assumes the objectifying posture of modernity. As Henry L. Gates Jr. suggests in his reading of *Cane*[12] and Catherine Gunther Kodat notes in her interpretation of Gates,

> Toomer explodes notions of privileged consciousness by deploying a privileged voice [. . . .] That [he] accomplishes this through a recognizably African American idiom provides the political point that distinguishes *Cane* among modernist works; Toomer shows how *Cane*'s modernist autonomy is rooted in, and indebted to, repressive social power structures. (Kodat, "To 'Flash White Light . . . ,'" 5)

Cane thus manipulates its modernist aesthetic to perform a self-critique of the dialectic between liberation and domination. And it is through this critique and this struggle that Toomer makes clear the tension inherent in modernist art and its tendency to enact the forces it critiques.

But even in its recognition of this problem of modernism, at different points *Cane* enacts the terms of its modernist social critique and struggles to find an aesthetic approach through which to articulate the history of exploitation and domination it is trying to represent without enacting that same domination in terms of its aesthetics. The difficulty, as exhibited in a number of *Cane*'s sketches, has to do with finding a position from which to speak. The form that is most representative of the characters' broken lives—modernism—will not relent in its tendency to exact what Kodat calls the violence of aesthetic dominance where the aesthetics take over the text. Arguably, Toomer's choice to use folk culture overtly and to use black life as a driving theme attempts to reject the modernist mandate to dominate his subject and, instead, to critique high modernism even as he acknowledges and uses its power and form. That he is somewhat successful is evidenced in the ultimate freedom he gives the characters in his longer sketches. Paul, Avey, and Kabnis, rather than imposing their will (or their aesthetics) on their foils, allow others simply *to be*.

Forrest makes a similar attempt to equalize nature and culture with form in his fiction, which fails in *There Is a Tree* and is perhaps most successful in *Divine Days*. Even in its use of African American folk culture and a distinctly African American theme of oppression and suffering, *There Is a Tree* leaves the reader feeling more dominated and oppressed than liberated. *Divine Days,* however, uses black life and survival so heavily as a theme that culture, not aesthetics, takes center stage. As an aspiring artist and the novel's central consciousness, Joubert, in fact, makes it clear how difficult it is to articulate the complexity of black life and folk culture through traditional forms and aesthetics, which ignore folk culture. His desire is to write a play that captures the essence of two of Forest County's most complex characters—the trickster Ford, who appears throughout the Forest County Sagas, and his biggest rival, Sugar-Groove, who makes his first appearance in *Divine Days*. Throughout the novel, Joubert seeks ways to dramatize the two men's lives, and his struggle mirrors Forrest's and other authors' difficulty in finding an aesthetic approach that adequately captures African American life and culture. But unlike *There Is a Tree,* where Nathaniel is in too much pain to order his thoughts and, subsequently, to avoid oppressing and alienating the reader, *Divine Days* is structured as a jazzlike rendering of Joubert's journal entries and is much more inviting to the reader.

In the sense that it rejects the omniscience of realism and has the narrator involved in the narrative situation, *Divine Days* can be likened especially to Zora Neale Hurston's *Their Eyes Were Watching God,* among other modernist texts. This use of an intradiegetic narrator, one in which the narrator is involved in the narrative situation, helps to dissolve the barrier between the reader and the narrative. It also helps create what Philip Goldstein describes as *critical realism* or *black modernism* in his reading of *Their Eyes*. Blending realism and modernism, Hurston's text, Goldstein argues, adopts many of the rhetorical devices of modernism and, to some degree, fosters modernist absurdity, but it still engages social life and historical reality. While Goldstein sees this as one of the novel's supreme achievements (since, despite being a modernist text, it avoids the withdrawal from social and historical reality which Georg Lukacs viewed as inherent to modernist texts), Brian Carr and Tova Cooper suggest that Hurston's achievement as a modernist writer rests in her ability to exploit a critical misrecognition within modernism (commodification of the marginal) and her corresponding willingness to undercut "modernism's elite and heroic self-fashioning" (303). In doing so, she shows modernism's critical limit and modifies it by participating in modernism's internal critique, "but only to the extent that [she] revises modernism's most routine self-fashioning as willfully non-complicit" (305). As I have suggested earlier, both Toomer and Faulkner (particularly in his racially driven texts) similarly highlight modernism's critical limit. Race, then, it would seem, is one of the critical factors that encourages the internal critique of modernism.

The relationship of the Harlem Renaissance and modernism is especially telling in this regard. As Carr and Cooper note,

> While the self-fashioned modernists aspired to exist outside of commodified circuits, Harlem Renaissance writers, because of the commodification of African-American bodies and cultural forms persisting as slavery's legacy, were acutely aware of the inevitable cooptation of their self-representations within a system of capitalist exchange and racialized patronage. (288)

Thus, modernism as rendered by African American and other ethnic authors (and some authors whose texts are driven by highly racialized situations) is inevitably and necessarily modified to accommodate these authors' sociopolitical and aesthetic agendas. In this regard, Forrest is no different. He adopts techniques from modernism's form, but he invokes pertinent African American experiences to authenticate its content. After making its internal critique, this invocation helps move modernism beyond its critical limit.

Like a number of the Harlem Renaissance artists, Ralph Ellison could see the relationship between modernism and black aesthetics and culture, particularly jazz. And it is from Ellison that Forrest learns, among other things, to use black music, especially jazz, as an aesthetic through which to reshape modernism. Jazz is a distinctly modernist art form, particularly its obsession with "making it new." Yet it draws from a largely black American experience. Thus, it allowed Ellison, and later Forrest, to balance his attraction to modernism's principles of high literary art with his awareness of the many aesthetic possibilities of jazz. Like the juxtaposition characteristic of montage, swing and the improvisational techniques of riffing and voicing offered the would-be modernist writer an alternative aesthetic through which to express the ineffable. Additionally, for Forrest, "the improvisational genius of jazz" was the metaphor that best captured the "the cultural attribute of black Americans to take what is left over, or conversely, given to them [. . .] and make it work for them, as a source of personal or group survival" (Forrest, *Furious Voice*, 23). Thus, a jazz narrative—which by definition would be highly innovative, experimental, and improvisational—would be the functional equivalent of a modernist one but would have the added benefit of signifying upon rather than distancing itself from black culture.

In many ways, modernism and black folk culture have always been related, since the latter emerged in large part in response to forces similar to those modernism critiqued and claimed to abhor. Berndt Ostendorf suggests the following of Ellison's awareness of the survivalist tendencies of black folk culture and its relationship to modernism:

> Whereas Eliot and Joyce achieved poetic complexity by using myth as a structural scaffolding and as a way of ordering the "chaos of modern history," Ellison mockingly invites the country cousin of myth, black folklore, into the salon of Modernist intertextuality. For him the black vernacular holds a store of repressed values that need to be made conscious through literacy. (109)

Though Ostendorf is clearly referring to Ellison, the statement could as easily and accurately reference Forrest and his fiction. For Ellison and Forrest alike, the therapy modernism seeks to offer for the fragmentation caused by modernity is simply an aesthetic attempt to do through narrative what black folk culture—black religion, signifying, masking—had done earlier as a means of practical survival, with black music—jazz, the spirituals, gospel, and the blues—as its aesthetic equivalent. Thus, for many African American authors, making these traditions literate has its own survivalist tendencies. And modernism's attempt to use literature to construct new ways of being that might offer alternatives to a failing system by using exploratory language and narrative forms offered authors such as Toomer, Hurston, Ellison, and Forrest the freedom to investigate racialized identities and corresponding techniques that might be useful in helping their characters survive the highly charged racial experiences they encounter. But, again, the problems inherent to modernism, which are especially heightened for African American authors, plague these modernist narratives. Oftentimes, the reading audience is so consumed with the authors' literary technique that the form covers the narratives' rich cultural tradition; it isolates and alienates the reader and makes the narratives prone to misunderstanding.[13] Yet for authors who saw writing as a means of participating in "high art" and who were similarly committed to writing what they considered "serious literature," a modified version of modernism, one which overtly invoked black cultural traditions, was a compromise that allowed them to be inspired as artists by modernism but also to draw from black folk culture and its traditions.

Few authors achieve this balance of simultaneously critiquing modernism and using it to investigate distinctly black experiences with greater success than Forrest's former editor and contemporary Toni Morrison, who completed her master's thesis on the modernist writers William Faulkner and Virginia Woolf. As her work on Faulkner and Woolf indicates, Morrison is well aware of what modernists were doing in their writing, and she adopts any number of these techniques in her own narratives. But what is of special interest here is her critique of modernity in *Beloved* and her adoption of modernism as a form to do so. Kodat astutely observes:

> In writing *Beloved*, Morrison was faced with a choice: to creatively deploy a "realist" narrative discourse so that its complicity with racial terror became clear, or to enter into a dialogue with "psychological" modernism [. . .] by exploring the ways in which modernism simultaneously inscribes and unmasks its complicity in social justice. In fact, Morrison does both: revising realism through *Beloved*'s content (especially through the figure of Schoolteacher, the sadistic scientific racist) and modernism in its technique and form. ("A Postmodern," 193)

That her attempt to combine realism (as primarily historical) and modernism (as primarily aesthetic and ahistorical) is successful is a significant literary achievement, one that is facilitated by the novel's content. The driving force of the narrative, a mother's choice to kill her child rather than allow the child to be returned to slavery, simply cannot be consumed by an aesthetic form. Rather, Beloved's resistance to commodification and her desire for *being* all but justify the novel's strategies of indirection, its ruptures in narrative, and its difficult syntax.

But, as Kodat indicates, the novel critiques modernism even as it uses its form. Among the most significant parts of this critique is of modernism's and modernity's failure to acknowledge the influence of black *being* in any meaningful way. Thus, both *Beloved* as novel and Beloved as character offer

> a historical perspective on the importance of African-American *forms* in the emergence of American literary modernism. ("Forms" here has a double charge, indicating both those African-American aesthetic practices that have influenced American modernism, and the bodies of African-American themselves, so often invoked as characters or symbols in modernist works). (184)

That Morrison is purposeful in her critique of modernity and modernism in *Beloved* is made clear in her collection of essays *Playing in the Dark,* where she notes the significance of slavery and an *Africanist* presence to the initiation of modernity. Beloved, then, can be read as an incarnation of the *Africanist* presence that is at the center of modernity and modernism but has been denied *being* and form.

While Forrest is not as overt as Morrison in his critique of modernism and modernity in *Two Wings,* he similarly uses an interpretation of the neoslave narrative[14] as a form through which to (re)present slave history through the eyes of Sweetie Reed, who is only a few years removed from slavery. The novel opens with Nathaniel responding to Sweetie's summons to act as the amanuensis who will write their family's history onto *legal* pads. Adopting modernism as its form, Sweetie's narrative is "[t]old in slivers of recollection, [using] voices-within-voices, pauses for enquiry and recapitulation, [with] one time frame held in abeyance in order to complete the events of another (Lee, 111). But even as the narrative adopts modernist tendencies, it is critical of modernism's flight from history into myth. Like Morrison, who also uses modernism's literary techniques to recover lost history despite its traditional flight from history, Forrest adopts the form in part to critique it.

Despite its claimed disassociation from modernity, in truth, modernism too often mirrors its nemesis in its desire to forget. And while Sweetie suppresses the horror of her experiences as the daughter of a former slave who chose to stay in the house with his master rather than live with his family even after slavery had ended and who, later, contracted her to be married at fifteen to a fifty-five-year-old judge who saw her only as a replacement for her mother, whom she had seen be brutally raped and killed by patrollers, she temporarily "forgets" history as a means of surviving. But she knows how important it is for her to tell her story from memory and then to have it written down, instead of allowing it to remain buried and forgotten. Failing to remember and then to tell her story would have been tantamount to modernity's and modernism's attempt to escape history in an effort to naturalize it. Under such circumstances, the negative experiences she is forced to overcome would simply be par for the course based purely on her existence as a black woman. But by simultaneously using modernism's form and critiquing its ideology, the narrative encourages history to acknowledge its role in Sweetie's suffering and in her being doubly negated by race and gender. Thus, central to the narrative is her insistence that (her)story, too, is written down and given its rightful place in history.

As is the case with Sweetie in *Two Wings,* literary modernism as Forrest most often interprets it makes room for history and attempts to avoid enacting the domination it critiques. Thus, throughout his fiction he embraces select modernist tendencies and modifies others, depending on their sociological and political implications. While these modernist narrative situations oftentimes leave his novels unread or misunderstood, modernism is one of the few literary forms that can accommodate the complexity of African American life as Forrest saw it—its failings and its fragmentation, its tragedies and its triumphs. But modernism alone is not enough to facilitate his investigations. The cultural underpinnings that serve as springboards for his novels, when coupled with modernism, help Forrest achieve that which he wanted most—to be a writer who could sing in the language of African American cultural, oral, and vernacular traditions.

chapter two

To Survival and Beyond: The Journey Motif and Transcendence in *There Is a Tree More Ancient Than Eden*

From Odysseus to Stephen Dedalus to the Invisible Man, major characters from a variety of world literature traditions have embarked on journeys that allow readers to experience these characters' cultures, their struggles, their failures, and their triumphs. Leon Forrest's *There Is a Tree More Ancient Than Eden* adds Nathaniel Witherspoon to this list as he journeys through significant moments in African American history and through cultural traditions that offer him ways to negotiate the contemporary moment. As he sends Nathaniel on an odyssey of self-identification and definition, Forrest creates a seamless juxtaposition of the personal, the communal, the historical, and the spiritual experiences the African American has endured and transcended over the years, and he investigates crucial distinctions between survivalist and oppressive forces of African American culture. The novel, then, articulates the experiences of this journey through a narrator as the centralized African American consciousness (but focalized through Nathaniel), rather than through Nathaniel as a character. This innovation of articulation is arguably one of the novel's greatest artistic accomplishments, but it is, conversely, the very thing that limits its easy comprehension.

In the sense that it encourages Nathaniel to consider the historical and contemporary events that create his agony (and that of the African American experience his life represents) and exposes him to sustaining cultural traditions, the journey offers an impressionistic portrayal of certain aspects of the black experience that otherwise would not likely be rendered as effectively. Ultimately, after engaging any number of black cultural traditions on his dream journey, Nathaniel is endowed with the power to create a synthesis between the past and the present and between his personal life and the African American's communal experience of oppression as he seeks to create for himself and his representative group a viable identity. Accordingly, full appreciation of the novel and the author's intent is heightened significantly by reading the novel through the journey motif Forrest uses, first, to investigate the historical and cultural politics that inevitably shape contemporary African American identity and, second, to explore ways for Nathaniel (and the African American experience he represents) to move beyond the psychological fragmentation cultural displacement causes to the point of transcendence or survival of his spiritual agony. One of the most successful approaches to this transcendence, the journey motif reveals, is immersion into sustaining black (African American, African, and diasporic African) cultural traditions.

Thus, Nathaniel's journey and *There Is a Tree More Ancient Than Eden* begin the Forest County (the author's fictional locale which is suggestive of Chicago) Sagas and initiate Forrest's examination of the varied aspects of the African American self, particularly as such experiences relate to loss and to motherlessness. Experiencing the agony of a motherless child, Nathaniel is the editor of his life and of his family's history. His attempts to process fragments of biographical, sociological, and emotional information about his relatives, his ancestors, historical figures, and, finally, himself in order to cope with his mother's death serve as the unconventional plot of the novel. Because his mother's death also involves a break in his link to his ancestral history, he must find a way to establish his own connection to his history and to the past. Highly symbolic of the rootlessness experienced by an enslaved people removed from their native land and culture, Nathaniel experiences a sense of loss that can be rectified only by recovering and examining the past, particularly as it relates to the historical and cultural politics that now inform the present.

As he sits in the back of a Cadillac with Aunty Breedlove en route to his mother's funeral, Nathaniel, through the process of (re)memory, explores the inner conflicts that have denied his sense of wholeness. In the first section of the novel, aptly titled "The Lives," he begins to sort out the list of characters that have some bearing on his life. These biographical sketches include his family members as well as historical figures such as Louis Armstrong, Frederick Douglass, Harriet Tubman, and Abraham Lincoln, each of whom is culturally and personally significant to Nathaniel. He thinks of, among others, his Uncle Dupont, a New Orleans Creole who passes for white when it is convenient for him; his mentor, Jamestown Fishbond, whose ideology and ability to transform himself in order to survive a situation encourage him to reject assimilation for all out revolution; and, his grandfather, Jericho Witherspoon, the first Negro judge in Forest County, who is self-educated and who seeks to impose on Nathaniel his ideas of working within the limitations of American democracy as well as his contention that the African American should celebrate his struggle since it birthed his greatness. What each of these memories has in common is that they are responses to highly racialized existences. Part of what Nathaniel must do by the novel's end is decipher for himself which response is best for him and his condition.

In "The Nightmare" and "The Dream," Forrest reinforces the themes introduced in the first section, especially the motherless child motif, as Nathaniel attempts to resolve his inner conflicts. As he rides down the streets of Forest County, still in his mother's funeral procession, he imagines that his journey to her final resting place is the African's journey through the Middle Passage and, later, the African American's journey through the Underground Railroad. Jamestown's experiences of racial discrimination become Nathaniel's as he recalls times when Jamestown was rejected for his blackness and for being true to himself. Though he is unable to articulate it fully, Nathaniel's fear is, at least in part, that without his mother to guide him, he will "get lost on his own camping ground" and will hence be unable to live up to the standard of personal racial integrity Jamestown has set for him. He thinks over and over again of the lines from the spiritual "Jesus told me the world would hate me if he changed my name" until, finally, he emerges from his nightmare and drifts into a dream that involves Jamestown and Jericho. In a manner reminiscent of the elders and Scooter in Albert Murray's *Train Whistle Guitar*, which Forrest taught at varying points in his career, the two men argue about what information to pass on to Nathaniel and to the black community at large. While Jericho argues that suffering is universal and that it facilitates creativity, Jamestown suggests that the African American's struggle is somewhat unique and that they must teach Nathaniel to transform it to a much greater degree than they teach him to celebrate overcoming it.

The central action in "The Vision," a crucifixion/lynching/dismemberment ritual, revolves around Billie Holiday's "Strange Fruit," which details the lynching of black men. Particularly significant in this section is the resurrection of the lynched body, which occurs at the section's end. Despite being crucified, lynched, and dismembered, the unnamed man achieves wholeness again after angels collect his bones in a sackcloth and release him to the world, where he flies. Thus, by the end of the section, as he moves toward "Wakefulness," Nathaniel has achieved his own vision of how to cope with the agony of both his mother's death and his racialized existence. In the novel's final section, Nathaniel, having acquired a sense of identity for himself, is persuaded to emerge from underneath the bed, where he has been hiding in the midst of his confusion. Though he appears to have achieved some sense of self-identity, his journey toward reconciliation of the past and the present and their effect on the future continues.

In the 1988 edition of the novel, Forrest appended a section entitled "Transformation" in the form of an "Epistle of Sweetie Reed." It is a letter to President Lyndon B. Johnson dated May 7, 1967, and is intended to warn the president of the world evils to come, including the election of Richard Nixon and the assassination of Martin Luther King Jr. In relation to the original sections, "Transformation" contrasts Nathaniel's rootlessness to Sweetie Reed's wisdom. As the one-hundred-year-old Sweetie Reed is still alive at the novel's close, Nathaniel has found his link to the past in all her wisdom, and, in turn, his hope for a better future. Rev. Pompey c.j. Browne's commemorative eulogy of Martin Luther King Jr. upon the twelve-year anniversary of his death, which is also appended in the section as a sermon titled "Oh Jeremiah of the Dreamers," reflects the new frustration the African American feels now that he has survived Jim Crow only to find himself still marginalized. His agony is no longer focused on his being enslaved or legally disenfranchised and denied equal rights; instead, it emerges out of his disappointment of the slow or nonexistent progress that followed the civil rights and black nationalism movements. Though the world seemed to have changed immensely in the years that passed between Nathaniel's initial outcry upon his mother's death and the occasion of Pompey's address, in so many ways, the narration suggests, it had not changed at all.

Interestingly, Ralph Ellison intimates the significance of this reality of the changing same and Forrest's willingness to fictionalize it in Ellison's preface to the first edition of *There Is a Tree More Ancient Than Eden*. He notes: "[. . .] rather than confining his efforts to projecting a neat, minor slice of life, [Forrest] seems to assume that, whether we like it or not, the day-to-day, here-and-now life of American society is the only life we have to live, and that, as such, it is the writer's challenge and his task" (n. pag.) Frequently referred to as a literary heir of his mentor and friend, Forrest assumes the posture of Ellison and his belief that fiction is capable of capturing both the beauty and the horror of American society. Much like Ellison's Invisible Man, Nathaniel seeks to transcend the agony that plagues his life as a culturally displaced and disillusioned African American male. Since his life in American society is the only life Nathaniel has to live, Forrest sends his nontraditional protagonist on a journey that seeks to reconcile the past with the present and to heal, at least to the point of survival, Nathaniel's psychological and emotional scars.

First published in 1973, *There Is a Tree More Ancient Than Eden* speaks to, among other things, the uncertainty of the predicament of the modern man both in spite of and in the face of his seeming acculturation into contemporary American society. Hundreds of years after the first slaves arrived in the Americas, the *African American Genesis Saga*,[1] as Forrest termed it, continued to deny the African American self-definition. Accordingly, Forrest begins Nathaniel's journey with America's denial of self-definition to the African American, beginning with the onset of slavery. The novel's title is, in fact, the author's first attempt to call attention to slavery as a metaphor for the "Original Sin." But the title had so many other implications that he did not fully pursue its metaphorical possibilities until later.[2]

In an interview with John Cawelti at the University of Kentucky, Forrest admits that he had originally titled his first novel *Wakefulness*. At Toni Morrison's prompting (she was his editor at the time), he decided to title the novel *There Is a Tree More Ancient Than Eden*. He surmises:

> I can do a pretty good title as a newspaper man and was nifty at headlines for other peoples' stories, but the title of my own book was different. I suggested "Deep Rivers of the Soul." At one point we [he and Morrison] were calling it "Of Eden and Thebes." Eventually Morrison came up with the idea of *There Is a Tree More Ancient Than Eden*. I liked it very much. It seemed close to a Negro spiritual. For her, it may also have implied some African themes. (Forrest and Cawelti, 289)

Certainly at least one of these African themes involved the intimation that before slavery, Africans, as progenitors of civilization, were self-defined. That Nathaniel, as a descendant of slaves, now has to embark on a journey of self-identification suggests that his fragmented identity is directly related to the imposition of the West on both the native and the diasporic African. But as we will see later, the diasporic African is not completely disconnected from his African roots or black African cultural traditions, and he is often able to access the power of the African ancestors to survive racialized experiences.

The title phrase appears only once in the novel (though it makes recurring appearances in *Divine Days*), in a dream passage in which Nathaniel watches death pursue his mother. Like the novel, the passage is heavily layered with images of archetypal, historical, and personal ramifications as Nathaniel's dream fuses death's pursuit of the living, Satan's entry into Eden, and a master's pursuit of his runaway slaves:

> And who saw the deadly fingers, within the gloved hands of the pale rider, who swooped up into the very tops of the leaf-lost, blood-dripping, branch-wild, scarecrow ancient tree [. . .] (yet the land unconscious of the downing down and the flaking, and the yelping hound dogs) as the brooding black madonna [called Moses with the man's shoes] sat under the tree. . . . Waited under that tree that looked like a bleeding scarecrow while the rider, curled about the tree from its roots to its leafless tops, looking like the twisted vertebrae of a snake with its blood-red rose dripping from his lapel into the snow-laden *tree more ancient than Eden.* (Forrest, *There Is a Tree,* 83–84; emphasis mine)

Alluding to the trials of the black madonna called Moses being pursued by hound dogs, suggestive of Harriet Tubman and the Underground Railroad, Forrest strengthens his metaphor by declaring that the pale rider, whose blood drips into the *tree more ancient than Eden,* resembles a snake. The slave master in pursuit of his runaway slave becomes Satan or the serpent personified, reinforcing the earlier reference to slavery as the "Original Sin" in the narrative sketch of Abraham Lincoln in the opening section of the novel:

> **Abraham Lincoln**; 1809–1865. The Father upon whose shaky, shawled shoulders the engulfing, awesome burden of the *Original Sin* fell, whose vacillation and compromise were really a reflection of the psychic split of the Republic and was only equaled by his bald-eagle steadfastness and undying faith that by pursuing the role of healer and savior of the nation's higher dream of itself, he could avoid the hysterical histrionics of body-soul slave-marketing merchandizing-foundation upon which the dung-tarred Soul of the Nation hung/rocked like a sweeping pendulum—yet compromise itself had vaulted him into the seat of father over a house divided. (35; emphasis mine)

Here, and throughout each of the novels, Forrest argues that for the African American, history, group consciousness, and group memory begin with the saga of slavery, even as his pre-American identity predates it.

Birthed out of this peculiar institution, the African American recognizes his patrimony as the Original Sin. And Lincoln's attempt to rectify this sin and to pursue the "other side" of the truth of the Founding Fathers' dream for the nation renders him as little more than father of a house divided. His relevance to Nathaniel and to the contemporary African American, as Forrest sees it, is his ambiguous role as savior of the people and as the president of freedom. The challenge for the contemporary African American now becomes to rediscover the "other side" of history—slavery and the *African American Genesis Saga*—and its impact upon the souls of the ancestor and his heirs. And the best way to achieve this end and to transcend the agony that ensues is by embarking on a journey of recovery, participating in a version of what Robert Stepto terms the *immersion narrative* whereby Nathaniel engages history.

Though Stepto's narrative patterns of ascent and immersion typically refer to early narrative times in literary history—the classic ascent narrative usually involves an enslaved figure, for example—the immersion narrative is no less appropriate for Forrest's 1970s text. According to Stepto:

> [. . .] the immersion narrative is fundamentally an expression of a ritualized journey into a symbolic South, in which the protagonist seeks those aspects of tribal literacy that ameliorate, if not obliterate, the conditions imposed by solitude. The conventional immersion narrative ends almost paradoxically, with the questing figure located in or near the narrative's most oppressive social structure but free in the sense that he has gained or regained sufficient tribal literacy to assume the mantle of an articulate kinsman. (167)

Such is the case with Nathaniel. His mother's death, which represents his most intimate connection to the past, initiates his alienation and solitude. He hides underneath the bed and will not emerge until the novel's end, when he has completed his journey to a symbolic South facilitated by ancestral figures—his aunt Hattie Breedlove, Jamestown Fishbond, and his grandfather Jericho. He is still, indeed, present in an oppressive social structure (the alienation and cultural fragmentation common to the African American), but he has gained, through the process of (re)memory, sufficient tribal literacy to become an articulate kinsman and to finally emerge from underneath the bed where he is hiding.

Interestingly, Nathaniel is somewhat unaware that he is actually embarking on a journey toward self-definition. He is simply mourning the death of his mother and imagining how he will cope with such a great (and symbolic) loss. This unawareness, however, makes his odyssey no less effective. In fact, it is perhaps to his advantage, for discovery is virtually impossible when one actually seeks it. Discovery, in its purest sense, simply happens. So Nathaniel merely resorts to that which comes most naturally to him; he retreats to his place of comfort as a child and dreams. He thinks back to a time when he imagines he *is* Sugar Ray Robinson punching the bag his father purchased for him, or when he *is* Adlai Ewing Stevenson writing beautiful sentences while singing in Kenney's (of the Ink Spots) soprano voice, or even when he is allowing his soprano to rise and fall between his Nat King Cole alto sound and his Paul Robeson baritone. And this act of remembering initiates Nathaniel's journey.

As important as the act of remembering to Nathaniel's quest is memory's interaction with history. For Forrest, remembered history is an equivalent of the past, and since the past is ever alive and instructive in the present, the wandering soul must be aware of his past if he is to reconcile his fractured psyche and achieve a sense of identity. Thus, the impact of history-as-memoir upon the contemporary experience is in the foreground. Significantly, Forrest does not privilege history over memory but, rather, implies the interconnectedness of the two. Similarly, Robert O'Meally and Genevieve Fabre, in *History and Memory in African American Culture,* acknowledge that there must be interplay between history and memory if there is to be an authentic representation of reality. History, then, must be inclusive of those "black and unknown bards" or "historians without portfolio, who inscribed their world with landmarks made significant because men and women remembered them so complexly and so well that somehow the traces of their memory survived to become history" (8). Nevertheless, history is sometimes constructed in opposition to memory, and in such cases, history-as-memoir must be recovered before self-definition can occur. And Nathaniel's recollections of his personal experiences and the passed-down remembered experiences of others reflect such inclusion.

As Melvin Dixon contends in "Black Writers' Use of Memory," the conflict for black writers trying to differentiate between history and memory "is crucial, for it addresses the simple issue of control of the past as well as proper transmission of the past" (22):

> If history as story promotes narrative, then memory, which is often expressed episodically and through visceral imagery independent of chronology, very much like a dream, reveals itself as metaphor. The

tension between history and memory then can also be expressed as a
tension between narrative and metaphor. (22–23)

Nathaniel's varied experiences throughout *There Is a Tree* serve as the metaphor that seeks to dissolve the tension between the past and the present and between history and memory. He must learn to negotiate this tension, lest he succumb to failure like his father, Arthur, who, "rather than 'becoming anything' became nothing" (Forrest, *There Is a Tree*, 4), since he could not be everything. And it is this tragic flaw that Nathaniel must avoid. He cannot remain trapped in the unproductive liminal space between the past and the present moment. And he does not. Instead, he journeys through both familial and communal African American history and memory, considering the historical ramifications of issues of slavery, of racism and lynchings, of martyrdom, of opposing race ideologies, and of religion, without being overwhelmed by them.

Through Nathaniel's memory, we learn fragments of his family's history:

> Myself—*remembering* those parties where uncles and aunts and cousins as well, whose several ancestors had made and developed a small fortune on special white lightning [*sic*] bleaching creme, and whose grandparents had owned and sold slaves and educated all of the children—except Uncle DuPont who was my father's fifth cousin and mother's second cousin—at the Sorbonne, from monies accruing from those two self-serving enterprises; all of whom hated my father for remaining a fourth cook. . . . (4; emphasis mine)

His fair-skinned family is so obsessed with whiteness that they developed a skin bleaching cream, and since his great-grandparents had owned and sold slaves and educated the children, we can safely assume that one of the Witherspoon forefathers was white. In this sense, Nathaniel's family becomes, among other things, Forrest's reminder of the exploitation of black women and the miscegenation that was so prevalent during slavery. Though *miscegenation* as a term did not have come into being until 1863 (primarily to deal with the interracial sexual mixing that was bound to be more prevalent, Americans feared, if slavery was abolished), miscegenation as an act existed long before the emancipation. Throughout slavery, black women were exploited sexually and forced to bear their masters' children. The result was the creation of fair-skinned children, who were often privileged by their masters at an early age and later educated by them because of this biological relationship and their subsequent skin color. The more race mixing or miscegenation took place, the more important skin color became to the Negro—so important that darker-skinned members of a majority fair-skinned family were often shunned.

Such is the case with Jamestown Fishbond, one of the characters who has the greatest influence on Nathaniel and whose most visible identifying mark is his "unusual, deep, abiding blackness" in a community of near mulattos. And Forrest uses memory to broach the subject of color in the novel. Nathaniel muses:

> [O]nce upon a mulatto purity party as uncle dupont called them where my aunts and uncles and cousins sang in french blushing red and glowing in   the candlelight from the dago red wine and jamestown coming to the back door in tears and uncle dupont bellowing in a half-drunk bleary-eyed way . . . moon coon . . . and aunt dupont . . . coming to uncle dupont with a large piece of my birthday cake in her hand and saying you dirty motherless crap-eater you could let the little black bastard in his black wasn't going to rub off on your yellow white passing ass. . . . (53–54)

Uncle DuPont, who passes for white when it is convenient, refuses to have any part of Jamestown for no other reason than his dark skin. Nathaniel's memory of this occasion provides Forrest with an entrance into the influence of the past on the present.

Because these memories of the past and Nathaniel's recollection of them seem to exist concurrently, they exist in the same space. The frequent result is that time defies chronological bounds, and the past and the present merge, especially when memories are organized thematically or paradigmatically rather than chronologically. Such is the case with most of Nathaniel's memories of Jamestown, who has aliases ranging from Jefferson Davis to Nathaniel Forrest and whose "Wanted Dead or Alive" handbill identifies him as one who speaks impeccable French, average Portuguese, and passable German, and who has an IQ that has been listed as high as 175. Nathaniel recalls, however, that like Uncle DuPont, Jamestown has not always been true to himself.

A gifted artist, Jamestown once entered two paintings into an art contest in high school. The one that won first place, Nathaniel recalls, is the one Jamestown "pissed out of his Uncle Tom side," depicting Lincoln with his arm around a Negro slave. The painting that reflected the way Jamestown really saw the world, which he submitted privately, got him suspended from school. Reflecting the chaos and the complexity of the race, "Fear No More the Stench of the Dying Sun, for Heaven is a Reefer and Salvation a Lost Bottle of Wine, Worth a Wee Bit More than Thirty Pieces off the Eagle's Ass," depicts a huge black man with a broken crucifix and a wine bottle. As Nathaniel recalls,

> It was also rumored that the huge man with reddish, thick lips sat on top of a horse . . . and there was a flag with thirteen holes in it, a Bible going up in flames, two crazy clowns, a great bird that looked . . . like an eagle, a golden cord running all through the picture and a crazy-looking black man. . . . (55)

For years, Nathaniel and his friends wondered what the picture that Jamestown had "washed out of himself for love" and that had caused him to get expelled from school looked like. But even if they had seen the painting, as children, they could not have possibly captured the full significance of images such as the flag with thirteen holes (which symbolized the emptiness the thirteen colonies represented for the Negro slave) or the symbolism of the Bible going up in flames and the broken crucifix (which represented the Negro's misplaced faith in religion), or the "Thirty Pieces" (which signified on being "bought off" and on Judas's betrayal of Jesus). However, as an adult, Nathaniel uses memory to access the past and to detect the relationship between how one *sees* the past and how one *survives* in the present. Because Jamestown can see the world both through the rose-colored glasses of Lincoln's embrace and through the jagged glass of "Fear No More," he is a survivor and considered dangerous by whites who seek to contain him. Through his memory of Jamestown, Nathaniel is exposed to the black cultural tradition of masking. In order to survive, both literally and emotionally, Jamestown must be capable of being all things at once. He paints the picture of Lincoln as savior because he knows it will be embraced by those in power, and he is willing to mask his true feelings about the "state of the union" in order to appease them. But in the spirit of masking, he must also subversively reveal, even as he does so secretly, his true feelings about life as a black American. What he offers as a more authentic expression of his feelings is a somewhat carnivalesque depiction of black life which subverts the notion that all Americans have access to the American dream. Nathaniel's engagement with this memory, then, exposes him to masking as an option for survival. But as Jamestown's subsequent actions suggest (he reveals himself as the artist "Fear No More"), masking is not always the most viable option when self-definition is at stake. Instead, Nathaniel's invocation of Jamestown's past teaches him that he must be true to himself if he is to establish a working identity for himself. And thus he moves one step closer to becoming an articulate kinsman.

Another of Jamestown's experiences also offers Nathaniel pertinent exposure to a sustaining black cultural tradition—the belief in the power of the ancestors. In his description of Jamestown's life in "The Lives," Nathaniel fades into and out of Jamestown's personal experience of nearly drowning and the historical experience of the Middle Passage. Describing an occasion where Jamestown was held under water long enough "to smell death," Nathaniel narrates the passage of Jamestown's consciousness, which, at the time of the incident, switches back and forth between his present personal experience and the past collective experience of the Middle Passage:

> The drumming and breast-beating and gasping sounds, and murder-mouthing eruption from down under was perhaps predictable ... even as he [presumably Jamestown] had dreamt of death and tasted its saltiness, even as he had learned no longer to live life by the inborn, contractual terms—even as he hungered, yes willed to not so much die, but rather, not to live, to sleep, but *outwilled* of that will, by a deeper urge from the ancestral bowels of the ship—in that bruised-blood cosmic cataclysm of all calamities; unable to walk, to taste, to see, to hear, to love, to die, and so had taken to water that *other* time, knowing that death was there in a pale-ghost fleshy presence and within a second could choke life off, take him whole, as it were, back back back to where many thousands were carried off [...] even as his bleeding ears recalled to him that a drowning man's shadow's been there all along, watching for him, waiting for him in those memory rooms of floods and periods of famine and days without light, nor substance, without names, stripped of them, yes and the blood in the ears, drum-haunted, amid the stripping of drums and the stripping of tongues.... (20–21)

This passage is rife with historical and ancestral significance. The Middle Passage, which carried an estimated 40 million Africans to Caribbean islands, Europe, and North and South America, left countless other millions dead before their arrival. Thus, their spirits, empowered by their goodness in a previous earthly life, are believed to be left in the water. Aware of the belief and presence of the ancestral spirits, Forrest writes that the "eruption from down under" (indicative of the spirits of the water) was to be expected, since the water is the home of the ocean goddess Yemoja. A deity in the Yoruba tradition, Yemoja has the power to protect or to harm. Similarly, the water of the ancestral spirits has the power to call the living unto itself or to release the individual back into an earthly life. In Jamestown's case, the *joto,* or the ancestor who, as the source of inspiration and protection, outwills his desire to surrender.

As important as the ancestral presence itself is Jamestown's new awareness of it. He knows that death could, within a second, choke his life off and take him to the place where many thousand of his ancestors had been carried off. Perhaps unknowingly, he has adopted the African belief that, at death, the shadow leaves the body and reblends itself with the *joto* (the ancestor) and *selido* (a new being) (Teish, 69). This belief explains why Jamestown sees a drowning man's shadow (he is the drowning man; the ancestor is the shadow) waiting and watching. What he sees and now becomes is the combined *joto* and *selido,* and from that moment on, for Jamestown, "the waters [were] suddenly sacred because of the lessons he had learned there" (Forrest, *There Is a Tree,* 23).

As Jamestown's character suggests, the belief in the power of the waters is not limited to Africans. Like so much of African culture that endured in spite of displacement, the belief in the power of the waters was retained by the peoples of the Diaspora even after their removal from their motherland. In fact, during the last weekend in July at Coney Island, many African Americans participate in a ceremony honoring the ancestors lost in the Atlantic Ocean in the Middle Passage. The ceremony, made in the name of Yemoja, is held in honor of the spirits of the lost ancestors, and it recognizes the power of the water. But more important, it maintains the continuum between the ancestor and the descendant. By embracing an African sensibility, Jamestown highlights the importance of ancestry and maintains the continuum between the African past and the African American present, and Nathaniel taps into this continuum through memory. By visiting Jamestown's site of memory, Nathaniel becomes more aware of the power of diasporic black cultural traditions and the importance of ancestry, and this knowledge becomes essential to the success of his journey.

As O'Meally and Fabre note,

> certain sites of memory were sometimes constructed by one generation in one way and then reinterpreted by another. These sites may [. . .] be revisited suddenly, and brought back to life [. . . .] [Sites of memory] are constantly evolving new configurations of meaning,

and [. . .] their constant revision makes them part of the dynamism of the historical process. (8–9)

Such is the case with Nathaniel and his visits to multiple sites of memory on his journey toward identity when he reinterprets the two contrasting ideologies of race constructed by Jamestown and Nathaniel's grandfather, Jericho. Both views seek to determine the importance of the past to the contemporary moment, particularly as the two men's different approaches to dealing with displacement relate to Nathaniel's attempt to transcend his present agony.

In many ways, Jamestown and Jericho are similar. They are both gifted men trying to overcome a system of injustice that misunderstands and seeks to contain them. They are both individualists. And they are both quite purposeful. They differ, however, in their beliefs about the role history should play as a passage into the angularity of the contemporary experience. Since both men think that their own ideology is the best one to be passed on to the younger Nathaniel, they must find a common ground or risk leaving the survival of the family and race "to seasonal chance, and other barometers of history" (Forrest, *There Is a Tree*, 109).

Jericho, the elder of the two men by a century, argues that misuse, suffering, and abuses are universal horrors not exclusive to the black race. He even sees some advantage to the suffering. He tells Jamestown: "You come from a people who have a history of never currying favor but rather making do out of the dust, transforming the most rudimentary thing into utilitarian survival kits of usefulness [. . . .] Only a Black man could have turned a peanut into a star" (110). The passage speaks for itself, but it also speaks for Forrest, who exalts the African American cultural gift of reinvention and transformation created in response to slavery. Though he sees the accuracy and usefulness of Jericho's position, Jamestown focuses on the uniqueness of black suffering and refuses to accept the horrors of slavery simply because it produced, in the Negro, the art of reinvention.

Jericho and Jamestown's argument (re)enters history as it mimics the ideological differences of Booker T. Washington and W. E. B. DuBois and of Martin Luther King Jr. and Malcolm X. Forrest acknowledges that the argument between Jericho and Jamestown is implicitly the argument of social equality and social responsibility going on in *Invisible Man* and that their argument is influenced by the contrasting ideologies of Malcolm and Martin (Forrest and Cawelti, 290). What Forrest seeks to do is to take each of the arguments of these four men (Washington, DuBois, King, and X) to another level, to do with eloquence on paper what these men did as talkers. And, as Forrest suggests, he is able to do so because he has the benefit of history and the benefit of literature.

Notice the lyrical eloquence of the following passage, which draws both from history and from Ellison's *Invisible Man*. Questioning whether everyone must suffer or whether the memory of some is suffering enough, Jericho questions: "[I]s there no way to infuse memory into the chapterless, rootless children . . . ?" (Forrest, *There Is a Tree*, 111). Jamestown responds:

> There is no hiding place, no real Rock. . . . And shock treatments [as those endured by the protagonist in *Invisible Man*] only burn out the coil-clasping memory fibers of the brain. . . . Bloodshed is the only infusion guaranteed to shock the slumbering spirit and fire the magical Soul-Furnace of FREEDOM. . . . (111)

Their debate continues:

> —Why then do you [Jamestown] mock the purposefulness of our journey and the promise of the boy . . . ?
> —I tell you the plow must be abandoned for the knife—Death must be wrought so that liberation and FREEDOM CAN RING, unless, UNLESS men can learn to contain the chain-bearing bloodhounds within their carnivorous souls and become the masters of their own spirits and not their brothers' enslaving chain keepers. . . . That's why I agreed once more to come with you and the boy. . . .
> [. . . . .]
> —But what kind of prologue are you suggesting that we set before the lad?
> —That there is no Rock to hide in. . . . And that hiding was part of the foul-faced heritage of our common history . . . that his eyes have tongues. . . . Let him see it all, so that he might become a man. . . . Yes and let the Light liberate his eyes, not fracture his resolve but embolden his fury for Freedom: YES and especially for continual *action*. . . . (112; italics in original)

In essence, Jamestown and Jericho agree to let Nathaniel see the world, in all its glory and gloom, for himself, since there clearly is "no hiding place" from the past. Ironically, however, Jamestown and Jericho (and the narration), in the tradition of patriarchy, preclude Nathaniel from seeing it all as they claim they will let him. Throughout this all-important dialogue, which allows the fictional world to encounter the historical world, the voices of women who are also engaged in these ideological debates are absent. It is not until much later, when Aunt Hattie appears as a traditional nurturer, that we see Nathaniel encounter a female voice, and even then, it is in a role limited by patriarchy rather than as an ideological thinker. Nevertheless, with the awareness of the breadth of the African American past he picks up from Jericho and Jamestown, Nathaniel must decide what aspects of history should and must be remembered in order to establish an identity for himself. Yet this identity cannot be static. Thus Nathaniel must adopt the art of transformation; accordingly, he moves through sites of memory that expose him to a black ethnic tradition for which transformation is inherent—folk religion.

The first of these sites appears in the section "The Vision," which opens:

> The lance rises and falls in the hands of a soldier, who seems to be practicing and testing its weightiness, and the crowds are moving down into the floor of the valley, with bloodhounds chained to their wrists. (115)

The lance is our clue to the crucifixion, while the bloodhounds are our clue to the lynching. And after the "golden-suited leader" brings the crosslike tree upon which the man will be nailed, the crowd cries out as he hangs upon the tree. Like Jesus, the man utters final "mumbling words." And as he is pierced in the side three times, his head droops "as if it were about to drop off and fall." The crucifixion evolves into a lynching when the crowd remains dissatisfied with merely nailing him to the tree. The racial significance of these acts becomes more apparent when "a beautifully attired man in quiet, immaculate pale linen" yodels out three times, "HE IS A NIGGER!"

Fusing together history and religion, "The Vision" draws attention to the racial specificity of the dismembered/lynched man's suffering. By recontextualizing race-based lynchings and suffering and likening them to Christ's oppression and the cross, Nathaniel realizes the relationship between the past, the present, and the eschatological future. In black theology, eschatology (both in spite of and because of its concentration on the final things) is related to protest against injustice in the here and now, and it acknowledges the need for revolutionary change or transformation in the present.[3] The reality of the resurrection and the promising future that God reveals through it are antithetical to any idea of contentment with present oppression, even in light of hope for a better afterlife.

Perhaps this is why Nathaniel's vision climaxes in a scene of transcendence. As the angels ascended with the soldier's dismembered body,

> the sack cloth exploded—the parts and members of the man cut down did rise Upwards and seemed to be TOTALLY COLLECTED INTO HIS ORIGINAL FORM [. . . .] The man's wings broken, storm-blasted like limb branches torn from their plantation roots; his feet bloody, his mouth twisted, his eyes bedeviled; his glorious head bloody; but LORD FATHER HE WAS FLYING FLYING FLYING [. . . .](148; emphasis in original)

Here, Forrest borrows from the African myth of the god Osiris to reorient Nathaniel with diasporic cultural traditions and to facilitate Nathaniel's transformation. In the myth of Osiris's dismemberment by the power of evil, Osiris is killed by his brother Set and then collected and reconstituted by the goddess Isis. In subsequent traditions that also interpret this myth, the Universal Daemon or supreme heavenly being is dismembered, robbed of its memory of its heavenly origin, and forced into individual beings as a fragment of a god. In these traditions, man has the potential to become a christ or a god if he but recognizes his ability to do so, dies unto his old self, experiences transformation, and is resurrected or recollected whole.[4] Reorienting himself with this tradition, Nathaniel accesses the power of transformation through contact with an ancestral past.

As a living embodiment of the past, Nathaniel's aunt, Hattie Breedlove, also offers Nathaniel access to transformation as a black cultural tradition. Significantly, she reminds him of his ancestral legacy of enduring oppression until transformation comes. Thus she tells him:

> [. . .] upon this earth young man you will learn to understand that there are some places where there are no seats to sit down in [. . .] but that's not a judgment upon you, or against you, rather it's a challenge to your vision [. . .] if your soul and spirit is anchored in the lord [. . .] you erect a wing of wisdom, delight and praise before him, so that you celebrate life, even as you feed his sheep, even as he bade peter to do [. . .] because nat you will one day give witness and voice to the glorious shape my jesus can give to the sun [. . . .] (155)

What she has to teach Nathaniel is that he must combine the ways of the world with ways of the spirit. All the while, he must constantly transform the *self*. This approach embraces the black cultural tradition best characterized as a gospel impulse.[5] Combining the sacred and the secular, the gospel impulse assumes the trouble of the secular world and engages it with the faith of sacred traditions in an attempt to offer hope to believers who are suffering from worldly (and frequently racial) oppression. Wit and cunning are combined with hope and faith, allowing believers to embrace the survival strategies of the blues without abandoning their faith in God.

Throughout the novel, Nathaniel debates the benefits of "changing his name" to overcome his struggles. Arguably, it is the gospel impulse that encourages him to see that changing his name would not change his struggle. Again, it is his *self*, not just his name, that must be transformed. For as Jamestown has already suggested in Nathaniel's dream, there is no hiding place. Nathaniel ponders:

> knowing and not knowing that by changing my name i could not change the track, or the switch of the train, or the splattered rainbow, the fleets at sea, the bombers abreast, the camping grounds turned against us, the trade route, nor the river's rumblings, nor the wheel, nor the harness of creation. . . . (154)

Instead of running from his past, he adopts the impetus of the blues and becomes determined to endure and to transcend his suffering.

As he is struggling to find himself in the present moment, Nathaniel hears a voice that tells him, "chile you working on his [God's] time now, not theirs [whites]—because honey this here's a rejoicing, jordan rolling train/hush i said 'cause you are confusing the misery of my history with the glories of our imperishably rugged cross" (153). The irony of this statement is that confusing the misery of history with the glories of the cross is the essence of gospel music. He seeks the transcendence that abounds after the blues confrontation, even as he acknowledges the worth of Breedlove's faith, so he adopts the gospel approach:

> god i know you got the woods and the warbles in your stubby hands and long fingers, but i need a cunning jesus down here on the ground to lead me around the bends and the cycles of the mountains, wrangling with lions, then wolves and sheep grazing and frothy-mouthed dogs and hounds over the river deep and river wide yes and moaning and groaning for power and light in the grotto-cave. (159)

Though he has faith, Nathaniel also possesses a sense of immediacy about his turmoil. He accepts the promise of heaven, but he wants some semblance of gratification on Earth to help him cope. And Breedlove's invocation of the gospel impulse offers him this temporary gratification; and temporary it is, for transformation is still essential. He can only rid himself of his blues long enough to get them again.

Eventually, Nathaniel concedes that even his mother was "born to die" and that, now, at least she has a "seat up in the kingdom" (156). He also begins to realize that even if his mother was still alive or if he could somehow convince Jesus to "change his name," his soul in agony would be the same. It is perhaps at this point that Nathaniel first becomes conscious and *fully* aware of the fact that his agony is not simply personal; nor is it limited to the recent loss of his mother. While it is, indeed, this loss that calls attention to the lack of wholeness that plagues him, by the novel's end (in its original form), he finally makes the connection and acknowledges that his personal loss is merely symbolic of the larger and more communal loss suffered by African Americans who, when forcibly removed from their homeland, were rendered motherless. Ideally, the reader, too, by the novel's end will have made this recognition that Nathaniel's experiences are as much representative of a centralized African American consciousness and feelings of motherlessness as they are of his personal agony. And this is why revisiting sites of memory involving Jamestown, contemplating the varying ideologies of Jamestown and Jericho, and embracing Breedlove's faith in religion are so key to Nathaniel's journey—because each of these ports of call into a symbolic South is thoroughly absorbed in African and diasporic African traditions and culture that may contribute to Nathaniel's and to the African American's ability to reinvent himself, oftentimes to the point of magnificence and, at the very least, to the point of survival.

The additional section in the amended version of *There Is a Tree More Ancient Than Eden* speaks specifically to this tendency toward reinvention and is aptly titled "Transformation." The section opens with a letter to then-president Lyndon B. Johnson from Nathaniel's adopted grandmother, Sweetie Reed, whose character takes center stage in *Two Wings to Veil My Face*. Unlike the previous instance of ideological debate, where women's voices go unheard, "Transformation" gives full voice to a woman as an ideological thinker. President Johnson had written to Sweetie to congratulate her on the occasion of her hundredth birthday, and the thirty-seven-page epistle is her response to his well wishes and her view of the success and failure of his administration. In a self-professed attempt to "set the record straight," she applauds him for the limited racial progress achieved under his administration. But she also admonishes the real value of his War on Poverty and programs such as Head Start that allegedly seek to create equality among the races. What Sweetie's epistle ultimately reveals is that despite the advances in civil rights America so proudly boasted of, many of which occurred not for the sake of humanity but as an attempt to *appear* to be more humane than its military enemies, little had changed over the years in the way of race relations. Thus, the most feasible response to the racially specific spiritual agony from which the community she speaks for suffers is still transformation. One of the figures who has mastered this art as well as anyone and who is capable of conferring it on the community is the folk preacher.

By sheer force of necessity, this spiritual and social leader, who evolved during slavery, excelled at the art of transformation. How else could he effectively console a displaced and enslaved people? Convincing African Americans to make a way out of no way and showing them how to reinvent themselves in the tradition of God and the Bible was his most significant gift. Arguably, it is the sermonic rhetoric that informs both Breedlove's everyday language (and, subsequently, her sermonette) and Sweetie's epistle (in the tradition of the apostle Paul) that moves Nathaniel to the point of "Wakefulness" and closer to transcendence. But he must learn the art of the folk preacher first, before his journey's end and before an ever-evolving self-identity becomes an attainable reality for him—hence, the appearance of Pompey c.j. Browne.

Introduced as the culminating event of a midnight mass that has been organized "to assess the meaning of Martin Luther King's life, upon the 12th anniversary of the martyr's assassination" (*There Is a Tree*, 204), Pompey's address is Forrest's first attempt at a full-length sermon in his fiction. The mass turns into a barroom potpourri of jokes, curses, tales and stories, and moments of celebration. Not until 5:15 AM does the six-foot-seven-inch Pompey c. j. Browne rise to give "the principal homily, sermon-address-obsequies," which is, in essence, bar talk couched in a sermon. The rhetoric of the sermon, appropriately titled "Oh Jeremiah of the Dreamers," reflects the transformation in Rev. Browne's character that Nathaniel has observed over the years. Though no description could ever "adequately capture the man behind the cloth, nor the mystery and meaning of the sermon he weaves" (205), Nathaniel describes him as a mix of Adam Clayton Powell, Martin Luther King Jr., Leon Sullivan, and Richard Pryor.

Violating all limitations of character confinement, Browne exploits his preacherly right to shift voices throughout the sermon as his voice fluctuates between husky, vibrant, gruff, and mellow. While Powell, King, and Sullivan share a somewhat similar rhetorical or oratory manner, Pryor, as a comedian, possesses an entirely different mode of expression. Pompey's adoption of Pryor's voice stands out the most, as the language Pompey uses in such instances is not very reflective of a preacher. The difference between the passage

> Oh the impermanence of paradise, oh ripped-off gallows of Gethsemane. This is my body and *this* is my blood. Oh missioned prophet in shattered temple of the merchandised Diaspora—body and soul . . . and Lord each   man riddled in the chambers of iniquity and the segregated metaphor of his own madness. (206)

and the passage

> . . . They say our politicians are whores and I believe them for I've seen them parting their asses like punk rock stars with acid in their wisdom teeth. And the patched-up one-eyed cop on the beat, spreads his legs for a pound of melted down, indivisible cure. (209–10)

calls attention to Rev. Browne's ability to transform himself and his word. Here lies the importance of his character to Nathaniel's quest for identity. He must learn the skill Pompey has mastered—the art of transformation. While he may not be able to capture "the mystery and the meaning" of Pompey's sermon, Nathaniel is able to recognize Pompey's never-ending transformation and the effect that each of these transformations has on Pompey's construction of himself and his rhetoric.

Pompey's sermon is also crucial to Nathaniel's quest in the sense that it highlights the fact that Nathaniel's individual grief parallels the larger historical reality of African American grief and suffering. As Cawelti suggests, the sermon

> becomes a weaving together of the two great strands of African-American culture. And as he evokes King's great crusades in Montgomery, Birmingham, and Chicago and then the terrible day in Memphis when the leader was assassinated, Browne rises to a whirlwind of eloquence out of which he cries for his hearers to take up the cross of King, whose voice still cries out in the wilderness. ("Leon Forrest: Labyrinth of Luminosity," 39)

Community wellness, then, becomes as significant as Nathaniel's individual quest. Like the jazz musician Ellison writes of, Nathaniel must find himself within the group, even as he fights to attain his own freedom and to assert his individual identity. This integrated existence already characterizes Pompey's sermon, which is a hodgepodge of facts and opinions that combines the past and the present, the personal and the communal, and the worldly and the spiritual. Importantly, it makes no attempt at definitive answers. It simply offers Pompey's varied interpretations of the past and its relationship to the present. Thus, Nathaniel must listen carefully to Pompey's sermon and decide for himself which variation of facts and opinions he will allow to stain his soil and impact him the most. And as Pompey's sermon is an address of limited formal sentences and recurring rhetorical questions, the narration reinforces the idea that no one interpretation of black experiences can be meaningfully articulated. Instead, the search itself, and not any pronouncements of truth, is where the meaning rests. Thus, Pompey ends his address with questions and not answers. But he has still functioned purposefully for Nathaniel, who must realize that while his struggle will and must continue, to survive it, he must transform it and re-create himself over and over again. In so doing, he must learn that the mystery is in the editing, and the meaning is in discovering what should be kept and what should be discarded. As newly endowed articulate kinsman, Nathaniel, then, in his acceptance of the role of Stepto's immersion narrative hero, must "forsake [his] highly individualized mobility [. . .] for a posture of relative stasis in the most oppressive environment" (167) while, paradoxically, changing within the stasis. Arguably, he does just this when he reemerges in the subsequent fictional world of *The Bloodworth Orphans*.

As the lead novel in the Forest County Sagas, *There Is a Tree More Ancient Than Eden* emphatically emphasizes the significance of culture to transcending spiritual agony and oppression and moving toward self-identification for Nathaniel and for the community. And the novels that follow—*The Bloodworth Orphans, Two Wings to Veil My Face,* and *Divine Days*—further develop this theme and attempt to show what happens when characters fail to experience cultural (re)affirmation or when the truth of history is obscured and then reclaimed. We all learn from the narrator's adoption of a centralized historical African American consciousness as its main character and from Nathaniel's journey through which this consciousness is focalized, and it is because we do that *There Is a Tree More Ancient Than Eden* achieves its success as lesson in history and struggle and survival.

chapter three

"Salvation Is the Issue":
Black Music as Metaphor in
The Bloodworth Orphans

In a 1988 interview with John Cawelti, Leon Forrest notes that "[a]lmost as an answer to the critic of *There Is a Tree More Ancient Than Eden* [he] wanted to create a novel filled with characters and a lot of character development. That was the impetus for *The Bloodworth Orphans*. The other was the idea of doing something with families" (Forrest and Cawelti, 299). Combining these two of Forrest's desires, *The Bloodworth Orphans* uses a variety of characters, most of whom belong to the same family, to continue to develop the themes of fragmentation and alienation initiated in *There Is a Tree*. In fact, *The Bloodworth Orphans* picks up where *There Is a Tree* left off, engaging in inquiries about experiences that predate the latter novel and that heighten Forrest's use of motherlessness as a metaphor through which to read African American experiences in America. *The Bloodworth Orphans* departs from *There Is a Tree*, however, in its use of many characters to offer a more tangible and less impressionistic rendering of the consciousness of the African American and of the African American experience.

As Forrest's most metaphorical novel, *The Bloodworth Orphans* adopts at least six pivotal characters who represent varied facets of African American life and whose diverse responses to racial oppression and to the Bloodworth curse allow Forrest to investigate the usefulness of certain black cultural traditions and institutions as means of survival. First is Rachel Rebecca Carpenter Flowers, the saintly church mother whose response to all life's difficulties is religious. Then, there is Regal Pettibone, a hipster whose response to the chaos not knowing his biological heritage creates is primarily musical. Next is Abraham Dolphin, a black physician who encourages his patients to get involved in the civil rights movement but who ends up killing himself because he cannot find an ideology or a tradition to sustain him. Then there is Saltport X, the former leader of a Muslim mosque who resorts to drug trafficking after he realizes that Black Islam is a farce. And closely linked one to another are Noah Grandberry and Ironwood Rumble, both of whom are sages of sorts who adopt jazz impulse's techniques of transformation to reinvent themselves in an attempt to bring order to their chaotic experiences. By examining these characters' lives as somewhat representative of broader African American experiences, Nathaniel Witherspoon, who returns as the saga's central consciousness, simultaneously explores individual and communal agony and subsequent responses to it. In his new role as observer, Nathaniel shifts his focus from his personal angst, which shapes *There Is a Tree,* to the spiritual agony of a community of African Americans whom Forrest dubs the Bloodworth orphans and who symbolically represent that slice of African American life which suffers from motherlessness because of its disconnection from Africa. A major attempt of the novel, then, is to tell the African American story of being orphaned in America. But as James Baldwin reminds us in "Many Thousands Gone," "It is only in his music [. . .] that the Negro in America has been able to tell his story" (65). Thus, the narrative adopts black music's impulses, especially jazz, and uses music as a metaphor to do that which Gayl Jones suggests jazz allows like no other—to reintegrate the "whole of American experience in a 'rainbowed' text" (*Liberating Voices,* 53). Using music as its guiding metaphor for cultural integration, the novel ultimately suggests that the contemporary African American must align himself with his new home if he is to survive. Thus, despite the fact that his tragic experiences of oppression and discrimination are clearly and distinctly African American, the Americanness of these experiences cannot be denied.

Such inferences can be drawn both from the novel and from the author. In an interview about the novel, Forrest tells Cawelti: "[. . .] in the most marvelous ways and in the most horrible ways black Americans are at the center of this society. I don't say this in any bragging [. . . .] This whole theme of family chaos and disruption seemed to me suggestive of a broad range of American life" (Forrest and Cawelti, 307). Thus, when read as an attempt to place the African American experience at the center of American society and literature, *The Bloodworth Orphans* makes two significant and complementary advances—it examines various rituals and responses that have been adopted by African Americans as survival techniques, and it investigates the effectiveness and consequences of these responses, ultimately suggesting that attempts at maintaining one's cultural essentialism, especially in a society as diverse as America's, must yield to cultural integration if survival in a contemporary context is the ultimate goal. For, as H. Nigel Thomas suggests in *From Folklore to Fiction*, "A forward-looking, self-liberating people cannot tote along defenses that were appropriate when they were a subject people. To do so would negate their freedom" (102); in the case of *The Bloodworth Orphans*, doing so propels them toward their impending doom. This is not to say that the orphans' culturally specific responses (primarily religious and musical) are wholly ineffective. In fact, without these, the orphans could not have sustained themselves at all. However, if they are to move beyond their fragmentation, they must adopt the integrative impulse of black music, which acknowledges that it is American experiences—particularly conflicts between America and the Negro—that birthed the genius of the black music tradition.

We are first introduced to the novel's theme of orphanhood through Rachel Flowers and her adopted son, Regal Pettibone, whom Nathaniel admires as a harmless hustler. Despite the fact that Regal appears in church with her only once a year for their Easter duets, Rachel adores her orphaned child, who seeks to order his chaos and to move beyond not knowing his biological parentage. Also orphaned are Rachel's two children, Industrious and Carl-Rae Bowman, who are never acknowledged by their white father, Arlington Bloodworth III, who also slept with sheep. Rachel, too, we later learn, is an orphan who was abandoned as a child and found by a shepherd who rears and, later, seduces her. Similarly, LaDonna Scales, who turns out to be Regal's half sister, lacks a relationship with her biological parents. As a result, she has a variety of dreams, each of which highlights her fear of abandonment and her desire to have acceptance and a home. Through Reverend Bass, we learn that LaDonna and Regal, who are lovers, are two of three Bloodworth siblings who were separated at birth in an attempt to escape the Bloodworth curse (that the children would slay their parents and commit varying levels of incest). Bass, too, suffers from loss and abandonment; he was separated from his mother at the age of six. Through intense therapy, he realizes that his relationships with his each of his wives have failed because the women could not imitate his mother. Through Bass, we are also introduced to Dolphin, who was abandoned (in Moses-like imagery) as a child by his Bloodworth father and his black mother and raised as one of the family by Governor Masterson's daughter. After transforming his life on more than one occasion, Dolphin ultimately shoots himself, and Nathaniel finds him.

Shortly after Dolphin's death, Rachel dies, and, again, Nathaniel is the first to find the dead. While Rachel is dying, LaDonna learns that Regal (her lover) and Amos-Otis Thigpen are her brothers. Thinking that Regal is attacking LaDonna, Amos-Otis accidentally shoots them both and then, in despair, turns the gun on himself. Regal, however, does not die from the gunshot; he dies later at the hands of the congregation, which he temporarily pastors and which dismembers his body.

After identifying Regal's body, Nathaniel feels the need to retreat but does not, instead responding to Saltport's mother's request that he visit her drug-addict son. Saltport was once a respected Muslim leader, but after accepting a medal of honor from the president, he is resented by the powers that be as one who has the potential to be greater than they. Thus, they devise a scheme to undermine his character, spreading the rumor that Saltport has been caught in the mountains with a white blonde. Saltport is devastated by his revelation that Black Islam is a farce and turns to drug use. While Nathaniel is visiting Saltport, the building is raided, and Nathaniel awakens at the Refuge Hospital, where he is locked in a room with Noah Grandberry, who later informs him of the myth of the serial hermaphrodite and trickster Ford. Noah and Nathaniel find ways to survive as they listen to the jazz great Ironwood, and they stay "holed up" in the room until they are able to escape from the city, which is experiencing massive chaos. The novel concludes with a series of deaths reminiscent of a Shakespearean apocalypse.

As a reconstructed origin myth, *The Bloodworth Orphans* investigates the source of being for its tragic characters and examines their varied responses to a curse that plagues them from birth. Whether or not they can survive this curse depends almost wholly upon how they respond to it. Take the obsessively religious Rachel Flowers, for example: As the lover of Arlington Bloodworth III, a patriarch of the infamous slaveholding Bloodworth clan, Rachel falls victim to the Bloodworth curse when she learns that Arlington also slept with sheep. But she learns this only after she has two children by him—Carl-Rae and Industrious—whom she leaves to be raised by a preacher named Bowman. Both children suffer tragic deaths, but Rachel does not accept this as punishment enough. Instead, she engages in extraordinary self-sacrifice (including marriage to the grotesquely obese Bee-More Flowers and adoption of Regal Pettibone, whom she does not know is a Bloodworth) and in religious obsession as her response to her agony.

Though we are introduced to Rachel in the opening list of characters and in chapter one as Nathaniel rides with Regal, who has picked up his adopted mother from church and who must now practice songs with her before their annual Easter concert, it is through a flashback of Reverend

Packwood's exorcising sermon that we learn the most about her. According to Packwood, Rachel was sired through an adulterous and incestuous relationship. Her parents were, allegedly, brother and sister, and her grandfather had tried to have her aborted. But God struck the grandfather with lockjaw, while her mother went mad; she was raised by a shepherd, to whom she was to belong upon her thirteenth birthday. According to Packwood, from time to time, Rachel's grandmother would sneak to see her to nourish "her upon the lessons of survival and how to walk and how make food out of what was left over [. . .] and how to make offering of words from those lessons unto someone called the God Almighty; and how to hold on" (Forrest, *Bloodworth Orphans,* 31). Rachel's grandmother had taught her the art of improvisation as a survival technique to the point of "honor." But when Rachel began to see less and less of the grandmother— both because the grandmother had grown old and was barely able to walk and because the shepherd had begun to recognize Rachel as a woman, not a child, and forbade the grandmother's visits—Rachel had not yet learned enough to sustain herself. The shepherd began to sleep with her, claiming that in doing so, he was releasing her from the curse of her birth. Confused and unknowing, she went along with it until in a "kneeling moment the Lord God said unto her,"

> Upon the morning say to your Master: "Yea, Shepherd and Master, let us now arise and go unto the mountain and lay up a sacrifice of a sheep upon the plateau." But when he then commences to lifting the sacrifice unto the burning timbers, my child, as you are kneeling and yet praying, you will hear the spearlike voice of a trumpet upon the wind, birthing fire and smoke, and then the horn-blowing—but you and you alone will hear it, and then you will know my Word and will know the hour and know what to do, and what to be, and not be. . . . But if I free you, you must pledge to be a witness, whatever the price, wreckage, ruin, or joy. . . . (34)

When the "spearlike voice" commanded her to push the shepherd into the flames of the pyre, Rachel killed him. And, in keeping with her covenant with God, she became a self-sacrificing lamb. She does the best she can to raise her children, and she even tries to make another pact with God to protect them. But this time, "in a dream the God appeared to her, faceless but with a raging voice" and proclaims, "NO DEALS" (42). So she must accept their fate as Bloodworth orphans. This revelation leaves her crawling and babbling and all but speechless (and she has already begun to lose her sight). When she recovers, she chastises herself for thinking that she could make a new covenant with God, and her faith grows stronger than ever. She becomes grateful for her sleeplessness, for it gives her more time to contemplate and to do work for God; and she considers her blindness a blessing, since she does not have to see the world as others see it. Ultimately, she becomes obsessed with the idea of sacrifice.

Significantly, Rachel's response to her agony and its cycle of abuse is facilitated by a former "corked Minstrel" turned blues prince turned preacher. As minstrel, Packwood knows how to mask his responses to experiences; as blues prince, he uses music to express the agony he cannot otherwise articulate; and as preacher, he has the gift of reinvention and the ability to make new all that is old and otherwise familiar. Perhaps most important, however, is his ability to transform himself when circumstances demand that he do so. This is what he fails to teach Rachel, who, rather than remaining open to the idea of transformation, resorts to religious piety. She makes no attempt to reintegrate herself into society or into the community except as an overbearing servant who leads "the choir and everyone else" at River Rock of Eden Church in Forest County. Notice how she responds to Packwood's sermonizing:

> And now Rachel ran through the mud and the rain, back and forth, weeping and hugging the sisters, and falling and kissing the hem of the preacher's long garb—and crying and singing: "I'm running on, I'm running on/I done left this world behind/I done crossed the separating line/I done left this world behind." (39)

The problem, of course, is that while she may be able to suspend time temporarily to overcome her agony, "leaving the world behind," as she claims she will do, she ultimately creates a detachment that only strengthens the power of the Bloodworth curse. As is the case with most, if not all, of the orphaned characters in the novel, Rachel's difficult childhood and poor upbringing represent the cultural displacement from which the diasporic African suffers because of a lack of connection to the African homeland and the subsequent feelings of homelessness or motherlessness he experiences at the hands of American society, which never fully embraces African Americans as surrogates but, rather, abuses them unconscionably. Even so, abandoning the world offers no real escape, only a feigned one.

Unfortunately, rather than providing salvation or transcendence of her literal and symbolic agony, Rachel's religious experience is rendered almost absurd. By the end of the sermon, both Packwood and Rachel are crawling in the mud and climbing a tree in ecstasy as the rain pours and the lightning flashes. Her moment of liberation is at the same time enabling and limiting. It saves her for the moment, but once that moment has passed, she is left with limited possibilities of success and survival. As a result, she turns to the next most logical response—music.

Rendered with a voice that sent the listening congregation into conniptions, Rachel's "songs brought many as close as they could contemplate to a miracle" (18). And even Nathaniel "found himself aggrieved by the furious intelligence of certain of Rachel's songs," which he describes as an art form that muted her chaos (18). He later explains: "[W]hen Rachel sang 'City Called Heaven,' it was the pronouncement of an epic. It represented for her all the ordering of chaos, all the possibility of bringing together those extremes that were the lot of her body in its blindness to know and cry about . . ." (43). It would seem, then, that her adoption of musical impulses might help to order her chaos and to sustain her. But again, her problem is her inability to incorporate all the varied aspects of life into her music. She limits herself mainly to traditional hymns, which are more rigid than other impulses which might offer her greater freedom. Thus, she cannot develop a blues voice or a gospel impulse, either of which would force her to acknowledge a world outside her own personal struggles and religion. That she refuses to incorporate her brand of music into a larger reinvention and survival strategy marginalizes her experiences and decreases her potential for all-out transcendence or a meaningful healing.

Regal, on the other hand, is keenly aware of the need to bring his experiences to the center and to draw from them to ensure personal wellness. Like Rachel, Regal from time to time embraces religion and music as strategies for ordering his chaos and his feelings of displacement and motherlessness, for he, too, has been orphaned and is a victim of the Bloodworth curse. But unlike Rachel, Regal does not limit himself by turning exclusively to religion or by simply singing traditional hymns. Instead, he incorporates the varied aspects of African American and American culture into his existence. And though he still suffers a tragic end, he is undoubtedly a more successful character than most of the other Bloodworth orphans.

Like so many of the characters in the novel, Regal is "hungry for a branch-bearing, life-giving harmony [. . .] wail[ing] in his pitched silence for nourishing root connections, Lord, anything which would keep his spirit kindled yet temper his chaos" (6). And while Forrest offers no guaranteed formula for Regal—or any of the characters—to achieve this end fully, Regal, like Nathaniel in *There Is a Tree,* is at least able to get rid of his blues long enough to get them back again. As a singer/songwriter/composer, Regal questions the feasibility of nonhybrid musical forms and seeks to create music anew. Thus, he performs music that draws from *Tosca,* gospel, and the spirituals alike. Though several of his songs are recorded by professional singers, most of his work is played and heard in Forest County nightclubs or cabarets because his lyrics are so complex that they can be mastered only by locals "who [are] boss powers in their own settings but rarely left town" (5).

Music orders Regal's chaos. The disorder that most plagues him is his ignorance about his parentage, for neither he nor Rachel knows that he is the biological son of Pourty Ford Bloodworth. Though he "always felt proud of his unknown, unscaled pedigree in which he envisioned himself an orphan of royalty" (70), Regal feels fragmented and less confident when he imagines that his origins are more humble than "royalty." In fact, he has nightmares in which he is denied his inheritance by his father and dreams of becoming a hero who destroys a boar to save his siblings until they, in turn, stab and kill him with the same knives he used to save them. Even his siblings become lost in the woods and are unable to find their way home, which suggests that finding a home is not even achievable in his dreams. The best he can do is make music.

So once a year, on Easter Sunday, Regal is in concert with Rachel at the River Rock of Eden Baptist Church. The power of their music is so overwhelming that Sister Marvella suggests that Rachel will use her voice to replace Gabriel someday. And Nathaniel thinks back to Easter Sundays past, when the congregation was both petrified and awestruck:

> [. . .] souls fled from the church when this final act was either in flight, descending or consummating [. . . .] Once the ushers and three deacons had to carry seven sisters and, surprisingly, one brother out upon stretchers [. . .] finally it seemed the church was engulfed in a tidal wave of glory and that to even listen or witness the renderings was life-destroying and yet life-giving [. . . .] It was as if the foul world had been destroyed before their eyes and then re-created. (11–12)

For Regal, Rachel, and the congregation, music is a powerful language of survival. It is life destroying yet life giving; it is re-creation; it is harmony, literally and figuratively; it is the only thing that Regal can order. But after Rachel, the only mother he has known, takes to her bed with cancer, even the ordering power of music is not enough. So Regal, too, turns almost wholeheartedly to religion. Thomas suggests that in order "[t]o cope with the psychic disorder that Rachel's illness creates in him, Regal picks up her sacrificial quality by undergoing instant conversion, by deluding himself into thinking he is a preacher, and by finding in Sister LaDonna Scales [. . .] Rachel's surrogate" (169).

Regal's role as temporary and grief-stricken preacher is quietly, though no less thoughtfully, contrasted with Reverend Foxworth's role as permanent and self-enhancing preacher. Foxworth, unlike Regal, knows how to manipulate all situations to his benefit. Though he knows that Regal's new-found evangelism will dethrone his own reign as prince of River Rock of Eden, Foxworth also knows that the congregation's (particularly the women's) fascination with Regal will not last long. So, instead of viewing Regal as threatening, Foxworth sees Regal's presence as "an opportunity to allure new members, to revive his apathetic flock to bind up the highly fragmented church, and even to shock the divided, corrupt Board of Deacons out of their machinations [. . .] seizing Rachel's son, as the force and source of that miracle of church transformation" (Forrest, *Bloodworth Orphans,* 212). And in all of Forrest's fiction, transformation is key. That Foxworth can access it almost at will is essential to his success as an ordered being in a county where chaos abounds.

Significantly, in spite of his new, overwhelming affinity with religion as ritual, Regal never disconnects himself completely from the larger world. In fact, he integrates the world into his religious music and creates a gospel impulse that brings him closer to transcendence than most of the other orphans can even imagine.

> It was as if all of the fury of his music, singing and the love-making magic of his lyrics consummated in the quarrel over the very nature of love, the defeat in love, and the total rebirth-salvation in the suffering quest for what was left of love (in the flooding ruins and canceled hopes) had finally culminated and found a home in God, and the sweep and epic language of the Bible. Some of the women claimed that "those old songs were just too narrow to hold Brother Regal down, he needed something to throw himself into, body and soul." And Regal's new music and singing gave a renewed range and power to the Gospel he sang, and the new Gospel music he was now composing for the church. (212–13)

At base, gospel music shares many of the traditions found in the spiritual, such as syncopated hand clapping, call and response patterns, and the use of scripture for lyrics. The most basic difference between the two is the tendency of gospel music to leave room for stylistic improvisation (a primarily secular technique), using the text of a song as a mere skeleton from which the musician may deviate at will. Because this improvisation avoids strict boundaries, it allows both the lead singer (Regal) and the congregation the freedom to maneuver and to integrate different forms into the music to create a sustaining tradition. Neither Regal's nor the congregation's life is exclusively religious; thus, neither entity's music can be. And because gospel music is closer than the spiritual to everyday life experiences of the secular world—hence gospel's resemblance to the blues—it was the ideal musical form. In gospel music, Regal finds a home, and his music and his life ultimately symbolize "the royalty of the blues" (his agony) and "the richness of the spirituals" (hope to escape it), made new again (transformation and transcendence).

This impulse orders his chaos, and he thrives in its midst until the congregation learns of his incestuous relationship with LaDonna Scales and the members decide to kill him, supposedly to rid themselves of the curse he allegedly brings upon them. So, despite finally being successful at integrating his personal experiences with the broader experiences of the world, Regal still meets a tragic end, as does Rachel, who dies from cancer. At least part of the reason they are unable to escape their fates, Thomas argues, is that they spend far too much time (a lifetime, in fact) trying to expiate curses they did not create. He contends that "[t]he implication [of their inability to break the curse] is that blacks are not responsible for the existential problems of Americans, and yet they have allowed themselves to believe that they are and have adopted ghastly rituals to cope with the burden" (161). As the burdens they seek to rid themselves of did not originate with them, African Americans seeking to cast off such burdens cannot do so without acknowledging the Americanness of their burdens and the subsequent need for at least partly American responses to them. Their suffering is indeed a consequence of their African American condition, but, more significantly, it is also a consequence of their human condition as Americans. Thus, the orphans need both to understand African American history and human history and to negotiate survival techniques that can adequately accommodate the Americanness of their experiences. And few forms negotiate this tension of being African American in America better than black music.

The necessity of negotiating this tension escapes those who partake in Christian and non-Christian rituals alike. As a Black Muslim, Maxwell (X) Saltport does at least acknowledge that African Americans are not responsible for their motherlessness or their fragmentation, and thus cannot fully relieve themselves from a curse they did not create. However, the Black Muslim's affinity with essentialist cultural nationalism renders him as much a failure as his devotedly Christian counterpart. Saltport eventually comes to realize this, but by the time he does, it is too late.

At Saltport's mother's prompting, Nathaniel goes to visit the former minister of a successful Muslim mosque. Though Saltport was once loved and respected among Muslims, when he received and accepted a "Medal of Honor" from the president (presumably of the United States), a number of his fellow Muslims began to resent him. He was then set up and accused of going to the mountains and sleeping with a blonde white woman. Allegedly, there was a tape recording and pictures. But Saltport knew that he had gone directly to California from Washington. When his friend Gladstone revealed the organization's intent to ostracize him, Saltport finally acknowledged that the organization is a farce, with a tendency to eliminate any man who has the potential to garner more power than its leaders. Devastated by this revelation, Saltport "descended back into the underworld life of narcotics traffic" (Forrest, *Bloodworth Orphans,* xxxviii).

Through Saltport, we see Forrest's not-so-subtle mockery of Elijah Muhammad and the Nation of Islam. As the last non-Muslim editor of *Muhammad Speaks,* Forrest had privileged insight into the Nation and Muhammad's role as a trickster-like character. Forrest writes of his relationship with and knowledge of Muhammad, particularly as it relates to Muhammad's ideas about culture, in an essay titled "Elijah" in *The Furious Voice for Freedom:*

> Stripped as the new-world Africans were of their cultural and religious life supports, during the early stages of their enslavement, Elijah believed that they must now be further stripped again, but this time of all the impure materialities and properties they had gathered in consciously or unconsciously through their three-hundred-year encounter with the value system of the white West [. . . .] Elijah absolutely believed that if the tribe were ever to awaken from the nightmare of wearing the white man's mask over their consciousness, the blacks must not only drop this mask but must be disembodied of the poisonous fluids and properties of Negro Culture and consciousness: the blues; the premium placed on rhythm; all forms of the dance; the rowdy power in jazz [. . . .] Also on the hit list were: all species of unbridled laughter of the cracking-up variety; hyperbole of expression, and signifying; most of the folklore; novels and literature [. . . .] (68–69)

Clearly, Forrest disagrees with this nationalistic idea of de-Americanizing the African American, as Saltport's interaction with the fictional version of Muhammad's Nation of Islam highlights its insufficiency for dealing with American experiences. By likening Saltport's expulsion from his Muslim organization to Malcolm X's expulsion from the Nation of Islam, Forrest makes allusions to his former employer easily traceable throughout the novel. Like Malcolm X, who was at first temporarily suspended from the Nation and removed from his position of mosque minister and later expelled completely, Saltport receives word that he is no longer an assistant minister at his or any other mosque and he is suspended, first for nine days and then indefinitely. Unlike Malcolm X, who was allegedly suspended for his "chickens coming home to roost" comment, made just days after President John F. Kennedy's assassination, Saltport really has no idea why he is being suspended. But he quickly realizes that he was guilty of the sins of Icarus—he had become too powerful in his flights too close to the sun for the "lamb's" liking. Notably, "Icarus" is the title of the chapter in Malcolm X's autobiography about his break with the Nation of Islam. Thus, Forrest's allusion to Saltport's Malcolm-like expulsion becomes even clearer, as does his suggestion that Islam's essentialism is more devastating than it is nurturing. Because Saltport has followed the "lamb's" dictates, he has discarded any Negro (read: American) cultural traditions that might have helped him cope with his expulsion. Instead, he finds himself lost in the only other world with which he is familiar—drug trafficking—where he self-destructs before Nathaniel can convince him to do otherwise.

While he is visiting Saltport in his apartment, Nathaniel is taken captive during a police raid and later forced to stay at the old River Refuge Hospital, where he encounters another Bloodworth orphan, Noah Ridgerook Grandberry, and legendary jazz musician Ironwood "Landlord" Rumble. Their ritual of choice is music, not religion. And unlike Rachel, who disavows all music except traditional and sacred forms, and Regal, whose blues and gospel impulses sustain him but do not allow full transcendence of his agony, Noah—the only Bloodworth orphan who survives the city's tragedy—is able to do so largely because of his ability to work within the jazz impulse, which he adopts from Ironwood.

As Forrest observes in his unpublished notes, jazz, as it is best known today, came to be when Negro musicians, who were heavily rooted in the folk traditions, and Creole musicians trained in classical music, who could often pass for white and thought themselves above the Negro, were forced together by Louisiana's black codes of 1894, which dictated that any man with any known Negro heritage or as little as one-sixteenth of Negro blood would be considered Negro. If the Creole musician wanted to work, he had to play Negro music. And, ultimately, the Negro stylized useful elements of the trained Creole's music and created jazz. At least part of what this history reveals is the Americanness of jazz as an art form, for it is undeniably American experiences that birthed the music. Thus when used as a metaphor in *The Bloodworth Orphans,* jazz again calls attention to the Americanness of the orphans' experiences and the incessant need to respond with an art form that acknowledges and accommodates these specifically black and American experiences. In short, not only is Ironwood's music aesthetically pleasing, it is also the embodiment and experience of history and race.

Throughout chapter eleven, where the narration focuses on Nathaniel's interaction with the other men who populate the old River Refuge Hospital, the musical genius of Ironwood's jam session frames their "philosophying" on the meaning of life. They can hardly get through their conversation without digressing to signify on Ironwood's playing. He starts out playing "St. James Infirmary" on his tenor sax, and by chapter's end he has played bagpipes, bass clarinet, a flute, and even the violin with his left hand, while playing the tambourine with his right. He moves easily between "Limehouse Blues" and Duke Ellington's "Solitude," while the men exclaim:

—"ALL NIGHT LONG."
—"PRECIOUS AS A PEACOCK."
—"CREAM OF THE MORNING, SUM IN THE WARM VALLEY."
—"FLYING ACROSS THE MOUNTAIN RANGES . . . WHY JESUS CHRIST COULDN'T HANDLE HIS [Ironwood's musical] CHANGES."
—"LORD, MISTER TICKET-MASTER, EASE THAT WINDOW DOWN."
—"DEEP IN THE CUT—TO THE BONE, JIM, TO THE BONE."
—"Thermongenesis."
—"Translucency."
—"Transbluency."
—"Transfusion!"
—"Thermo-junction?"
—"Mean Boss Solar-Time!"
—"Hey now, Double-Barrel, is this the Funky-Butt?"

—"I may be crazy, but I ain't no Fool."
—"I thought you looked like Buddy Bolden." (305)

Ironwood's ability to access a variety of traditions guides the men toward discussions that illusively (and allusively) intimate, again, the Americanness of the African American. So when Nathaniel corrects one of the men, who calls him "Foamy," and tells him that his name is *Nathaniel Turner Witherspoon,* the man asks if the "Turner" he is claiming is Joe Turner, the white landowner who used to steal black men and force them to work on the chain gang. When Nathaniel replies that "*that* Joe Turner is a mythical character out of [his] people's history," another man mocks that Nathaniel is probably "claiming kin with Nathaniel Turner, THE [NAT] TURNER" (309), who led a revolt against white slave owners. At various points during the conversation, the men integrate Shakespeare, T. S. Eliot, Dante, Elvis, Ovid, Faulkner, Orpheus, and Eurydice into their machinations, which ultimately suggests the inevitable reality of the interconnectedness of human history. Eventually they are led back to American history, generally, and African American history, specifically, again by Ironwood's interpretations of black music and, interestingly enough, thoughts of the reinventive magic of black basketball greats like Earl "The Pearl" Monroe, Doctor J, and Elgin Baylor, all of whom, according to the men, play to the tune of the Duke Ellington's "The Twitch."

Ironically, though he is "mentally unstable," Ironwood is still the conductor for the masses in the Refuge Hospital. He transports his homeless patrons from the "forest on fire, through Job's—tear grass; wisteria; cotton fields and patches of maize; through the tumbledown razor-strapped gospels and epistles of tracks to glory of chained stars" (295). Through Nathaniel and Noah's interaction with Ironwood, Forrest solidifies his metaphor of jazz as one of the most viable rituals of survival and transcendence of racially specific agony. Once he, too, becomes institutionalized, Nathaniel hears Ironwood's music in a different light. For the first time, he realizes the full implications of the renewing power of Ironwood's music, and he looks to Ironwood "for nourishment, [for] reviving the spirit, like the church that never was" (83). Before, he had never "really listened" to where Ironwood's music took him, but being locked in the basement with Ironwood and the other wards "forced [Nathaniel] to listen with a new set of ears, or to unstop those old ear-tubes of hearing back into the ancestors, from whence Ironwood's power issued" (299). After this revelation, he views Ironwood as the "wounded musical blind bard-warrior, out of whose prophetic, fountain-basin voices poured the denied soul, and now towards whom poor banished children turned for sustenance, in the cataclysmic mutilation of life" (302). In short, Ironwood's music is the only possibility for regenesis out of his and Noah's "calamitous perdition-condition." According to the narration, Ironwood, as the "wizard-chef-warlock, high-priest-musician[,] mixed trumpet, trombone, tenor sax, alto sax, bagpipes, bass clarinet, flute, drums, violin" until he reclaimed, through his music, "a nourishing buried treasure of stormy cauldron served to the supping, sucking patrons, in their pitched nakedness" (294–95). In this sense, Ironwood takes on the status of jazz hero, or what Sherley Anne Williams describes as "the black musician as light bearer":

> The musician is [. . .] an archetypal figure whose referent is Black lives, Black experiences and Black deaths. He is the hope of making it in America and the bitter mockery of never making it well enough to escape the danger of being Black, the living symbol of alienation from the past and hence from self and the rhythmical link with the mysterious ancestral past. (145–46)

Ironwood is, indeed, the light bearer for Nathaniel and Noah at the end of the novel, as they find in his music the empowering act of transformation and enough understanding to deal with the tragedy of their feelings of displacement. The act of transformation in Ironwood's jam session serves as a metaphor for the act of transformation, which the orphans must learn if they are to escape the curse and which Nathaniel must be willing to undergo if he is to learn anything on his ad hoc journey.

Ironwood repeats the theme of displacement through the end of the novel as he riffs on lines from the blues, gospel, and the spiritual such as "God bless the child," "a long way from home," "nobody knows," "Motherless," and "Limehouse Blues." Just as his solo reaches its climax, Ironwood begins to quake and is taken away by the guards and placed in chains.

> He was a tumultuous wreckage. He was exhausted, and ever so wasted, a solitary figure, full of trouble. And they [the guards] were easily able to shift and shape his body upon the ancient rack, after divesting him of his horns. Those horns, which he had turned into stunning orchards of beauty and power, now appeared to take on the visage of corroded chains, as they were carted away in huge moneysacks. (Forrest, *Bloodworth Orphans*, 315)

In addition to reflecting Ironwood's troubled existence, this passage demonstrates Forrest's use of interpolation to weave independent allusions without interrupting the flow of his initial idea. Ironwood's troubled existence is highly symbolic of the torn and troubled black musician who was, too often, "torn apart . . . by the very complexity and brutality which he has helped to ameliorate" (Williams, 143). His horns, once the source of beauty and power, return to their point of origin (pain and suffering), which is symbolized by the image of chains. That Ironwood's horns are taken away in money sacks is no coincidence, either; rather, it speaks to the exploitation of black musicians and their music by commercialism and a white-controlled music industry. Yet the lesson the history of jazz teaches Noah and Nathaniel is still present—jazz's impulse is still a viable ritual for survival when it remains in the right hands. Its very origin and nature reflect key elements of survival—a working integration of the useful elements of the past with the present, improvisation and transformation, and an audible response to racially specific fragmentation. Forrest suggests the necessity of accepting these same ideas throughout the novel if agony is to be transcended, since, for the "lost-founds" who are trapped in the old Refuge Hospital and for motherless children of *The Bloodworth Orphans,* black music—particularly jazz—is one of the few sources of self-definition and self-affirmation. This is perhaps why they see music in all that they deem true and self-authenticating. As Veena Deo notes, "Forrest's characters continuously search for means of self-invention. For them, language which is fraught with contradictions is often inadequate to express intense emotional experience and yearnings. Approximating music is one way" they successfully liberate themselves (191). The notes wailing from the saxophone of the blind musical genius who has been institutionalized help all of them conceive of ways to escape (mentally if not literally) the fatal curse of being lost in the only place they know to call home.

If Ironwood's music is emotionally redeeming to the lost-founds Nathaniel encounters in chapter eleven, then Noah's storytelling of his childhood experiences with W. W. W. Ford and their relationship to the infamous Bloodworth clan in chapter twelve is as close as Nathaniel can come to salvation by the novel's end. Notably, Noah's storytelling is a variation of the novel's use of music as a metaphor for cultural integration. Noah's storytelling, in fact, takes on incredible significance for Nathaniel and the narration alike because it positions otherwise marginal experiences at the center and highlights these experiences' connectedness to broader experiences and traditions. Through Noah's musings, Nathaniel learns the family history of his friends LaDonna Scales and Regal

Pettibone (and of their triplet brother Amos-Otis Thigpen). As it turns out, Noah is their half brother, since he, too, was fathered by Pourty Ford Bloodworth. More important, however, is the lesson Noah's storytelling teaches Nathaniel about the undeniable interconnectedness between all men and between the past and the present and the subsequent limitations of essentialism. It is more fruitful, Noah's storytelling suggests, to find ways of placing African American experiences at the center whenever possible and of integrating these experiences into other human experiences of the past and present when necessary.

The narrative establishes this belief as it creates dialogue with traditional myths to acknowledge African American experiences. It is the myth of Cronus,[1] in fact, that Forrest alludes to as he shapes and complicates the primary diegesis of the final chapter of the novel. Significantly, Forrest does not simply recreate an old myth; he creates a new one, even as he invokes Cronus's fate to castrate his father and to be killed by his offspring. The core of the Bloodworth curse centers around an unnamed adopted Bloodworth son who is the last of his brothers to train-rape their mulatto half sister. Furious at his sons but blaming only the adopted one, old man Bloodworth banishes the unnamed youth from the plantation, "telling him that if he ever had a child, that offspring would physically murder him, just as he, the old man, was 'murdered spiritually' by the foster son" (Forrest, *Bloodworth Orphans*, 341). After years of trying to escape the curse by avoiding women and reproductive sex, the unnamed Bloodworth (whom Noah later identifies as Pourty Ford, or P. F.) fathers triplets with his dark-skinned wife. Still convinced that the children will kill him, he sells his wife into body slavery for thirty dollars to a traveling minister/salesman. She, in turn, kills herself, leaving her husband to rid himself of her body and their children. He gives the first son to an unemployed garbage man, along with thirty dollars in silver, with instructions to dump the child in the city garbage heap. The second child, the girl babe, he gives to a sharecropper, along with thirty dollars in silver, to leave in a pig's sty. The last child he gives to a prostitute with instructions to destroy the child in whatever manner she sees fit. When none of the children is destroyed, as the unnamed one had hoped, the curse of doom is borne upon these orphaned children. Their smaller truth of hereditary doom becomes highly symbolic of the larger truth of the chaos caused by the African American's orphaned status and his fragmentation. And the narrative becomes a rendering of their search for order in the midst of this chaos. Forrest's use of myth intentionally complicates this search.

Unlike in *There Is a Tree More Ancient Than Eden*, where the ordering of chaos and survival hinges largely on the characters' (especially

Nathaniel's) ability and willingness to access cultural traditions that can sustain them, in *The Bloodworth Orphans* folk traditions alone, especially when asserted in isolation or outside of broader human traditions, do not suffice. There must be an awareness of multiple cultures and multiple traditions. The tension between these often warring ways of life must be negotiated, not ignored or denied. The significance of the necessity of this negotiation is again buried within Noah's storytelling and in the narrative's signifying acts. Noah adopts the African oral tradition of storytelling to convey information and to teach Nathaniel the art of survival, but he coopts a jazz impulse and a Western voice in his telling.² Nathaniel notes, for example, that when Noah finally reveals the truth, as he knows it, about the infamous clan, Noah sounds "so professorial and muted—more like an academic humanist . . . rather than a sterling vagabond [. . .] a hobo summa cum laude!" (343). Noah is aware of his doubleness, so he mutes those elements of his Africanness that do not sustain him. And he is even more aware of the chaos in the world to which the two men are about to return. He also knows that this chaos is birthed primarily out of the tension between the Afrocentric and the Eurocentric. His task and his skill, then, is to negotiate and to survive it.

From his memory, Noah gives Nathaniel a history of the Bloodworth clan as the seer, Ford, who is also Noah's great-grandfather, has told it to him. The spoken word, reminiscent of the oral tradition, the folktales, and the riffs, provides Noah with the root of black survival. Jeffrey Renard Allen makes a similar observation when he contends that "the waters of Noah's voice are the source of direction" that "must not be allowed to 'wither,' to dry up, to be rendered speechless" (182). Because he has learned to adapt to the chaos and deception he has encountered as a black man and as a Bloodworth orphan, and because he is aware of the urgency of integrating history and cultural memory with human memory and history, Noah survives his tragic fate.

Ironically, one of the sources from which Noah learns this lesson is from Forest County's most infamous trickster, Ford, who is, at least in part, responsible for both men's imprisonment (the authorities suspect that they know something about Ford's whereabouts). Revealing to Nathaniel the story of his childhood, Noah tells his young apprentice how he was raised by Ford after his mother killed his father, Pourty Ford Bloodworth, and then hanged herself. Because he has a personal fascination with orphaned children (perhaps he recognizes their especial vulnerability), Ford reared Noah and employed him as his accomplice. Ultimately, Noah grew tired of Ford's schemes and recognized that Ford was simply using him as a pawn. As he grows older and wiser, he realizes that Ford's success was based almost completely on his ability to transform himself (he is, after all, a serial hermaphrodite) and to integrate his reality (all versions of it) into broader realities. This is perhaps why the story Ford tells of his origins situates him in the center of the Eden myth. According to Noah, in at least one of the versions of Ford's origins, he takes on the form of a serpent who, through Eve, "cracked open Adam's will" (Forrest, *Bloodworth Orphans*, 318). Later, when Ford, in his human form, kills a female snake, he is "almost immediately transformed into a female" (374). But after seven years, he kills another snake—this time a male—and he is transformed back into a male. Eventually, a god took pity on him and

> [. . .] added to his powers extra attributes of prophecy, and eternal life—one, however, which would be lived out in constant metamorphosis . . . that he would have seven years of sight, and seven years of blindness; that the seer would have seven years of male life, followed by seven years of female life. (375)

Notice Nathaniel's response. Instead of absolute disbelief, he muses:

> This recalls to mind, Noah, a story I've heard all of my life, of a youth, a kind of modern-day Peeping Tom, who peered over a ledge to watch a beautiful goddess, as she bathed. He was caught and the goddess immediately blinded the lad. But his dutiful mother—who was one of the goddess's attendants, desperately beseeched for him. The goddess heard the grieving mother's petition and gave the son special powers of prophecy and understanding. (375–76)

Ford, through Noah, places himself at the center of multiple myths. He refuses to limit himself (or his origin) to one tradition, though he is, at times, visibly African American. For Ford, survival is the issue. And if he is to survive, he must be capable of transformation, improvisation, and integration.

Eventually, Nathaniel, too, learns this lesson, and he begins to invoke experiences from his familial past in response to Noah's story. When Noah tells Nathaniel of Pourty Ford's difficult relationship with his father, Nathaniel connects Pourty's story and the Bloodworth name to his grandfather Jericho, who, as a former slave, escaped his "savage father's whipping lashes" by running away, only to be "hunted down and wanted dead or alive by his own uncle, who claimed [Jericho] was a dangerous ingrate"

(342). And when Noah tells him how Pourty stole books from the library and learned about "bookkeeping and accountancy," Nathaniel retorts: "'Well, my grandpappy educated himself, too, but he rose to become a lawyer and then a judge'" (342). So not only does Nathaniel assert *his story* into the main *history;* he all but privileges it over that which would otherwise exclude him. Forrest's statement to Cawelti about the novel warrants repeating here: "[. . .] in the most marvelous ways and in the most horrible ways black Americans are at the center of this society" (Forrest and Cawelti, 307). Again, he does not "say this in any bragging," yet, Nathaniel makes it clear that his grandfather's achievements outrank those of his white counterpart, who was a member of the slaveholding family that once owned Jericho.

Education and socioeconomic status are not, however, the factors that render Jericho successful. As Nathaniel learns in *There Is a Tree More Ancient Than Eden,* Jericho, too, knows how to integrate the past with the present and how to reinvent himself when necessary. Otherwise, success would be due Abraham Dolphin, who is the epitome of Negro success within white society inside and outside of Forest County. Yet he meets disaster because he cannot bring order to the chaos that informs his life. Dolphin is a doctor who was forced to leave the South in 1952 for attempting to arouse his patients to take political action for their civil rights. Despite his professional achievements, his search for identity is unsuccessful, to a large degree, because he is unable to negotiate his unknown past. He does not know he is the son of Arlington Bloodworth II's mulatto son William Body. After years of living with his chaos, Dolphin retreats to the mountains to hunt for his soul. All in one year, one of his daughters goes insane, his other daughter is killed by her lesbian lover, and his wife leaves him. These events join with his inability to sire a son (and his belief that this is punishment from God for the many illegal abortions he has performed), along with his uncertainty about his origins, to drive him mad. His only recourse, he thinks, is to go away, "not to face the blood upon his hands, but so that he can record, or get [Nathaniel] to record, this side of his splendor. . . . To record, standardize [. . .] these last days [. . .]" (Forrest, *Bloodworth Orphans,* 176). Armed with a tape recorder and other minimal necessities, Dolphin ascends to the mountains. On the seventh day of his forty-day exile, "the physician turned to his battery-generated tape-recording equipment [. . .] and sought to retell himself his life story—to find his own true voice" (177). During the course of his recording, he realizes that instead of really finding his voice and communicating with God, he has become enamored with "the shadows his voice made as he tumbled back into the past" (177). When he realizes he is achieving little more than a "boxed-in voice" that only God might recognize, he admonishes himself to stop: for staging his "re-entry into the world of civil men of Godly confrontation" and for "failing to confront God and himself" (177). He is ill-equipped to order his unordered past because he does not know how to integrate it into the present. Nor can he achieve what Ellison labeled *antagonistic cooperation,* where the soloist and the band are, all at once, individual and group. At least part of Dolphin's failure as a character is that he is isolated and can never quite become one with the community. Eventually, he returns home one last time before his intended lifelong exile to the mountains, where he will deny any relationship between himself and human experiences and, hence, concede to failure. But before he can return, he is attacked by thugs, and he unknowingly kills the young man to whom he had sent Christmas care packages for years. Three weeks later, despite having "the whole wide world in a jug and the stopper in his hand" (194), Dolphin kills himself.

Each character, then, investigates a different option for survival, thus revealing the viability (or lack thereof) of a variety of responses. Rachel and LaDonna try religion, Regal tries religion and music, and Amos-Otis relies purely on biological ancestral ties that continue to escape him, while Dolphin, a former civil rights activist, stands in contrast to Saltport as Black Nationalist Muslim. By the end of the novel, Forrest has taken on slices of African American history—from slavery to the Great Migration—and seeks to give an ordered voice to the unorderable by using music as a metaphor that suggests the importance of cultural integration. A. Robert Lee, in "'Equilibrium Out of Their Chaos: Ordered Unorder in the Witherspoon-Bloodworth Trilogy of Leon Forrest," suggests that

> [g]iven the initial diaspora out of Africa and the Middle Passage, the ensuing ranks of illegally fathered and mothered offspring, and all the ancestral enigma, curses, and sexual bans and transgressions of color, which have passed riddlingly down through both black and white American history, perhaps no literary form, finally, can ever pay anything like complete imaginative due. (102)

Forrest's "difficulty," his own "circling style of modernism," Lee continues, "nonetheless makes the attempt" (102). And at its center is the much-needed balance between cultural integrity and cultural integration and the one art form that has historically been recognized as capable of telling the African American's story in the African American voice—music.

Though the novel takes on the fullness of a variety of literary traditions and cultural myths, it reinterprets them as distinctly African American experiences and offers new breadth to black literary and cultural traditions. The potential effectiveness of this integration is why we can be optimistic about the future, in spite of the seemingly apocalyptic chaos that has overtaken the city when Noah and Nathaniel make their reentry into the world in the final pages of the novel. As the two men flee the city where the burning mayor is hanging on a pole and people are rioting and fighting each other, Noah stumbles upon "a boot box with a screaming babe inside" (Forrest, *Bloodworth Orphans*, 383). And as caregivers to the next generation of lost-founds, the two men are seemingly equipped to teach the babe how to survive and to transcend the agony that (s)he will inevitably encounter. Significantly, the babe, who is "wailing with fear and life," reaches *upward* with its trembling hands toward the "two sad-faced sobbing men" (383). It will be a lost-found but embraced, orphaned but not fatherless and alone, unordered but not unorderable—because for the next generation of Bloodworths, who have hopefully learned the art of transformation and of integrating their experiences into broader human experiences, "salvation is the issue,"[3] and survival is a real possibility.

chapter four

"Learn it to the Younguns": Bearing Witness to the Blues in *Two Wings to Veil My Face*

Like all of the fiction in Leon Forrest's canon, *Two Wings to Veil My Face* is concerned with examining the relationship between the past and the present and, correspondingly, with suggesting means through which the contemporary African American can avoid being trapped in and by an oppressive past. In *There Is a Tree More Ancient Than Eden,* Nathaniel, through the process of (re)memory invokes his family's ancestral past to begin to imagine how he can function successfully in the present following the death of his mother. In *The Bloodworth Orphans,* Nathaniel observes the various cultural traditions the title characters adopt in their attempts to survive the fragmentation they experience because of the racist past that shapes their present existence. In *Two Wings,* Nathaniel is both observer and participant as he prepares to take over his family's history. Part of that history involves slavery. His great-grandfather I. V. and his great-grandmother Angelina are slaves on Rollins Reed's plantation, and the slave experiences they have, which directly impact Nathaniel's grandmother, Sweetie Reed, are detailed throughout the novel. Thus, at varying points, the *Two Wings* can be read as a neoslave narrative.[1] Having beckoned Nathaniel to her bedside altar to bear witness to her reasons for rejecting Nathaniel's grandfather, Jericho Witherspoon, and for initially refusing to attend his funeral, Sweetie Reed goes back to slavery, or to "the beginning times" as she calls them, to help Nathaniel understand her actions and to make him more aware of his family's history. To a large degree, the story Sweetie tells is a blues narrative, detailing how the men in her life—her father, I. V., who neglected her to serve his former slave master, and her husband, Jericho, who fathered a child by another woman after her numerous attempts to have his child failed—did her wrong. Thus, two traditional African American expressive forms—the slave narrative and the blues—shape the novel structurally and thematically. The combination of these traditions allows Forrest to create a freer form for the novel and, perhaps more important, it helps to facilitate successful negotiation of the tension between orality and literacy, freedom and oppression, and the past and the present. This feat gains special significance for two reasons—it allows Sweetie Reed to achieve a sense of self by reconciling her internal conflicts, and it reminds Nathaniel and the reader of the survivalist capabilities and tendencies of black cultural traditions (in this case, the slave narrative and the blues).

The blues and slave history are logical bedfellows. As Booker White explains: { . . . } the foundation of the blues is walking behind the mule in slavery times" (quoted in Oakley, 6). And, as Houston Baker suggests in *Blues, Ideology, and Afro-American Literature,* the blues has been of such great value in African American culture historically because the blues is capable of affirming humanity in even the most dehumanizing of circumstances (190), and no circumstance was more dehumanizing than American slavery. In its affirmation of humanity, the blues is an agent of healing. And this, in addition to its aesthetic function, is Forrest's attraction to the blues as a structuring device in *Two Wings.* Sweetie must bear witness to her family's slave history before she can assert her own *self* and before she can be fully healed. Because she is concerned with her *self,* her contemporary blues dialogue with slavery as narrative also assumes the form Angelyn Mitchell, in *The Freedom to Remember,* astutely dubs the *liberatory narrative.* Mitchell writes:

> While [the] term [neo-slave narrative] suggests that contemporary writers are inventing fictional slave narratives that revisit the historical period of slavery in much the same spirit historical novels describe past lives, there is a more appropriate term for the[se] cultural productions [. . . .] [T]he focus of these narratives [. . .] is not [. . .] on the experience of enslavement but, more importantly, on the construct we call freedom. In other words, they do more than narrate movement from bondage to freedom. The narratives analyze freedom. Accordingly, these narratives are *liberatory narratives.* (3–4; italics in original)

She defines the liberatory narrative as "a contemporary novel that engages the historical period of chattel slavery in order to provide new models of liberation by problematizing the concept of freedom [. . . .] [Its] primary function indeed is in describing how to achieve freedom" (4). In addition to describing how to achieve freedom, the liberatory narrative focuses on "the protagonist's conception and articulation of herself as a free, autonomous, and self-authorized self" (4). While Sweetie is not a former slave, her narrative can be accurately characterized as a liberatory narrative for two reasons.[2] First, the story she tells about her father's neglect of her and about her mother's rape and death at the hands of patrollers is shaped almost exclusively by these characters' slave history. And second, her purpose for invoking the historical period is in dialogue with key functions that characterize the liberatory narrative—to articulate herself as an "autonomous self-authorized *self*" and to provide for Nathaniel and the reader new models of liberation that can effect a release of slavery's historic pain and, correspondingly, to describe how the contemporary African American can achieve a reconceived and usable concept of freedom.

That the African American is unclear about exactly what freedom after slavery entails is perhaps best depicted fictionally in the prologue of Ralph Ellison's *Invisible Man*. After the old woman in the narrator's dream tells him that she killed her master, who is also her children's father, because she loved freedom more than she loved her master, the narrator asks her: "*Old woman, what is this freedom you love so well?*" (Ellison, *Invisible Man*, 11; italics in original). And she responds, "*I done forgot, son. It's all mixed up. First I think it's one thing, then I think it's another. It gits my head to spinning. I guess now it ain't nothing but knowing how to say what I got up in my head*" (11; italics in original). Though she claims to love it, she is unclear about what freedom is. The closest she can come to describing it is as the ability to articulate her blues. Then, when the narrator awakens from his dream shortly after this imagined conversation, he immediately hears Louis Armstrong singing his jazz-blues song "(What Did I Do to Be So) Black and Blue." Thus we see slavery, freedom, storytelling, and the blues intimately connected as Ellison's attempt to construct new and useful notions of freedom. And like the woman in the Invisible Man's dream, whose struggle with freedom involves sexuality and gender, Sweetie's struggle in *Two Wings* with reconceptualizing freedom to achieve *self* involves gender and sexuality as well. Thus, she must adopt a blues impulse for her storytelling, since the blues discourse is one of the few forms that precludes gender and sexuality from limiting her attempts to subvert patriarchy and, subsequently, to be self-authorized.

At first, Nathaniel assumes that Sweetie is telling the story because, as the only grandchild, it is his turn "to take over the memories." But he soon comes to realize that she is telling stories of the past not just for the sake of perpetuating them but also to assert her place in a narrative that has repeatedly excluded her. But her attempts to give voice to her own gender-specific blues must wait until Nathaniel returns the narrative to her. Though *Two Wings* is clearly Sweetie's tale, Nathaniel, as focalizer and part-time narrator, largely controls it until she finally and fully achieves her blues voice during the course of the novel. Thus, as she renders her song, Nathaniel as character and Forrest as author unwittingly displace her again, as Nathaniel regresses to memories of a talk he and Sweetie had when he was seven years old. But even as he interrupts her tale and begins one of his own, the memories he engages help develop her theme of female sexual exploitation. He asked his grandmother the meaning of the word *rape,* and Sweetie, abiding by her premise "if you were old enough to ask a question, then you were old enough to get an answer" (Forrest, *Two Wings,* 81), explained rape to Nathaniel in the context in which he has heard the word. He had overheard a group of men talking about a newspaper report of a woman in the South being raped while her husband was forced to watch and then was lynched. He heard the gory details of how the man was stripped naked, lifted to a platform, yoked at the neck, and bound at the stump to a poplar tree. As the men raped the hanging man's wife, he nearly tore the tree from its roots in rage—only the more he moved, the more he hanged himself.

Unsure exactly of what *rape* meant, Nathaniel knew that "it was so fierce it seemed beyond murder in what it did to the mind and spirit of a woman (and a man, too, if he loved her); he also knew it was something men alone did to women; and he also knew enough not to ask the men in childish shame about what he didn't understand" (81). So, he turned to Sweetie, who explained it to him (telling him what she wants him to know, he adds) so clearly in its articulation of betrayal and hurt that, by the time he is twenty-one, "the close, perverse connection between rape and sexual aggression tormented him body and soul" (82), and he feels guilty about engaging women sexually. Ultimately, his confusion about lovemaking, mixed with his worshipful feelings for women, frequently render him sexually inactive and the object of his friends' amusement. They tease:

> —Man, Spoons be in there working out, doing some down heavy third finger work and all of a sudden when he's supposed to be copping his plea and popping the loaded question, his mind goes acrobat, his soul goes berserk, and his hard-on goes iceberg slim on him. . . . (82)

Though Nathaniel denies the truth of the frat boys' story, he cannot deny the influence of his knowledge of historical exploitation on his present-day interaction with women. He makes no attempt to; instead, he willingly admits that when he hears young girls whispering "no no no," he translates it into the voice of a representative victimized woman. He understands their blues. He finally settles down and becomes engaged to Candy Cummings, but Sweetie's past experience as excluded woman influences even the outcome of this situation. Though she does not tell Nathaniel until the end of her story why she dismisses Candy, who then dismisses Nathaniel, sending the engagement ring back to him by messenger, she does so because Candy reminds her of Lucasta Jones, who, as we shall see later, is a vital, though unacknowledged, part of Nathaniel's ancestry.

Having unwittingly introduced her theme of exploitation, Nathaniel, after returning the narrative to Sweetie, learns of his grandmother's role as a woman who has been exploited and wronged by a man. Born only two years after slavery ended, Sweetie goes back to this "beginning time" as she explains her hurts to her grandson. Though her blues themes of lack, loss, and love are repeated with variation throughout the novel, we hear it first as Sweetie tells of the lack she feels from the absence of love from her father. Almost from birth she had a strained relationship with her father, I. V. Reed, who was a house slave to Rollins Reed on a Mississippi plantation. On his deathbed, I. V. attempts to explain his life to Sweetie. Thus, again, a male narrative interrupts Sweetie's attempt to achieve subjectivity. But because I. V.'s life as a slave is so vital to Sweetie's identity as a displaced woman, she accepts the importance of his tale and includes it in her blues narrative.

One situation that informs I. V.'s slave experience and is particularly relevant to his deathbed confessions to Sweetie about why he neglected her as a child is his role in the death of another slave, Reece Shank Haywood. The only reason I. V. tells Sweetie this story is that he has been mandated to do so by one who knows the power of orally narrating slavery's blues. In an attempt to gain revenge on Shank after I. V. saw him with the bonnet I. V. had given to his love interest, Minnie-Bea, I. V. told Shank that Rollins Reed, their owner, was at Jubell's shack. Knowing that Shank would lose his temper and confront Rollins, since Jubell was Shank's woman, I. V. hoped that Shank's actions would warrant a beating. Instead, Shank waited until Rollins left the shack, choked him nearly to death, and left him after I. V. hit Shank with a slingshot to keep Shank from killing him. Since he knew that the death of his master would cause more trouble than good, I. V. dragged Rollins to Jubell's African great-grandauntie, Foisty, "who [knew] a mite of everything 'bout anything in the way of bringing people back from the dead and how to help the living to keep on holding on" (106). She restored life to Rollins but punished I. V. for his part in the ordeal. I. V. confesses to Sweetie:

> Auntie Foisty told me [. . . t]he sole way I could ever hope for salvation was to tell the whole story out loud before I died out to each of my children and each of their children's children unto my last breathing gasp. . . . Me personal, not through any third hand, but by my very own lapping tongue. (139)

Thus, before he dies, he confesses his sins to his daughter, much like she confesses her past to her grandson—out loud and firsthand (she even tells I. V.'s story in his own words). By requiring I. V. to "tell the whole story out loud" until his "last breathing gasp," Foisty, from beyond the grave, asserts the power of oral history and intimates storytelling as a cultural cousin of the blues.

The only living African left on Rollins Reed's plantation, Auntie Foisty was especially known for her memory and her uncanny ability to recall facts. I. V. marvels:

> Auntie Foisty's mind seems to get sharper, more supple, deeper with each fork-turning in the long woods of her days; so much so, Master Rollins himself bends to her for recollecting 'bout the rightness of Old Master's records on the crop books [. . .] what his pappy, Old Man Rollins Reed, kept fifty-odd years before, in the beginning time. Those books partly burned in a fire, so who do they turn on, Auntie Foisty, who can't even read or write; even asking her what each slave was sold for, hour, day and year of the auction. Most of the time she ain't for sure about the money part of it; but knows where each and every one of 'em was sold off to [. . .] when they come into this world and how they went out: backwards and forwards. (111–12)

Though she is not always able to recall what is most important to the master—issues of money—Foisty is always able to recall what is most important to her—issues of humanity. As Keith Byerman notes, "[s]he knows, not the putatively neutral record of the ink marks, but the human traces behind those marks. She knows *how* slaves died rather than just *when*. She knows the *whole*, instead of merely its economic significance" ("The Flesh Made Word," 205–6; italics in original). She is at once both a product and a teller of history through memory. As oral historian, she foreshadows blues wisdom where cultural knowledge and understanding are sought in the community rather than in white power structures.

Sweetie, however, understanding the interplay between written history and orally transmitted memory, knows that success also turns on the ability to master both history and memory as modes of expressing the past. So she insists that Nathaniel commit their family's history both to memory and to paper.[3] When Nathaniel suggests that he bring a tape recorder to their storytelling session, Sweetie says simply:

> *No. Just bring along a pen and pad, not a pencil, either, because too much has been erased in time. Nor an indelible pencil. Write it all down in longhand, with blue-black ink on the pad, in your notebook, and then it all will be recorded on the tablet of your memory and in your heart, as it's transformed from your longhand to your short memory. It's time we moved from listening and half hearing to listening and recording in longhand.* (Forrest, *Two Wings*, 7; italics in original)

In the tradition of the blues, Nathaniel, as blues artist, must now sing his own version rather than a verbatim recording of Sweetie's and his family's song. At its base, it will be the same tale, but Sweetie bestows upon him the power of interpretation. Nathaniel recognizes this gift and embraces it as he smiles upon the legal pads that flow with his family's history, bestowed "unto the fifth generation," and which he desires "to spin [. . .] into an eternal gold beyond the radiance of the here and the now of men's eyes" (245). He knows that he must take his role as singer of his family's history seriously, since "none of the family history was put down in books, in the way it was for the families of the Hebrew children, Great-Momma Sweetie Reed said" (8). So, at the very least, it must be sung.

Though part of the purpose of Sweetie's oral lesson is to give Nathaniel the gift of ancestry she receives vicariously from Foisty and to make sure that future generations do not forget the "ustea be" ways of their forebears, in order to achieve her blues voice Sweetie must first deal with a number of historical betrayals—whites' betrayal of blacks, blacks' betrayal of blacks, and men's betrayal of women. Her willingness to describe these betrayals to Nathaniel is what gives her narrative its ability to be liberating. By bearing witness to her blues, she frees herself from the residuals of slavery's legacy and its shame. The betrayal that shapes Sweetie's relationship with I. V. the most is one that does, indeed, shame I. V. and causes both Sweetie and her mother pain. After Sweetie is returned to him after being kidnapped along with her mother, Angelina, by men who plan to sell them into forced slavery, I. V.

is unable to love her. Angelina is raped and killed, and Sweetie, who witnesses these acts, becomes a living reminder to I. V. of his powerlessness to defend his wife. Since Rollins Reed does not have enough money to pay bounty hunters to return his daughter and granddaughter, he writes to Jericho Witherspoon, an affluent Negro lawyer who remembered Angelina from the time he saw her on the Reed plantation as he was escaping to the North. Jericho agrees to pay the ransom, and as punishment for I. V.'s role in Reed's ordeal with Shank, Reed plans to betray I. V. and give his wife to Jericho. When she is killed, I. V. betrays Sweetie and allows Reed to arrange her marriage to Jericho. We soon learn that Sweetie blames I. V. for being so obsessed with Reed that I. V. was underneath his former master's bed instead of with her and her mother when they were kidnapped. But she is powerless and all but orphaned. So she accepts her fate as her mother's replacement and, at the age of fifteen, she marries Jericho Witherspoon, Forest County's first Negro judge, who is fifty-five.

Her primary purpose is to produce offspring for Jericho, and when she fails to do so (after numerous miscarriages and infant deaths), he betrays her and fathers a child with his mistress, Lucasta Jones. As it turns out, Nathaniel's father, Arthur, is this child. Much to Nathaniel's surprise, Sweetie, the woman who was "vitally linked to everything in his world of remembrances" (244), is not his grandmother at all. She does not reveal this fact to him until the end of her narrative, because he must begin to discover who he is in relation to his communal ancestry, which has little to do with blood, before he knows the truth about his biological ancestry. Yet she also feels obliged to tell Nathaniel the "whole truth" because she does not want him to feel the pain of betrayal she felt when her father told her only a "side" of the truth. She tells Nathaniel:

> [. . .] to hear the satanic one's [I. V.] voice allowed to bear witness to history was something that I had to get used to because amongst other things I had so grown used to being called upon as the counsel for the wretched. I'd forgotten how it is always a fool, or a wise fool, who gives us a quarter of the truth, turned inside out. So that out of the voice of the serpent came coiled memory but what spat from off of his tongue in its mockery was the base truth and a side of my truthful history. (91)

Out of this history, Sweetie remakes her *self*, and her willingness to bear witness in her liberatory narrative subsequently enables Nathaniel to use what he has learned about his family's slave history to negotiate the contemporary moment more successfully. In the sense that it is based in large part on her memory of how she gained command of her life after Jericho betrayed her, Sweetie's blues narrative, even with its element of lamentation, is more importantly about her liberation.

The most logical way to acknowledge one's agony without conceding to it, of course, is to adopt a blues aesthetic, which Sweetie does hesitantly. She would much prefer the more sacred gospel aesthetic, but she knows it cannot accommodate her secular trials. Nor would it acknowledge her gender-specific hurts. The blues, however, as Angela Davis notes in *Blues Legacies and Black Feminism,* has historically "constitute[d] a privileged discursive site" in a culture where there were "stringent taboos on representations of sexuality" and on a woman's desire to chose her own sex partners or to determine her own sexual value (xvii). Sweetie's conflict with Jericho is that he insists on defining her worth as a wife and as a woman exclusively in terms of her ability to give him a child. Thus, she must adopt a form that will not only allow her to express her trials as a member of an oppressed racial group but will also offer a rebellious response to the patriarchy that denies her worth based on gender. And the blues is this form.

But, again, Sweetie's desire to articulate the wrongs she has experienced at the hands of the men in her life and, subsequently, liberation is not the only objective of her storytelling. Like the grandfather in *Invisible Man,* who, also on his deathbed, insists on the significance of passing down ancestral wisdom, Sweetie knows that, as an elder, she must structure this wisdom and "learn it to the younguns." Thus, as Nathaniel listens to Sweetie's liberatory narrative, he also participates in the progression of his own soul. Once he discovers that he is both editor of and participant in Sweetie's narrative, he realizes that in listening to "her hurts, her wrongs, and her history," he can see the hurts, the wrongs, and the history of the African American. Seeing "what went wrong, from the beginning time," Nathaniel can "look into the mirror" and find himself (Forrest, *Two Wings,* 21). But first, having become aware of familial and communal history and discovering its relationship to his personal experience, he must now learn to order the chaos that informs black experience. Admittedly, this is a difficult task:

> in the ABC's you went from A to B to C. But in these stories of the family, the boy [Nathaniel] felt he often went from A to C to E and then maybe later on learned of B. But often, maybe not. Learning to play the piano as he was now doing, the boy thought of how you skipped notes to Every Good Boy Does Fine. *E G B D F.* And it took perhaps forever to learn what those notes could do, when brought

> together in different combinations. One day he would learn the meaning of the chords [. . .].(11)

Sweetie intends to make the day in which *Two Wings* takes place the day that Nathaniel brings all the notes of the past together to create his own song. And he must choose what aspects of the past are vital and relevant to his success and discard all others, lest he be destroyed by an inability to free himself from those harmful aspects of the past and its chaos. Instead, he must adopt the blues aesthetic, which allows life's inherent contradictions and ongoing problems to coexist, rather than pretending that they can be easily solved or succumbing to them.

Among the most important lessons Sweetie teaches Nathaniel with her storytelling-as-blues is the lesson that is at the heart of all of Forrest's novels—that survival is hinged on one's ability to reinvent the past and to transform the self. For, as Nathaniel finally realizes, in order to reestablish a working identity he would have to integrate the past and the present, and

> he would have to be many kinds of men brought together as one, in one flesh, and soul, and mind. Each man must re-create himself [. . .] out of all that's given to him and placed upon his shoulders; Great-Momma Sweetie Reed had contributed to that shaping of the young man. You could not escape from the yoke of history, ancestors, lovers, and the demons and gifts of living, only transcend and remake yourself through all of it as a man. (5–6)

And by learning, through Sweetie's narrative, the power and wisdom that evolved from African American traditions such as the blues, which not only expressed communal woes but resolved to overcome them, Nathaniel stands a chance of recovering from the horrors of the past and of functioning well in the present.

Forrest repeats this theme, suggesting the significance of transformation to survival as he has Rev. Pompey c. j. Browne discuss this characteristic of Jericho in his eulogy of Jericho. Pompey begins his eulogy testifying about the lessons he learned from his grandmother and Jericho Witherspoon. Both characters knew how to mask their true selves in the presence of threatened whites. From Grandmother Browne and Jericho, Pompey learned "[to] constantly reinvent life out of whatever material of chaos that came [his] way" (184). Pompey also points out how Jericho's life reflected broader African American experiences. He tells the congregation of mourners:

> . . . The very odyssey of this grand, audacious man traces the outline of our story with such vivid visage that the longevity of his preservation seems a tapestry stitched in the agony riddles and wonders and tribulations of our Great Awakening from slavery to freedom to quasi-slavery. (180)

Thus, African American group history is as much a part of Pompey's eulogy as is Jericho's life activity. From the brand *JW* on Jericho's back, put there by his own father, to Jericho's work on behalf of newly freed men, the former slave's life was intricately linked to the African American and his quest for equality. As Pompey astutely recognizes, Jericho's life was a walking, living, breathing explanation of what the African American desires:

> [. . .] all Mr. Asa [Philip Randolph] had to do would be to bring Jericho Witherspoon to the White House and take off his shirt and let the President of this Divided House see what a white father did to his own mulatto blood and then he'd stop asking why the Negro wants to be free to be, to work for equal pay, and yes, Lawd, to *Fly*. (182; italics in original)

Notably, these are many of the same desires articulated in traditional blues. But as Sweetie's response to Pompey's eulogizing of Jericho suggests, in many ways these blues fail to acknowledge women. So she modifies Pompey's eulogy by offering one of her own.

Although she had vowed not to attend her estranged husband's funeral, Sweetie enters the parlor chapel, approaches Jericho's casket, and picks up where Pompey has left off. When Nathaniel's father, Arthur, questions why she must disgrace Jericho's death with this interruption, she reminds him that even still waters "don't run deep enough" and that such waters need to be troubled to stir up "the appearance of calm" and to clear the path for healing (192–93). In other words, Sweetie needs to assert herself into this male narrative if she is to fully achieve her blues voice. After continued arguments with Arthur, who, in his patriarchal way, attempts to mute her, Sweetie responds that what she is trying to get at is "a confession, mixed up with a transformation" (21). Through Jericho, God reveals to her that a "soul can't be rested until it's bathed in the pool of trouble-faced water, cracking the calm—that you got to stir up" (210). Jericho's voice implores Sweetie: "Preach if you must, but teach and lacerate you will, into our sheer enchantment with aggravation—making us the sheer monotony of trouble" (214). Here, Forrest's authorial voice rings out clearly as Jericho suggests that trouble is ordering and purifying. Arguing that "spiritual agony at the core" is what was missing from contemporary writing when he began writing fiction, Forrest, commenting on the aesthetic and healing impulse of the blues, notes that "[t]rouble is always at your back door and, if you would but look, at your front door as well. Out of this you can recreate your life, by constantly crafting out new doors in the menacing mansions and old house of life" (*Furious Voice,* 26). Sweetie, in the tradition of the blues, crafts new doors for herself and, like Pompey, reminds her listeners that they, too, must understand the power and necessity of transformation as it relates to healing and to survival.

Though Sweetie's modification of Pompey's eulogy is, at points, in line with Pompey's representation of Jericho, the points of departure where she is critical of Jericho and, correspondingly, of patriarchy are of grave importance to the narrative. Sweetie has spent most of her life finding ways to overcome her status as a displaced woman. And though she eventually defines her *self* without regard to her father or to Jericho (she becomes known in the county for her mission work with Lovelady Breedlove; the two provide food, shelter, and nurturing to the needy), she still feels the need to disrupt the master narrative and to infuse her own. And she does so with the ambiguity sometimes characteristic of women's blues. Davis observes:

> What gives the blues such fascinating possibilities of sustaining emergent feminist consciousness is the way [blues-women] often construct seemingly antagonistic relationships as noncontradictory oppositions. A female narrator in a women's blues song who represents herself as entirely subservient to a male desire might simultaneously express autonomous desire and a refusal to allow her mistreating lover to drive her to psychic despair. (xv)

Such is the case with Sweetie, who never denies her affection for Jericho, even after he brings home a child he has fathered by another woman. And even though she still loves him and is hurt by his mistreatment of her, she finds the strength to live her life without him rather than succumb to despair over his betrayal.

She is similarly ambiguous about her relationship with her father. Though she refuses to let her hurt destroy her, she can never completely release the theme of loneliness and lack of love the narrative repeats. She tells Nathaniel early on in her narrative:

> When I. V. Reed was on his deathbed, I went back to the Rollins

Reed plantation to say goodbye; fifty-two years ago to this very day; after all, this was the father, I said to myself. I had not seen him since I left that plantation, twenty-four years before. Maybe I wanted to hear him say just simply *I tried to love you, Sweetie* [. . . .]

Yet I knew his word would be a foundling lie, so maybe not even that; but to give me a portion of recognition as his child, that never sprang from his tongue while I was there. In turn I had pledged myself to give out a show of the daughter's gift of feeling, even though I knew it only came from a hurt and father-cut-off heart. (Forrest, *Two Wings*, 45; italics in original)

In spite of herself, Sweetie seeks to be told that she is loved. She craves the feeling of belonging. But even as her feelings toward her father and Jericho are wrought with ambiguity, her use of the blues as a site where she can articulate her protest against male dominance is clear. As Davis notes of Bessie Smith, especially, women blues singers "countered the Christian monopolization of black spirituality" and its corresponding patriarchal ideology and established themselves as equal to the church's patriarchs (129). The blues became scripture, and its presentation became the sermon. And Sweetie disrupts Jericho's funeral, much to the patriarchs' chagrin, in this tradition. She places her eulogy of Jericho side by side with Pompey's and attempts to enforce egalitarian gender relations by asserting her *self*.

By the end of the narrative, it is this action and the date *June 5th* that Sweetie must ultimately explain to Nathaniel. When he notices Sweetie's delay in explaining the date to him, he could hear "his soul commanding him if not to take charge then to charge forth with his question" (Forrest, *Two Wings*, 250). Sweetie complains that the burden of the date is still too fierce for her "to center down upon," but he insists:

> Great-Momma Sweetie, it's not for the story alone that I need to fill out that date and what it meant to get the story right. But to get right what is missing from you and me. Between us, too. For myself and my own troubled mind within. I came upon those dates in your Bible long ago. And now I want to know what is hidden from me and what you have hidden maybe from yourself, as unspeakable in the long ago. (250)

Ultimately, Sweetie reveals that June 5th is the date Jericho brought home the son he conceived with Lucasta Jones. The child of this union, of course, is Arthur, Nathaniel's father.

By telling Nathaniel the whole of her story, Sweetie finally achieves her blues voice, though, ultimately, she releases her narrative, including its distinctly female aspects, to a male. The implications of this release can be read in one of two ways—either Sweetie feels empowered enough by the success with which she articulates her liberation that she is indifferent about handing this narrative over to her male descendant, or she concedes that she cannot escape patriarchy completely and thus manages only to shape rather than to control her narrative. No matter the case, she inevitably becomes a part of the feminine blues tradition of Ma Rainey and Bessie Smith, a tradition that allows women to speak for themselves and to create dialogue between their desire for subjectivity and their role as objects of sexual desire, even though she does so almost surreptitiously. Her lack of resistance to this rests perhaps in the fact that her purpose for telling the narrative in the first place is so that she can show Nathaniel, as representative of the contemporary African American, how to survive and how to achieve selfhood. The characterization of Sweetie's narrative as a blues narrative then becomes only as significant as its characterization as a liberatory narrative, which, again, invokes slavery and its subsequent historical period for the express purpose of communicating to its listening/reading audience ways the contemporary African American can free the *self* from the residual legacy of slavery (Mitchell, 3). Thus, though Sweetie is concerned with achieving a blues voice that validates her experiences as a female, she is as concerned with using this voice to provide a model of liberation for those who are to come after her. By telling Nathaniel her story, including the fact that she is not his biological grandmother, Sweetie attempts to prepare Nathaniel for his own blues burden and, by empowering him with the truth, to show him how to transform the themes of loneliness and lack to a theme of survival by making a way out of no way.

Like its gospel namesake, *Two Wings to Veil My Face* is concerned with survival. In the traditional hymn, the singer chants: "two wings to veil my face, two wings to veil my feet, two wings to fly away, so the world can't do me no harm." In Forrest's novel, Sweetie Reed seeks this angelic protection from historical and worldly hurts, but is forced to borrow from the blues tradition in order to overcome them. To ensure her healing and to encourage Nathaniel's subsequent wellness in the contemporary moment, she combines two closely related black cultural forms of healing and sustenance—the slave narrative and the blues. The stories she tells and the blues she sings investigate ideas of freedom, provide a model of liberation for the contemporary African American, and bear witness to what she believes must be *learned to the younguns*. At the novel's end, Sweetie finally removes the two wings that have veiled her face. Now the world can't do her no harm.

chapter five

Though I Am Many, I Am Yet Still One: Reinvention in *Divine Days*

As early as 1934, people watcher Zora Neale Hurston observed at least twelve characteristics she deemed typical of and, in some cases, peculiar to Negro expression. Among them were angularity (nothing about the Negro was straightforward, monolithic, or one-sided, she claimed) and originality (everything the Negro touches is reinterpreted for his own use). Fifty years later, Leon Forrest adopts Hurston's language as he comments on the "angularity of the contemporary experience" and on the African American's gift of originality. It is this gift, in fact, that he argues is one of the

> literary constants of Afro-American literature [. . .] the Reinvention of life. Or, the cultural attribute of black Americans to take what is left over or, conversely, given to them [. . .] and make it work for them, as a source of personal or group survival, and then to place a stamp of elegance and élan upon the reinvented mode; to emboss, upon the basic form revised, a highly individualistic style, always spun of grace, and fabulous rhythms [. . .] Of course the improvisational genius of jazz is the epitome of what I am getting at here [. . .] Or in athletics Doctor J, Jackie Robinson, and Willie Mays, to name but a scant few. (Forrest, *Furious Voice,* 23)

As Forrest recognizes, reinvention, as a black cultural tradition, manifests itself in many ways. But in terms of own writing, reinvention is the basic hallmark that enables him to reveal his appreciation for the "angularity of cultural expression and the existentially rugged independence of [his] oppressed but not destroyed characters" (23). And while the technique of reinvention surfaces in each of his first three novels and contributes tremendously to their success as survival narratives or narratives of transcendence, his use of reinvention as black cultural tradition of survival and as narrative strategy reaches its pinnacle in his fourth novel, *Divine Days*. If the effectiveness of *Divine Days* as a great African American narrative rests in its orality, its imaginative storytelling, its willingness to grapple delicately and aggressively with the beauty and the horror alike of the African American experience, then its effectiveness as a literary masterpiece and as Forrest's masterwork rests in the author's use of reinvention as a black cultural tradition that allows him to revise, to resist, and to rewrite ("in the light of likeness—transformed") prescriptive types and aesthetics. Together, African American literary traditions and Forrest's transformation of them create new aesthetics that take reinvention as a central technique and as the only means through which the contemporary writer can express the fullness of the African American's angularity. In addition, reinvention gains its significance in *Divine Days* because it provides Forrest with a technique through which to present a critique of black intellectual history in the context of the novel. With its likeness to a literary jazz motif, reinvention creates shifting visions of both characters and themes, ultimately suggesting that meaning, particularly the meaning of blackness, is not fixed but variable.

Structured as a week's worth of Joubert Jones's journal entries, *Divine Days* is most heavily informed by the conflict between two culture heroes—Sugar-Groove and W. W. W. Ford, who resurfaces in Forest County after making less pivotal appearances in the preceding sagas. This structure affords Forrest access to any number of black cultural traditions (some of which are devastating, some of which are healing) and subsequently allows him to highlight the variability of blackness. As one of the culture heroes Forrest reinvents, Sugar-Groove is, on the surface, representative of a standard stereotype of blackness that was popularized during the 1970s, which middle-class African Americans constantly tried to subvert for fear that white America would accept the hustler as the prototypical African American. In addition to reinventing this character type and giving Sugar-Groove layers of complexity uncommon to a black street character, Forrest offers his vision of what makes black literature interesting and meaningful as Sugar-Groove becomes both our means of accessing a fictional plot and a repository for the author's critique of the world, as well as one who is not simply a repository but who constantly remakes himself to accommodate the ever-changing contemporary experience. By toying with who Sugar-Groove is as a fictional character and as a representative of blackness, the author suggests that, contrary to popular 1970s rhetoric and thought, blackness could never be limited to being static or marginal.

Unlike Forrest's first three novels—*There Is a Tree More Ancient Than*

Eden, The Bloodworth Orphans, and *Two Wings to Veil My Face*—which take Nathaniel Witherspoon as central consciousness, *Divine Days* adopts aspiring playwright, journalist, and bartender Joubert Antoine Jones as its narrator. Arguably, the shift in narrating consciousness from Nathaniel to Joubert is the novel's first reinventive task, for as John Cawelti suggests in "Earthly Thoughts on *Divine Days*," Joubert is a reinvention, of sorts, of Nathaniel. Though the two young men share several characteristics, Joubert is "much more sophisticated, reflective, and self-aware than Nathaniel" (233). And while Nathaniel is more than adequate as character in and consciousness of the early novels of the Forest County Saga, the complexity of experiences Joubert chronicles in his journal during the first eight days of his return to Forest County from Germany exceeds the limits of the types of experiences Nathaniel is capable of interpreting and, subsequently, narrating as effectively as Joubert does. But instead of abandoning completely the intradiegetic narrator, who renders, at different levels of consciousness, the events he observes and which intrigue him, Forrest simply reinvents his narrator, in the author's terms, *in the light of likeness, transformed.*

Forrest first coins this phrase in a collection of essays (originally titled *Relocations of the Spirit* and reprinted as *The Furious Voice for Freedom*) that reveals reinvention and transformation as key tenets to understanding the art of his fiction. The quest is to embrace a theme, a character, an idea, and then to transform it into something new yet recognizable. It still maintains the general qualities of its origin but with its new seal of personal élan. The example Forrest cites as representative of reinvention involves another art form—dance—and Alvin Ailey Dance Theatre's Judith Jamison and her dance tribute to black women titled "Cry." He writes:

> Miss Jamison employed a huge cloth as the symbolic agency in order to reenact—through ceremonial stages—this migration of the soul, this epic story of the black woman in the Western experience. With a section of her cloth pressed into service—*durante vitae* [sic]—we see Jamison as the black scrub woman; then again, using her cloth as a "carriage" for the nursing of everybody's babies; then as a shawl of adornment; now as a cotton sack; later as a wraparound, Northern Muslim woman's headgear, etc. (22; italics in original)

Clearly, the cloth is presented in the light of its original likeness; yet it is as clearly transformed.

Suffering from a writer's very natural anxiety of influence, Forrest acknowledges a desire to outdo the masters (including Shakespeare); one of the ways through which he seeks to achieve this—to cut his own path—is by transforming, in the light of likeness, that which the master writer only suggests through clues, which Forrest then expands and broadens. This is certainly true of his reinvention of the culture heroes who emerged in early African American literature and have evolved over the years. To a large degree, the plot of *Divine Days* turns on the actions and antics of three characters who escape broad definitions of and, in some cases, the limitations of culture heroes, but who resemble them tremendously. At least to some degree, the African American culture hero goes undefined in a detailed sense both in the world and in the literature that seeks to re-create him. But generally, he follows the basic ideas of the hero purported by Lord Raglan, Joseph Campbell, and Kenneth Burke, each of whom summarily move through the following progressions: purpose, passion, and perception (Burke); death, life underground, and rebirth (Raglan); and departure, initiation, and return (Campbell). More often than not, the African American culture hero repeatedly experiences these miniodysseys on a less-than-mythic level and is best known for his tendencies toward perception/rebirth/return. The primary difference between the more traditional mythic hero—Odysseus, Prometheus, and the like—and the African American culture hero is that he is born (out of necessity) within African American culture and subsequently returns the boon to this community. In addition, his passion/life underground/initiation are often racially specific and involve some racially motivated tension or conflict. He also looks to history, tradition, and culture to survive this conflict, at which time, upon his success, he receives his apotheosis from those within the culture, with whom he shares the boon.

In a 1996 interview with Forrest, Madhu Dubey calls attention to Forrest's rejection of prototypes for heroes as he develops *Divine Days*' most interesting character, Sugar-Groove. She writes:

> [. . . a] striking example of what one can call a gumbo method of mixing cultural forms in the novel is the character Sugar Groove, whose cultural ancestry includes Oedipus, Icarus, the black folk figures of the trickster and the badman, and even the legendary flying African [. . . .] Sugar Groove [also] recall[s] Luzana Cholly from Albert Murray's Train Whistle Guitar. But [. . .] despite all the parallels, there are clear differences [. . . .] (Forrest and Dubey, 596)

Acknowledging Sugar-Groove's affinity with these characters, Forrest suggests that his reinvention of these folk types is born out of his desire to write against figures he admires without repeating them. He tells Dubey:

> [. . .] there are a lot of things about Sugar Groove that are symbolic of a certain generation of African-American hustler, and drifter, and a man who collected everything along the way [. . . . There exist] personality attributes within the community that are just waiting out there for some artist to come and seize and give a shape to. (597)

Writing distinctively out his Chicago heritage, Forrest seeks to capture the city's essence as a hustler's town. Hence, one of the characters waiting for the artist to seize his actions and, thus, serve as springboard is, inevitably, the hustler. Though his presence was never doubted, he had yet to appear in African American fiction in any complicated manner. He had appeared on a surface level in blaxploitation films of the seventies. But even then, he was more of a pimp and a fighter than a fully explored drifter or a hustler. And what sets Sugar-Groove apart from the character types Forrest is writing against is the fullness of his complexity. While he is as much pure folk figure as gentle badman, Sugar-Groove is also college educated. Similarly, he could appear as easily in the spirit of romance as Janie's beloved Tea Cake in Hurston's *Their Eyes Were Watching God* as among John Henry in Sterling Brown's "Strong Men." We see in Sugar-Groove the "interior loneliness [. . . the] interior cry of the soul" (597) of all the characters—the badman, the drifter, the hustler—whose bravado and outward appearance define them in the community. Through Sugar-Groove, however, their internal conflict emerges to the surface and, accordingly, complicates and reinvents our image of him.

Joubert first introduces us to a sustained metanarrative about Sugar-Groove two days after Joubert's return to Forest County, which also happens to be the day he goes to Williemain's barbershop to get a haircut and to get "the truth of it all" about Sugar-Groove's death. As the "vernacular university with an invisible library," the barbershop becomes the center of storytelling. Of his love for barbershops Forrest writes:

> [. . . [T]here are so many of these voices, so much intelligence, so much lying that goes on in there. [My] barber told me the other week, he said, "You know what I want you to do? I want you to help

> me do a book, Forrest, because you know there's so much bullshit out here and lying." I almost fell out. I said, "Matt, don't you ever contemplate cutting off the lying going on in this barbershop." In these exaggerations we come closer, of course, to something that's greater than any attempt to pinpoint truth—all these stories and fables and so on. And out of that you develop something. (Forrest and Rowell, 351)

Out of that he developed Sugar-Groove and much of *Divine Days*. Though he knows that Williemain will surely exaggerate the "truth," Joubert, like Forrest, has more faith in his barber than in alleged historical truths. In an attempt to authenticate his role as the novel's storyteller and his barbershop-storytelling experience, Joubert, introducing one of his many metanarratives, notes:

> It was always extremely difficult to trace the actual genesis of a story in Williemain's Barbershop, but apparently somebody had asked the question [. . . .] Whatever [*sic*] happened to the body of Sugar-Groove, the scavenger, *after* he vanished *that last time* before this one? And this really ripped it open.
> After he tied the collar of that red, white, and blue apron about my neck, and pumped the handlebar of the chair so that my head was at a workable level, Williemain declared: "Well, Sugar-Groove went for a joy ride. Not the kind you fools thinking about. I sure ain't spieling on Mary Poppins, nor am I riffing on them flying nuns. There's a word for it too, but I'm not telling you dudes doodle-squat—not yet." (Forrest, *Divine Days*, 97; italics in original)

As storyteller, Williemain exercises his right to delay beginning his narrating act until he deems the time appropriate. And in the spirit of the jazz artist, he plans to begin his story with one idea and to expand and to improvise on it as he sees fit. Hence, the narrative takes on a sort of jazz orchestration, which reflects Sugar-Groove's tendencies toward reinvention and improvisation.

According to Williemain and to legend, Sugar-Groove had violated the restrictions placed upon him by the divine proclamation that confounded his status in paradise. He enters the War-Room to meet with St. Peter, who has just returned to heaven from a working vacation out west and who is very upset with Sugar-Groove because of his stylized flights through and around heaven.[1]

> Casting his eyes down upon his Supersonic Over-Soul timepiece, St. Peter started off: "Negro have you lost your cotton-picking mind? You just got here on a wing and a prayer as it is. Your grand aunt prayed you into Heaven and apparently struck some shady deal between herself, her boss man and Gabriel, behind my back. But limitations were placed upon your status in the beginning. And your travel was curtailed. Now you are breaking every rule in the good black book. So help me God, I don't think putting you on milk and honey would be a difficult penalty I'm thinking seriously a cutting down on your spare-ribs, Sugar-Groove. (99)

At least three elements of black folk culture are at work here: the language, which is as authentic as any written replication of black folk talk; the tradition of black maternal figures constantly praying for their younger male descendants; and black humor that plays on the black American's love of barbequed ribs. All three elements complement each other and contribute to the many culture markers (including the original folktale of the flying hero, which Forrest reinvents) that inform the text. Sugar-Groove's aunt Gracie-Mae has a direct line to God; Gabriel has the authority to admit souls into heaven; St. Peter takes working vacations and deals in securities; and Sugar-Groove can leave heaven and visit Mississippi and Harlem on a whim. And all of this is presented by Joubert and Williemain as plausible truth, as the barbershop patrons (and the reader) listen anxiously to learn about Sugar-Groove's latest escapades.

After he reminds Sugar-Groove that he only "got to heaven on a wing and a prayer" and threatens him with punishment, St. Peter whispers:

> But tell me how are you—doing it? Particularly the way you do that little sweep around under a cloud pocket, carry up through cross-around corkscrew—outside—in a floating fashion, back hipbone motion transfer over and under super sublime sail, without shaking a tail feather, breathlessly—meantime you are actually going so fast you're threatening to break the sound barrier; meanwhile you are floating backwards and doing it all on the left-hand side of the road, while you seem to be zigzagging right [. . . .] (99)

When Sugar-Groove tells him that he just "wings it," St. Peter responds, "Sugar-Groove, between us, now. Don't you have a magic musical score on rhythm tucked away in one of those wings—to pitch you in time, out of time, on time, in your own time?" (100). Just as St. Peter is about to kick

Sugar-Groove out of the room, he tells St. Peter that if he only knew of Sugar-Groove's previous condition down in Sugar-Ditch, Mississippi, he would not be surprised that Sugar-Groove could outfly a sparrow so fast God could not spot him "on the head of a pin, dancing, and with more power than a back-stroking Eagle, on a sun-shiny day, using Vigil Residual" (99). Frustrated that Sugar-Groove will not reveal his secrets of "flying-high," St. Peter decides to clip Sugar-Groove's wings. Finally, Sugar-Groove confesses:

> You see when I died, and they cracked this deal to send me up in here, I was issued an old patched-up set of shattered wings thrown in the Catholic Salvage section and over in the Free Will bin where other angelic vestments were tossed away and cast asunder [. . . .] You see Mister Peter, Sir, they (them officials) plucked up the worst of the discarded wings for me [. . . .] Not to ruffle your feathers, Mister Peter, Sir, but you see part of the deal they struck to let me in . . . [was] I'd have to fly about Heaven all of my days, with one wing tied with shipyard rope behind my right shoulder, whipped about my belly [. . . .] (103–4)

Nowhere does Forrest celebrate reinvention and Sugar-Groove's improvisational style more than in this lyrically constructed episode between Sugar-Groove and St. Peter. Though he knows that St. Peter is incapable of seeing the *how* of his reinvented mode, Sugar-Groove, at least, tries to explain the *how come*. He makes it clear that it is his tendency to overcome struggle—the "particular preparation in the eye of the storm of life he flew through before getting to heaven"—that accounts for his adaptability. And it is the Negro tendency to reinvent and to emboss what little inheritance he is given that explains Sugar-Groove's gift of pageantry. So he not only survives, but he stylizes his survival.

A Bloodworth by birth, Sugar-Groove experiences the horror that plagues the accursed family, as detailed in *The Bloodworth Orphans,* along with the agony of being a motherless child, since his mother, Sarah-Belle, died in childbirth. But unlike the other Bloodworths of Forest County, who fail to transcend their agony, Sugar-Groove, as the reinvented badman–turned-hustler-turned-drifter-turned-jazz hero, masters his blues and adds to it the improvisational style of jazz, subsequently acquiring an overwhelming capacity for self-regeneration. It is this ability to transform himself constantly that creates his mythic status and that drives Joubert's attempt to dramatize Sugar-Groove's soul. Joubert's fascination with Sugar-

Groove is also related to his own reliance on Sugar-Groove as a sage of sorts. As a young boy trying to understand why his Aunt Eloise (who had become his guardian after his mother's death and who, shortly after, married his father) insisted that he make consistent visits to "old man Tobias," who had never repaid money he had borrowed from Joubert's grandmother Daphne, Joubert asks Sugar-Groove to help him understand his aunt's actions. The scenario reminds Sugar-Groove of his own childhood and his scheduled visits to receive an allowance from his white father, who never openly acknowledged Sugar-Groove as his son but who agreed to see him periodically because of a promise he made to Sugar-Groove's Aunt Septima. Like Aunt Foisty in *Two Wings to Veil My Face,* who demands that I. V. Reed tell his children, firsthand, the history of his evil deeds, Septima demands that Bloodworth at least privately and repeatedly acknowledge Sugar-Groove before she will restore the old man's sight, which he had lost after being devastated by Sugar-Groove's mother's death during childbirth. After implying that Joubert's Aunt Eloise, like Sugar-Groove's Aunt Septima, simply wanted to force the betrayer to see the face of the legacy of the one betrayed, Sugar-Groove swears Joubert to secrecy and begins to tell Joubert the story of his existence.

From the badman, a folk figure in African culture, Sugar-Groove adopts an ability to attract women, though he is not as uncaring or as unfeeling as his counterpart. Thus, he frames his story around his actions following an episode of lovemaking with his lady love. He has left his lover, Maybelle, and is heading to his father's house to receive the first installment of his unofficial inheritance when he discovers the body of his sister Roxanne underneath a tree. As he recalls that his first instinct was to run immediately to his father, he is distracted from telling Joubert the details of Roxanne's death when he recalls that his desire to experience the simplest familial acknowledgment from his father continually went unmet. As he digresses further from the story of his sister's death, he tells Joubert of one of the episodes that distances him from his father.

Bloodworth had agreed to pay Sugar-Groove's tuition to Tuskegee, since the old man believed firmly in Booker T. Washington's vision and his idea of Negro success. But when Sugar-Groove learns of Washington's "scripture" which reads, "The Negro will advance when he learns that there is as much honor in tilling a field as there is in writing a poem," Sugar-Groove decides firmly against Tuskegee, realizing that Washington's "vision would keep him from ever flying very high" (Forrest, *Divine Days,* 318). When Sugar-Groove decides on a college in the southwest, his Negro kin despise him, since to disavow Tuskegee was to disavow Booker T. Ironically, they blame Roxanne for creating DuBoisian notions in Sugar-Groove's head, which subsequently, in their opinion, decrease his potential for success. As he is, indeed, influenced by Roxanne, Sugar-Groove looks forward to telling his sister, who had taught him to read, all about his two years away at school. But instead, he finds the only Bloodworth with whom he finds affinity dead underneath a magnolia tree. Throughout all the years when he was forced to come to the back door of his father's house on the first of each month to receive his allowance, all without any acknowledgment as a son by his father, it was Roxanne who embraced him. Eventually, Sugar-Groove learns that Roxanne has fallen victim to the Bloodworth curse and was killed by their brother Paxton, who commits both incest and murder because he can no longer control his infatuation with his sister. Sugar-Groove tells Joubert how he, too, almost committed incest, in the Bloodworth tradition, when he fell in love with Tilly Taylor before realizing that she was actually Bella-Belle, the daughter he left to be raised by Sweetie Reed and Hattie Breedlove years before in an attempt to avoid the very thing that almost happens.

Perhaps the event that informs Sugar-Groove's life most heavily, even more than his devastation over Roxanne's death and almost personally experiencing the Bloodworth curse, is the fight he has with his father, who blamed Sugar-Groove for Sarah-Belle's death. Bloodworth tells Sugar-Groove that his mother chose her own death to ensure his life, leaving his father loveless and heartbroken. After he tells Sugar-Groove this story, Bloodworth leaves the room, and the Bible he has been reading attracts Sugar-Groove's attention. When he turns the Bible face up, Sugar-Groove sees, for the first time, a picture of his mother. She is not naked, "but half-dressed to show off her body" (331). Angry at his father and disgusted with his mother for taking the picture, Sugar-Groove begins to cry just as Bloodworth reenters the room. Sugar-Groove attacks his father, and a fight ensues. As they fight, they both hear "seven whispered words, from a female voice in the wind: *How can you destroy what we created*" (336). And it is these seven words that plague Sugar-Groove's existence for the rest of his life. In Oedipus-like fashion, he dreams of killing his father, and though he continues to take the allowances from Bloodworth, Sugar-Groove struggles to forgive him. Since Sarah-Belle has power over both men, even from beyond the grave, they are reconciled, but only to the point of tolerance. Thus, without ever receiving acknowledgment from his father, Sugar-Groove leaves for college and, eventually, evolves into a wanderer.

Significantly, Sugar-Groove explains his inner conflict to Joubert. Otherwise, Sugar-Groove is little more than a culture hero who experiences rebirth repeatedly. Instead, by sharing with Joubert the complexity of his character and being, as well as his survival strategies and secrets of transformation, Sugar-Groove escapes the limitations of the traditional culture hero, reveals the fullness of a culture hero's experience, and returns the boon—survival—to his community through Joubert. Though he has reservations about whether or not the thirteen-year-old Joubert is old enough to hear the tale, Sugar-Groove hopes that Joubert can "[m]ake some sense out of it in the long run" (312). During his second session with the young lad, he continues his lessons of transformation with his apprentice: "Look Joubert, there is a river of time, more ancient than Eden, where every form of waste and wonder has been discarded, past all parchments of recorded time" (765). Out of waste, one must create wonder: "you are tossed adrift, or hurled asunder [. . . .] Told to swim [. . . .] Get lost. Or die" (765–66). So Sugar-Groove creates his wonder constantly, primarily because it is the only means of ensuring his survival.

Seven weeks later, much to Joubert's surprise, Sugar-Groove returns to his story. The connection the two men share, Sugar-Groove points out, is that they both have family members who lie and "seal up" the truth. Joubert's aunt kept the truth about his grandmother Daphne and Tobias from Joubert, and, as a Bloodworth, Sugar-Groove's heritage is filled with his paternal family's incessant lies and deceit as they attempted to escape the Bloodworth curse, which is detailed fullest in *The Bloodworth Orphans* but which Sugar-Groove condenses as he tells Joubert how his sister was killed. Learning of the familial curse also has personal significance for Sugar-Groove, since it is Sugar-Groove's arch rival and seer W. A. D. Ford, a trickster variant of W. W. W. Ford, who makes him aware of it. Sugar-Groove tells Joubert how he went to the seer after the fight with his father in hopes of contacting his mother, Sarah-Belle (much in the same manner that Noah visits Ford to contact his dead mother in *The Bloodworth Orphans*). Instead, he was tricked by Ford, who hung a scarecrow from a tree and threw his voice "in a soprano-female shrillness" (809), pretending he has made contact with Sugar-Groove's mother. When Sugar-Groove sliced the rope that held the scarecrow on the tree, he discovered that the figure was not his mother, and he tried to destroy Ford. But this is only after Ford has informed Sugar-Groove of the curse that strikes Roxanne and Paxton.

Having come to believe in the power of both Ford and the curse, Sugar-Groove resolves to survive his chaos at all cost. Out of his chaos, then, he births the gift of transformation and reinvention. And unlike his nemesis Ford, Sugar-Groove uses his art for good—to save himself and to offer to the community a hustling, drifting hero at whom to marvel. Again, he departs from the more traditional characterization of the hustler or drifter, for, as Professor Jamesway tells Joubert, "Sugar-Groove is mythic. Yet different from other Negroes who believed this about themselves, he doesn't [. . .] believe in himself as the religious center of a heroic worship ceremony" (90). Thus, in an attempt to recreate Sugar-Groove as the hero might see himself, Joubert seeks to gain access to Sugar-Groove's inner conflict, and Joubert realizes that it is the voice of Sugar-Groove's own soul, not his actions (as we will see is the case with Ford), that is worthy of being dramatized.[2] It is, in fact, Sugar-Groove's soul-spun epiphany that helps Joubert realize the meaning of it all—that *the greatest thing you'll ever learn is just to love and be loved in return.*

The irony of Sugar-Groove's revelation is that it comes to him, in part, through his dealings with the trickster-like Ford, whom Sugar-Groove despises and at whose hand he finally experiences death. Like a number of other characters in the novel, Ford is no stranger to Forest County. And while he has a full presence in *The Bloodworth Orphans,* his character is developed most completely here. He is undoubtedly a part of the broader trickster tradition; yet he, too, resists stereotyping. Unlike most African American tricksters, particularly Ishmael Reed's infamous collection of characters, each of whom "is driven by a mocking wit that subverts white authority and destroys white illusions of superiority while simultaneously promoting numerous value-laden symbols of black culture" (Lindroth, 185), Ford garners his attention in *Divine Days* from his interaction with and trickery of other black characters. While he does subvert white authority—his carefully selected mistress and sidekick is a white blonde from a prominent Jewish family who offers Ford vicarious protection since the authorities are unlikely to risk damaging her family's reputation, and he is wanted by the CIA, FBI, or KGB—Ford's character as a kind of trickster is shaped more around the tradition of a Chicago hustler and confidence man who has trickster tendencies than around the actual tradition of the trickster tale. Thus, we first see Ford in relation to the disillusioned black characters in Forest County who need to see him as all-powerful and who, as a result of the horrors society has shaped as their reality, all but crave the false reality or boon he offers them.

Notably, Ford is a spoof of Black Muslim W. D. Fard, whose effectiveness rests in his ability to reinvent and to recreate. As the last non-Muslim editor *of Muhammad Speaks,* Forrest had great familiarity with the Black Muslim tradition. What he admired of this tradition—its ability to recreate myth and to shape it to fit the specific needs of a people—is the gift he bestows on Ford. In one of the conversations he has with Joubert, who formally observes Ford's work as the leader of Divine Days, as his flock is called, the seer-turned-preacher tells Joubert:

> The constant problem for every great leader, my young friend, is to keep his flock convinced through cycles of new horror and ecstasy, that they are part of a new covenant with God. But *you* spin this new covenant out of some old myths. *You* invert, convert, the meanings of these myths. The people (who are always wolves in lambs' clothing) come to believe that it is you who've righteously come to actually save those old, so-called truths; when really you are spinning out a new fantasy, in accordance with your own high sense of drama, your interpretation [. . . .] Meantime, you've got them believing in your credo, even as the old myths are not only being revised, inverted, but hell they are being mocked, subverted, and finally sacked. But you've got to use the old myths, in the beginning, as your springboard [. . . .] All of this is no simple enterprise [. . . .] More than anything else you must guard against the dangers of the intellectual life, which are almost as perilous to the true leader's purposes as life vaulted upon one current of emotion after another." (Forrest, *Divine Days*, 39; italics in original)

What Ford knows better than anyone, except perhaps Fard, is how to exploit people's need to live out fantasies of alternate realities. His success rests in his ability to re-create affirmations of black humanity in a world that denies it. As H. Nigel Thomas suggests, in terms of the expectations of others, Ford is "the secular equivalent of that force that gives magic flesh to the 'dry bones' in the desert of America—when blacks are not listening to their [traditional] preachers effect the reincarnation" (105). Without ever fully acknowledging it, the congregation participates in perpetuating its own chaos by accepting re-creations of religion and its myths. And while re-creation is, indeed, a gift, at the wrong extreme and in the wrong hands, it is harmful.

Unlike Sugar-Groove, who also possesses trickster-like characteristics but who most often uses his gift for good, Ford exploits religion as a sustaining black cultural tradition and uses his powers of transformation and reinvention to corrupt and to destroy. Forrest admits to Dubey that Ford is the diabolical "trickster as demon" (Forrest and Dubey, 598), contrary to Sugar-Groove who, though sometimes selfish, uses his devices for healing. Like Ellison's Rinehart, Ford thrives on chaos. Yet, in the midst of the very chaos he creates, he sadistically resembles a healer or nurturer. Members of his congregation defend him wholeheartedly until they realize they have been duped. Claiming that he will "rise again" on Easter Sunday if he vanishes or is killed, Ford tells his congregation that only the "truly faithful" will be able to see his Transfiguration-Transformed miracle, while others may be able to see it from a "goodly distance" (Forrest, *Divine Days,* 141). While a limited few claim to see the "miracle," most of Ford's followers finally realize that he is a farce. But too many of them are unable to handle this reality, since they have lived Ford's fantasy of their reality for so long. A rehabilitated drug addict returns to the streets; one lady gouges her eyeballs with the knife Ford had given her for protection; and one member commits suicide. The reality of his trickery and his absence as the sustaining force in their lives overwhelms them. Thus, through the obvious void in people's lives, which feeds Ford's success, we hear Forrest's commentary on the desperation too many black people feel throughout their lives and even (perhaps particularly) in the 1960s, the time in which *Divine Days* reaches its peak. Though the civil rights movement was almost at its end and war against Jim Crow had been waged head-on, the search for a viable identity or a reality that validated black humanity and subsequent equality permeated black communities, especially urban communities, where the potential for equal access to the good life was largely visible but heavily denied. It is this denial off of which Ford feeds. As long as he can give the people what they ask for or create the illusion that they are fulfilled, his strength is untouchable. Their need for validation is so great they accept it in whatever form it emerges. And, oddly, Ford as preacher-trickster becomes an agent for black survival.

If such were his only claim to fame in the novel, perhaps Ford could garner some sympathy for his role as facilitator of pseudohealings. But as Sugar-Groove's chief antagonist, Ford dispels any notions of sympathy when he moves beyond tricking his needy flock to seeking ways to destroy Sugar-Groove. As far as Joubert knows, Sugar-Groove is the only person who had ever given chase to Ford and lived to tell about it. And though the event occurred many years before (when Sugar-Groove, as a child of fourteen, attempted to attack Ford for faking contact with Sugar-Groove's dead mother), the two men still despise each other. When Sugar-Groove rises to fame and becomes a rival and the biggest threat to Ford's mythological status, Ford pursues Sugar-Groove to the mountains, where the latter has gone to seek the meaning of life. As a serial hermaphrodite whose father was a god and mother was a lioness, Ford goes to the mountains to seduce and impregnate a mountain nymph, to ensure perpetuity of his lineage. According to legend, as revealed in the two men's diaries, Sugar-Groove defends himself by shooting Ford seven times. Ford does not die but, instead, restrains Sugar-Groove with a rope and commands a trained eagle to pluck out Sugar-Groove's eyes as Ford looks on and laughs in "foul-faced mockery" (1084). What Ford reveals later in his diary is that he was envious of Sugar-Groove because he had *seen* too much. So he had to be struck down because Ford "could not let another potential seer remain in this world, unmaimed" (1086). And since Sugar-Groove was on the "precipice of coming into an advanced stage of sight," Ford felt impelled to rob Sugar-Groove of his sight and leave him for dead. Thus, he moves away from preacherly trickster as pseudohealer to demonic trickster whose target is not white America and whose perniciousness is somewhat unprovoked. As a result, he escapes the confines and limitations of the more traditional trickster and emerges as reinvented confidence-/bad-man with hustler-, preacher-, and trickster-like tendencies. In short, as major characters, both Sugar-Groove and Ford are "type" resistant and, instead, emanate from multiple traditions but are limited by none. Accordingly, their resistance to restrictive roles or confining types highlights the novel's message of reinvention as a means of survival.

While Joubert is nowhere near as prolific a character as Sugar-Groove or Ford, the two men whose lives he seeks to capture in plays, he is, nonetheless, a reinvented culture hero of sorts as well. He is a storyteller, but he is far from Uncle Remus; he resembles a griot, but he is as much an observer of culture as he is a preserver of it. Thus, the importance of his role as teller of tales should not be overlooked, for it is through his astute observations and soulful renderings that we learn of Sugar-Groove and Ford. In so many ways, Joubert is the artist as healer. He is the artist who, Toni Morrison would argue, is responsible for telling those stories we hear no more, an artist whose art "should be beautiful, and powerful [. . . having] something in it that enlightens; something in it that opens the door and points the way. Something in it that suggests what the conflicts are, what the problems are" ("Rootedness," 341). The latter is precisely what Joubert's playwriting seeks to do.

From Williemain, the local barber and bard, Joubert learns the art of storytelling. And what better place to learn to tell stories than in the barbershop? As Trudier Harris notes in "Barbershops in Black Literature,"

> In addition to its status as a gathering place, the black barbershop also functions as a complicated and often contradictory microcosm of the larger world. It is an environment that [through storytelling]

> can bolster egos and be supportive as well as a place where phony men can be destroyed, or at least highly shamed, from participation in verbal contests and other contests of skill. (113)

But even the barber, Forest County's historian and bard, does not know everything about Sugar-Groove. And when Joubert inadvertently reminds him of this, Williemain responds: "Oh Joubert, Hell, I ain't no college man; and this ain't hardly no classroom. We just having us a little vibrating fun. Let things drop-out naturally; fall into place; pass in review. Or, let's drop it!" (Forrest, *Divine Days,* 864). This scolding from the elder teaches Joubert (and the reader, since he declares it in his journal) to believe in the primacy of story above all else and that

> [y]ou let the story hang, suspend, float—see what tomorrow brings—and you [take] parts down of it to reflect upon other troubles or glories from time to time, but not too damn much. Or, you [tell] the whole story all over again and see what might jangle forth, in a shimmering light; because you might ruin the spangling magic of it all. (865)

The spangling magic, of course, is Ford and Sugar-Groove's antics. As the shoe-shine boy at Williemain's, young Joubert grew up listening to the latest tales of both of Forest County's mysterious heroes. And though his Aunt Eloise tries to persuade him to pursue a career as a journalist, Joubert's real desire is to become a playwright. He has completed a play on Ford after observing him at Divine Days, which has since been transformed into Eloise's Night Light Lounge, where Joubert tends bar. And though the play disappears, then reappears with a "dead letter" stamp from the post office, and Joubert suspects that it has been confiscated by federal agents or Ford to search its contents, Joubert still feels he is "destined to dramatize [. . .] the soul within the voice of Sugar-Groove" (9–10). His desire to do so overwhelms him to the point that he constantly hears voices. He muses:

> Why am I so attracted to playwrighting [*sic*]? There alone can I [. . .] pen those voices upon the confines of two boards and a passion, deal with the distractions, and keep flying. I don't have to open my mouth to speak. Nor do I have to speak the words of those voices stirring from within me, out loud; because when I allow my mouth to utter their words, I get into deep trouble [. . . .] The danger is I'll become a talker, instead of a writer. (53)

Arguably, Joubert's fear that he will "become a talker" and not a writer is a subtle reflection of his disenchantment with artists who have begun to ignore their art and who have replaced it with rhetoric. His desire to be a *real* writer, in the traditional sense, contributes to his status as a myth-maker, culture keeper, neobard, and culture hero. He observes two almost mythic figures who have mastered arts of reinvention and survival, and his goal is to become the *artist as culture hero* and to return to the community the knowledge he gains about their magnificent existence, in hopes of ensuring similar success to the community. In this sense, he seeks to fill the void left in the community, which was in search of its identity and of a voice that was capable of articulating its experiences and of offering a viable means of surviving it.

In one of his first journal entries, Joubert examines his potential and desire to be a successful playwright. Part of this examination forces him to find ways to escape the shortcomings of another writer he knows.

> Sergeant Franklin Hamilton has written seven full-length novels of about 350 pages in longhand. Franklin Hamilton, the writer, is a man who hears voices issue from simple-minded cardboard characters [. . . .] He always hears voices, but he rarely hears them in their complexity [. . .] he is a tremendous oral story-teller; he and my uncle Roderick can imitate all kinds of voices [. . . .] But Sergeant Hamilton can't get that variety on paper. He has the great patience to write these stories out in longhand, the problem is he doesn't hear into the places where the voices lead; nor does he use the voices, as faint as they may be, to pick up their enriching mysterious echoes and overtones, nor as springboards for a new creation [. . .] my heritage is hounded by the voices of the oral tradition, literary tradition [. . . .] What must I do to produce a Black literary revival, in order to be saved? First of all shut my mouth up! And listen to those voices wherever that may take me. (16–17)

We hear Joubert's command that he quiet himself so that he can "hear into the places where the voices" lead. By this he means, at least in part, that he must respect the complexity of the experiences he seeks to recreate. And this means that he must not only include black cultural traditions in his literature, but he must explore their possibilities and use their complexity as springboards to create comparable literary traditions. The lack of complexity and artists' failure to follow and to capture the muse's voice are, in fact, two of the factors Forrest might conjecture contributed to the limitations of the black arts movement, which failed, in large part, to express the fullness of black experiences.

In an interview with Kenneth Warren, Forrest notes that the writers who have had the greatest impact in contemporary (post-1970) African American literature—writers such as Toni Morrison, Alice Walker, James Alan McPherson, and John Edgar Wideman—are those whose novels are complex and would not have been welcomed by the movement. Later, he tells Dubey that the narrows of the black aesthetic were never complicated enough for him and that he knew that there was "a whole lot about black life [. . .] that they had no sense of" (Forrest and Dubey, 592). Summarily stated, the black aesthetic was characterized by a demand for positive expressions of blackness and for a revolutionary reordering of Western cultural aesthetics; a rejection of protest literature, since it inevitably appealed to white morality, not black cultural values; the belief that the technical level of art must be natural and unforced and that art should teach; and an active resistance to anything that did not de-Americanize black people. It is, perhaps, the latter against which Forrest writes most aggressively throughout his fiction, but especially in *Divine Days*. In fact, Joubert becomes the novel's antiessentialism mouthpiece when he writes in his journal about the "thoughtless, mindless, souls" who fall prey to nationalism and Islam alike. They do not realize it, but

> it is the Negro in them that saves them [. . . .] What saved them from the dead was that some remnant, some streak was still there of Negro, not African, and not European, but Negro—with that fabulous impulse to reinvent, to make a way out of no way. The Negro American's will to transform, reinvent, and stylize until Hell freezes over. (Forrest, *Divine Days*, 1127–28)

The statement speaks against the very essence of the black aesthetic purported by the likes of Larry Neal, Hoyt Fuller, and Amiri Baraka. It is, in fact, in direct opposition to Addison Gayle's claim that "the price for becoming an American [is] too high. It mean[s . . .] to desert one's heritage and culture [. . .] to become part of all 'that has been instrumental in wanton destruction of life [. . . .]' [T]o be American is to lose one's humanity" (xxii). What Joubert comes to realize and to symbolize by the novel's end is that resistance to an aesthetic that seeks to deny the usefulness of his Americanness, and similar resistance to DuBoisian double-consciousness and to essentialist Black American Islam and Afrocentricity, is the only means of accessing the complexity of anything that can be accurately called a black aesthetic. The success or failure of many of the characters he observes is hinged upon how well they respond to and find balance among the varying definitions of blackness that surround them. Creating a viable identity is their preeminent struggle, as was the case for many African Americans during the late 1960s. The ultimate question was, Who are we?—not as we relate to others but as we define ourselves. Sixty years after DuBois coined the term *double-consciousness,* the African American still struggles with definitions of identity independent of others' view of him. In a postmodernist attempt to define the self as something other than a binary, and, instead, as in relation to no one except one's self, the postmodern African American experiences the frustration of such an impossibility. Physical limitations—skin pigmentation—and political limitations make it impossible for the African American to define himself outside of his past and his opposition to a more dominant non–African American world. And while the cultural aestheticians of nationalism, Afrocentricity, and the black aesthetic responded perhaps as well as they knew how under such tenuous circumstances, their responses were often too misinformed and myopic to be fully productive.

Take what happens to DeLoretto/Imani in *Divine Days,* for example. She is easily recognizable as and symbolic of the African American who has experienced the far-reaching effects of slavery on the black family—her biggest quest is to locate and to embrace her lost siblings—and who is incapable of creating an identity for herself. So she adopts one from popular culture only to be dismantled by it. Embracing wholeheartedly the impetus which drove a new wave of cultural traditions, in this case Kwanzaa, DeLoretto changes her name to Imani—the Kwanzaa principle that means *faith* in Yoruba—and she changes her son's name from Rhobert to Nia—the principle that means *purpose.* Had she learned to balance her new cultural traditions with the old *Negro* in her, at least some level of success might have been possible for the troubled character. Instead, she denies all that is American and loses herself as a result.

As Joubert's love interest, Imani seeks to "enlighten" Joubert with her mind rather than with her body. So the two engage frequently in intellectual debates about culture heroes and artists ranging from Lorraine Hansberry to Malcolm X. Again, a lack of balance becomes her tragic flaw. She is as dedicated to Malcolm X as she is to herself. Yet she refuses to acknowledge that even Malcolm experienced change after he realized the limitations and the falsity of essentialist beliefs and rhetoric. She virtually ignores Malcolm's return from Mecca as El-Hajj Malik El-Shabazz, and when she does acknowledge it, she does so only to excuse him from becoming less of an essentialist. Similarly, she loves Hansberry's Asagai passionately without considering his limitations. When Joubert points out that Nkrumah, Banda, and Azeikewe would crush Asagai in a power play and that he would be less vocal if he were in his native Africa, her response reveals her lack of foresight and her tendency to be captivated easily by shallow ideas, movements, and people.

At varying points in the novel, she and Joubert move through the major periods in African American literature, and her reaction to a variety of authors further reveals her shortsightedness. She refuses to see the beauty of Jean Toomer's *Cane* because of her distaste for Toomer's ambiguity about his heritage, when she is herself ambiguous about Countee Cullen's "What Is Africa to Me?" In a manner highly reminiscent of Zora Neale Hurston, Imani is similarly ambiguous about accepting sponsorship from her white patron, Mrs. Heinz, whom she imagines writes in a note that calls to mind Ellison's *Invisible Man:* "To Who It May Concern: Keep Sister Imani Running." She even sees herself as a part of a Brer Rabbit folktale, which Joubert reads from her journal after she has killed herself:

> Sis Goose swims in a pond where she does not belong. Brer Fox catches her. Sis Goose gets royally pissed. She had the right, after all to swim wheresoever. Took Brer Fox to court. At the trial she bitched and moaned. When all of a sudden Sis Goose looked about. Sheriff was a fox. Judge? He's a fox, too. Attorney? All foxes for Brer Fox's defense. Jurymen? You guessed it. Foxes. Sis Goose's fate is sealed. Her goose is cooked. Convicted, executed right there in the jury box. Soon they were picking her bones. Moral? Do you have to say anymore [. . . .] I'm the only nigger artist plucked for the city-wide show again. And again. World with an end, amen. (1001–2)

Arguably, because she has embraced a new-age Afrocentricity that denies the Negro's will to reinvent, she cannot outfox the fox and, instead, cooks her own goose. Ultimately, she becomes prey to the former hustler-turned-cultural nationalist Sambi!, who recognizes that the abusive nationalist rhetoric is a farce, but who uses it to attain success among the identity-starved characters in the novel. When Sambi! convinces DeLoretto/Imani to attend a retreat that will "put her in touch with her blackness," she retreats into failure and, finally, kills herself by taking an overdose of pills.

While Forrest certainly does not position Sambi! (who seems to be an evolved reinvention of Ellison's Tod Clifton) as hustling trickster to be admired, his cunning and his wit, which he draws from his heritage as an American Negro, saves him. But this cunning destroys all who take his placated salvation to be authentic. Imani is one such victim. From Fulton Armstead, the novel's exceedingly Afrocentric but well-meaning representative, we learn that Sambi! led Imani to a sociopolitical group that consisted of a bunch of young "hot-heads" who had broken off from pro-black movements ranging from black-power Garveyism to pre–Malcolm-exile Islam to CORE to black middle-class Marxism. Without any real sense of their own identity, the group members harassed Imani because she did not have an Afro; because she had worked within the civil rights movement; because she had been educated at Sarah Lawrence, the University of Hidelburg, the Sorbonne, and the University of Chicago; and because she had a white patron whose financial backing sustained her artistic career. As a member of this group, Sambi! has the potential to save Imani. But he does not consider doing so because her salvation could have come only at the expense of exposing himself as a fraud, for, as Joubert recognizes, Sambi!'s existence relied heavily on those "who were so desperate to assert a black identity, only if it was centralized and ordered by an African identity, which, in turn would allow all them to strip away a slave heritage; remove the force of the white man's vulture-culture out of their lives, and the life of their imagination, once and for all and forevermore" (1032). Sambi!'s success rested almost completely on his ability to control and to contain complexity. And while the black arts movement aestheticians may not have intended to control and to contain, the movement's limitations were only slightly less devastating. Arguably, Fulton is Forrest's example of this.

As the benefactor of the infamous double-As, Fulton bestows to those who are worthy "his especial linkage emblem"—a large A with a little a inside—which symbolically connects Africans and African Americans. His most favored recipients are African students who come to Forest County to study. On rare occasions, he dons African Americans with a double-A, but most others are unworthy. High on Negritude, Fulton fails to see the limitations of overcompensating for his slave heritage. He simply cannot see the benefits of his past. And though he is shunned by the students as frequently as he is accepted, he is largely clueless. Even after Sambi! openly criticizes Imani's weakness unto death and reveals how little he really cared about her, Fulton still fails to see the limitations of his own beliefs. For Joubert, Fulton's myopia is maddening:

> Listening to Fulton Armstead made me not only want a drink, Hell I needed a drink. Lord didn't I get sick and tired of all of this brother

> shit, and this sister stew-ball crap. In the mouth of Fulton it was not so much false, Bull-shit-3-6-9, as it was gullible bold face gall; naive on the one hand, ideologically burning bright in the forest county of the night; not shrewd but politically vulnerable and clever in terms of the manipulators of cultural-political ethos, who would pick up its latter-day stages from their own interests.
>
> Fulton Armstead getting his nationalism all mixed-up with his half-ass solidarity, and his quarter rump roast of Marxism; in the pot with a quarter slab of Muslim lamb shank. (989)

Like Imani, whose hope was to redeem the family so that they could all sit around together in a circle at Kwanzaa, Fulton refuses to acknowledge that only the Negro in him can save him—not the Yoruba, not the Islam, not the Afrocentric, and not the nationalist—only the Negro; for as Wilkerson, who claims to have dined with DuBois, tells Joubert, in spite of being "[f]orged, fucked, and dislocated into a new race of people wherein anything human and inhumane could happen,"

> [. . .] our human rage was always to make a way out of noway. And to create a synthesis out of all nightmares that our experiences kept throwing up at us. That will to synthesize was what DuBois never understood . . . to absorb and re-invent; to take it all in and to masticate it, and process it, and spew it back out, as lyrical and soaring as a riff by Father Louie [. . . .] DuBois never understood that with his double-consciousness theories. (1062)

What Forrest seems to imply throughout the novel is that DuBois is not the only cultural critic who failed to consider the Negro's will to reinvent. Aestheticians who followed the likes of DuBois chronologically also followed him ideologically. To the art of reinvention, synthesis is key. And while the black arts and Afrocentric founders did make minimal attempts at synthesis of the African and the American, the African was, more often than not, privileged. The shortcoming, perhaps, is a failure to recognize the African American, or what Forrest refers to as the Negro, as a culture in and of itself that is life sustaining. The success of James Weldon Johnson or Sterling Brown in earlier African American letters and of his contemporaries Toni Morrison or Toni Cade Bambara in later years emitted from these authors' acceptance of their ancestors' slave past, without ever romanticizing it. Each also acknowledges that while tragic and filled with horror, this past could not and should not be abandoned, but rather embraced for its cultural significance. Similarly, Forrest's novels attest to the significance of synthesis, as they embrace black cultural traditions as a way to segue into and as a point of transcendence beyond black literary traditions and ideas of cultural blackness.

Arguably, finding the language with which to express and to investigate these cultural traditions and their subsequent meaningfulness to contemporary black identity is a challenge *Divine Days* meets with more success than many of its contemporaries. The novel reinvents ideas from the black arts movement, nationalism, and Afrocentric thought, then ultimately defines for itself a black aesthetic that embraces the useful characteristics of these other aesthetic traditions and rejects outright those that are essentialist and, hence, stifling. Self-reflective throughout, the novel ends with Joubert as artist responding to the infamous exchange between St. Peter and Sugar-Groove. When he thinks of St. Peter telling Sugar-Groove, "I can't find the proper words to express the meanings of all your carryings on, your swerving cavorting . . . your," Joubert interrupts and responds, "No, St. Peter you can't [. . . .] That's my job" (1135). As the artist-as-hero, Joubert is, indeed, endowed with the task of finding "the proper words to express the meanings" of the "carryings on" throughout Forest County. Through Joubert, we learn of tricksters, hustlers, drifters, lovers, fathers, mothers, sisters, brothers, and combinations thereof. Perhaps most important, however, we learn from Joubert the role of reinvention as both a survival strategy and a literary technique available to the African American as a sustaining black cultural tradition. With reinvention as theme and as technique, *Divine Days* crafts a new aesthetic and declares reinvention the supreme medium through which to access and to re-create the fullness of an African American experience.

chapter six

"The Transformation of Grief": Self-Invention and Survival in *Meteor in the Madhouse*

As the culminating collection of narratives in Leon Forrest's body of fiction, *Meteor in the Madhouse* is charged with the admirable responsibility of bringing to closure the sagas of Forest County. Envisioned on the heels of the 1,135-page *Divine Days*, *Meteor* functions, at the very least, as a follow-up to Joubert Jones's adventures and to the lessons he learns and seeks to convey in Forrest's fourth novel. In the broader sense, the novellas that constitute *Meteor* continue to develop Forrest's themes of love and survival, of history and ancestry, and of abandonment and agony, all of which inform his earlier quest narratives. In each of the earlier novels, as well as in *Meteor*, total escape from agony and grief is impossible, because grief is inevitable. In *There Is a Tree More Ancient Than Eden* and in *Two Wings to Veil My Face,* Nathaniel's transformation of grief comes mainly from the ancestral wisdom of Hattie Breedlove and Sweetie Reed and their mandate that he access black cultural traditions to sustain himself. In *The Bloodworth Orphans,* the jazz impulse helps the characters make this internal transformation, while in *Divine Days,* reinvention—a literary variation of jazz—allows the characters to re-create themselves perpetually to transcend their agony. And while jazz and reinvention work for these characters as a means of temporary salvation, more permanent soul healing requires people to invent new and varied ways of being for themselves. Thus, in *Meteor,* the characters who experience tremendous amounts of grief at the hands of the outside world must shift their visions of transformation to look inward almost exclusively, while any outward projection of this transformation becomes almost incidental. Correspondingly, the novellas seem to be concerned foremost with issues of self-invention,[1] which Forrest presents in the form of memory, artistry or creativity, language, and myth as a means of internally transforming grief for survival.

Self-invention, as it appears in Forrest's fiction, is a coping mechanism that borrows from, among other things, black cultural traditions of survival.[2] For these characters, self-invention does not involve abandoning the old *self.* Instead, they remain largely true to themselves, but they find ways to transcend their grief or to manage difficult situations by creating alternatives that allow them to live within the context of their agony without being consumed by it. To some degree, self-invention can be likened to reinvention, which also emerges out of necessity and as a means of survival. The two differ, however, in the sense that self-invention as a black cultural tradition is foremost concerned with making a psychological transformation in an attempt to transcend agony or to "get over" something. Self-invention's internal transformation may or may not carry with it an outward display, for, again, it is largely psychological, while reinvention offers an outward display of an external transformation. The impetus of reinvention is to take what is left over or that which has been discarded and to make something new and useful of it. With self-invention, transformation does not typically involve changing or making use of something that has been left over or discarded. Instead, it involves adopting activities, survival strategies, or ways of being to find ways to cope with an unwanted condition and, subsequently, to transform grief and to transcend the agony this condition of grief has caused.[3]

Throughout *Meteor,* self-invention appears in a variety of forms, though Forrest presents the technique primarily in the context of memory, artistry, language, and myth. In "Lucasta Jones, in Solitude: Lives Left in Her Wake," Gussie Jones and Leonard Foster use their memory of past experiences to find ways to function successfully in the present. They also invent allegories of creativity, in the form of gardening and hat collecting, to help them avoid being consumed by their occasional grief. In the same novella, Gussie's sister Lucasta adopts ironing and the blues as her sources of self-invention and as her means of coping with losing her son and her lover. In "Live! At Fountain's House of the Dead," Joubert highlights the power of language as a technique of self-invention, while his cousin Leonard's failure to access this power results in insanity because of his inability to transform his grief. In "To the Magical Memory of Rain," it is the narration that offers the lesson in self-invention as it adopts fairy tales and myths to articulate Desiree Dobbs's grief. Without self-invention, the narrative seems to suggest, Desiree's experiences are otherwise exceedingly difficult to express with the same level of meaning and emotion that she experiences. Thus the narration enacts rather than simply tells of Desiree's experiences with agony and grief. And in the final novella, "By Dawn's Early Light," Joubert highlights the relationship of self-invention and reinvention as he accesses memory to describe Hopkins Golightly's gifts of self-invention and transformation.

Structured mainly as Joubert's remembrance of a number of fateful events between 1972 and 1992, each of the novellas deals with the soul condition of its main characters. Thus, the collection reminds readers that even after the death of Jim Crow, African Americans still experienced agony and grief at the hands of racism and classism. But as Forrest notes in an examination of William Faulkner's presentation of Mollie Beauchamp in *Go Down, Moses,* Mollie's success as a character rests in her internal transformation of her grief and her subsequent ability to deal with her situation. For Forrest, Mollie's concession that America would not soon change becomes the metaphor for the African American's coming to consciousness about options for survival in the contemporary moment (Forrest, *Furious Voice,* 208–9). Until America changed it laws and, more important, its heart, an inward transformation of grief, in the form of self-invention, was one of the few means of maintaining sanity and of surviving. If America would not change, then Mollie must.

This is the lesson Leonard Foster, one of the first characters we encounter in "Lucasta Jones, in Solitude: Lives Left in Her Wake," initially refuses to learn. Part of Leonard's grief has to do with the fact that he is abandoned by his parents. He is raised by different relatives, one of whom is Lucasta Jones, the woman Nathaniel comes to realize in *Two Wings to Veil My Face* is his paternal grandmother. But Leonard is also consumed by his race and his ardent activism during the civil rights movement. His refusal to participate in self-invention as he fights to make America change her heart and her laws renders him insane. Rather than create his own humanity when the world refuses to acknowledge that humanity is God-given, Leonard makes an outward rather than an inward attempt to transform grief. His attempt inevitably fails, and he is institutionalized. The first novella thus finds Joubert preparing to visit Leonard in the hospital, but before he does, he must visit his grandparents, who, unlike Leonard, have mastered the art of self-invention.

As representatives of the older generation of African Americans, many of whom lived through Jim Crow and its decline, Gussie and Forester Jones thrive because of their self-inventive survivalist tendencies. Though they had long since left Forrest County, Mississippi, for Forest County, Illinois, they maintained their sense of the past and even brought a taste of it with them. In the middle of their urban environment, they planted a "self-help vegetable garden" in their backyard and, with some success, encouraged others to do the same. The garden functioned on two levels—it provided them with nutritional nourishment, with "tomatoes, cucumbers, squash, mustard greens (and tulips, too)," and with emotional nourishment. As John Cawelti notes in his introduction to *Meteor*, Gussie "represents the solid peasant tradition of the southern Negro transplanted to the urban North but [who] never loses the 'grit and mother wit' that made it possible for her to endure and triumph over almost anything" (xvii). And "grit" and "mother wit," along with artistry of any sort, are at the heart of self-invention.

In addition to gardening, Gussie turns to loving hats. She knows that the need left unmet by the world's failure to acknowledge her humanity fully must be filled with a passion for something. So she falls in love with hats. In order to meet this need, Forester takes a job to earn Gussie's "hat money" at a brothel, which he renames the Doo-Doo Drop Inn. He knows how important it is to compensate for the slights imposed on her humanity, and he is also aware that he has a similar need. Ever efficient and practical about survival, his need becomes, quite simply, to ensure that Gussie's needs are met. So both characters are able to transform their grief internally by inventing humanistic alternatives for themselves purely in terms of their creativity.

Through the well-balanced Gussie and Forester we encounter the poet-gone-"mentally," Marvella. Fluctuating between functional insanity and potentially fatal depression, on the day Joubert goes to visit his grandparents, Marvella upsets the neighborhood with threats of suicide. She is a former civil rights activist who was also at one time a successful poet. Her mental stability took a turn for the worse when her fiancé, Paul, also an activist, was killed by embittered whites. What destroyed Marvella's already unstable sanity was that other members of the group (including Joubert's associate, Beefeater, and Marvella's sister) were apparently aware that there would be an attempt on Paul's life, and they did nothing to warn him or to prevent his murder. Though Paul has been dead for years, Marvella is trapped in the past and in the race battle that consumes her. Her inability to find the balance that could sustain her prompts the following astute and humorous exchange between Gussie and Forester, who clearly sympathize with her inability to function outside of the racialized existence that slowly overtakes her humanity, but who mock her nevertheless:

> FORESTER JONES: Awful to see how our young people (with the learning, the commencing, the breaks) . . . the ones who might and

could lead us to something better, they often be 'zactly the ones going 'round and 'round in circles like horses on a carousel, merry-go-round.

GUSSIE JONES: Others, educated fouls, I'm trying to learn you about. These days some high on horse, too. Riding for a sure fall; and ain't never visited no carnival. Don't do the kind of clowning anybody clothed in their right mind pay good money to see.

FORESTER JONES: Some of 'em high in the saddle, just like upstairs [Marvella]. Well, I ain't had but three grades of learning and one grade of bad hair, and now all these strands is divorced me to patches of baldness; but I got some meat on my head; mother wit all 'bout; five changes of underwear for work [. . . .] And my sweet Miz Honey-du-Melon Gussie at my side. (Forrest, *Meteor*, 28)

In short, Gussie and Forester have learned to transform their grief through self-invention and, correspondingly, by validating their own humanity.

Marvella, on the other hand, functions in racial spaces only. Even when she sweeps the street to beautify the area, she tries to get the residents to give her money for what she calls "tax for a block drive," since the city neglects to provide this black neighborhood with the services it needs. Though Marvella's proclamations of racial discrimination are true, the intimacy with which she deals with this reality borders on the insane. Just as her sweeping fails to create a coping mechanism to deal with racial discrimination, her threat of suicide fails to force the world to acknowledge the role of its race hatred in her lover's death. When Joubert approaches her to talk her down, she agrees to go with him only if he will represent her before the authorities and if he will force Beefeater to speak openly about his involvement with Paul's death. Her one desire is that the world knows just how guilty it is for its complicity in her lover's death and in its inaction against racial inequality. And although as a former singer and poet, she has access to music and to language as tools of self-invention, she does not use them to transform her grief internally but rather as tools to make the world aid her in transcending the agony it helped create.

After convincing Marvella to come down off of the roof, Joubert leaves his grandparents' home and heads to the hospital to visit his cousin Leonard, who, like Marvella, has lost his ability to transform his grief because he is consumed by the fight for racial equality. But before he tells of his encounter with Leonard, Joubert digresses to thoughts of his great-aunt (whom he calls his cousin) and Leonard's adoptive mother, Lucasta, after he is forced to explain to the hospital desk sergeant his family's version of the "extended branches of the Negro's complex family-fate" (37). What we learn is that Lucasta gave birth to only one child, Arthur Witherspoon, whom Jericho Witherspoon took from her, but she raised Leonard from time to time after his father, Roland Luke Foster, left her without taking his son with him.

From the age of twelve, Lucasta was employed as a "body washer and wardrobe mistress for the dead" (40). At varying points, she also danced with a local troupe whose final act climaxed with a self-choreographed performance by Lucasta. When T. C. Larkin, a professionally trained artist, sees her dance, he attempts to capture her motion on paper. Larkin initially intended to do sketches of the troupe Lucasta danced with, but he is so taken by her that "soon after his arrival, he began to draw in his large sketchbook 'the enchanting, brilliant, bizarre, deeply erotic, and moving twenty-minute-solo-dancer—this, Lucasta Jones's performance" (41). Her movements are so graceful and erotic that even her nephew Joubert is mesmerized by her. It is also her dancing that captures Jericho Witherspoon after he sees her at Memphis Raven-Snow Jr.'s semiprivate club. But because few dance companies are interested in black dancers, Lucasta is forced to continue to work for Raven-Snow at his funeral home, dressing the bodies of the dead. Rather than allow herself to be overcome by the denial of this artistic opportunity, and more importantly, by Jericho's denial of her worth as a proper mother for their son, Arthur, Lucasta chooses to process both denials mentally and, as an outward manifestation of her unwillingness to be defeated, puts her full energy into ironing, especially men's dress shirts.

Because Jericho had promised to return Arthur to her after the babe had reached the age of two, Lucasta commits to ironing Jericho's shirts free, "feeling certain that this *free ironing* would 'lay a claim on his heart'" (43; italics in original). When she realizes that Jericho has no intention of returning Arthur to her, she quits her job at the funeral home, since it was through Memphis Raven-Snow that she had met Jericho in the first place, and takes in ironing to sustain herself emotionally and financially. To transform the grief of the "three great heartbreaks in her life"—losing her son, Arthur, to his father, Jericho; losing Leonard to his father's Mississippi relatives; and losing her lover, Tuscon, to death and to another woman's heart—Lucasta, according to Joubert, develops "an inner power of living her life, as she willed it to be" (46) and governs her life by the religious philosophy she has tacked on her wall—LET NOT YOUR HEART BE TROUBLED. She knows that transformation of her grief can come only through internal means. The only heart she can transform is her own. So she takes up ironing as a means of self-invention through creativity.

Like Gussie's gardening, Lucasta's ironing, which she gives her full devotion and "all of her powers of thought and talent" (47), is, of course, in dialogue with Alice Walker's "In Search of Our Mother's Garden." Walker's contention is that because black women have historically been denied an outlet for traditional artistic expression, they tend to create an alternative expression of artistry that often goes unrecognized because of its domestic usefulness. And while Lucasta's ironing does not go unrecognized as a work of art (everyone raves about the beauty of her work), it must also be seen as an allegory of her unmet desires. The Nigerian seamstress who appears in the fourth novella, "To the Magical Memory of Rain," seems to recognize this and proclaims Lucasta's ironing an act of transformation. She recommends Lucasta to her customers, one of whom is Felicity Dobbs, whom the narration reveals thusly:

> Although she could not regard Lucasta Jones [. . .] as anything more than a laundress, Felicity was forced to admit that the way this woman Jones turned out her man's shirts was nothing short of magical. Why, even the way she sprinkled the clothes before her, with a flick of a wrist, reminded Felicity of the manner in which a priest joyously sprinkles his congregation as he comes down the aisle for High Mass. Where had she, this lowly Lucasta Jones, picked up this form of ritual-like adoration for the awakening of the litter of shirts at her elbow? (155)

Felicity wisely, though unknowingly, makes an accurate comparison between Lucasta and the priest. Both are concerned with the transformation of grief—the priest with his congregants, Lucasta with her own. What Lucasta could have told Felicity, had she but asked Lucasta, was that she "picked up this form of ritual-like adoration" as a means of self-invention and of survival.

In addition to dancing and ironing, Lucasta finds solace in one other form of artistry as self-invention—the blues. "[O]ut of the doldrums of despair, there in her dungeon of desolation, Lucasta allowed the music to creep in: the voices of Bessie and mainly that of Lady Day's singing 'Good Morning Heartache, here we go again'" (48): at times when she is too weak to re-create herself, she relies on Bessie Smith and Billie Holliday and their use of the blues as a site of self-invention and self-definition to cope with her constant experiences with loss and desolation.[4]

While Lucasta adopts black music as a sustaining cultural tradition, her adopted son, Leonard, rejects not only the blues, but gospel music and the spirituals as well. Instead of acknowledging black music for its worth as a coping mechanism, Leonard deems it one of many "perilous nostrums and opiates" (213) that keep the African American from overtly rebelling against oppression. Leonard, like Marvella, suffers, because he is so narrowly focused and dedicated to a single view of life that he contstricts himself. Black music especially, Joubert recalls having heard Leonard (mimicking Ron Karenga and other black arts movement aestheticians) say on occasion, "kept blacks 'sheltered from reality and blinded, even providing psychological disclaimers,' concerning the 'true nature of the police state and the reign of terror African Americans truly lived under'" (213). The irony of this belief, of course, is that insanity becomes Leonard's opiate, psychologically sheltering him from the madness that has become his reality, but never healing him of his soul's agony.

Though he never makes clear exactly what happens to Leonard during his days as an activist in Forest County, Joubert uses the narrating space of the second novella, "Live! At Fountain's House of the Dead," to suggest that it is intramovement corruption that destabilizes Leonard and nearly destroys his faith in living. By the time he realizes that he can control only that which is inward, "something deep within, something deep and fragile" has already snapped (16). Yet Joubert still accepts, though hesitantly, the role of healing agent, which Leonard's lover, Shirley Polyneices, bestows upon him. But his attempt to help heal Leonard fails, primarily because Leonard views himself almost exclusively in the context of others rather than in terms of a *self* that he has created independent of a binary other.

Even when Joubert tries to move Leonard away from allowing others to define him and toward self-invention, Leonard rejects it. Joubert attempts to lift Leonard's spirits by reminding him of their childhood antics; they recall Joubert's storytelling skills, even at a young age, and for a moment they laugh about it. But quickly, Leonard moves from laughter to anger and insults Joubert grandly. Leonard tells Shirley, who has been listening to and enjoying their storytelling all along, that Joubert's talent for inventing himself with words and through playacting disgusted him. Leonard claims that after he rounded up the neighborhood kids and listened to his cousin create "all kinds of characters out of lying tongue," he would go off to the end of the alley and throw up. He acknowledges Joubert's talent but also admits that Joubert disturbed something in him. The thing that apparently disturbs him most is Joubert's power to create and to redefine his environment through language and, correspondingly, to invent himself.

Adopting African and African American traditions of orality, Joubert realizes the power of voice and, thus, uses storytelling to his advantage. Rather than simply accept the experiences of agony and grief that surround him, Joubert redefines them through language and storytelling. The two thus become his coping mechanism since, as the teller of tales, Joubert, through his "mind work," has the power to include that which he wishes to include in his stories and a similar power to exclude that which might overwhelm him and his listening audience. And he uses these tales, rather than letting them use him, and gains power over them. This power is especially pronounced for Joubert in the novellas because Forrest removes all framing devices from Joubert's storytelling in all of the novellas but one.[5] Rather than have a narrator shape his stories, Joubert uses memory to access his experiences. He then relays them firsthand. By using language to recreate experiences, both through the spoken word (as a spontaneous storyteller) and through the written word (as a playwright), Joubert assumes the power that accompanies the presence of voice and thus has access to self-invention each time he engages in the act of storytelling or of playwriting. At one point, Leonard attempts to assume this power by writing poetry, but his friends from the movement discourage it because there is no room for artistry in activism. Later, when he becomes a preacher of sorts, he realizes that by rejecting the power of language, both the spoken and the written word, he also rejects access to self-invention as a coping mechanism and the freedom that ensues.

Following "Live! At Fountain's House of the Dead," which ends shortly after Joubert's visit with Leonard, is the more satirical third novella, "All Floundering Oratorio of Souls." While the two novellas that precede it present mostly serious characters who struggle with finding ways to invent themselves and to survive, "All Floundering Oratorio of Souls" re-creates character types whose souls are literally and figuratively floundering because the selves they invent are grounded more in fantasy than in reality and more in relation to others than to their desires for themselves. Thus, while they seem aware of the power of self-invention, they have less awareness of its limits. Self-invention cannot act as a substitute for reality; it simply allows one to create alternatives as a means of coping with reality and, subsequently, to move beyond agony and grief. We find these overly self-invented characters thrust together as Joubert's housemates in Mrs. Titlebaum's apartment building, which was inspired by Chicago's notorious Avon where Forrest once lived. According to Joubert, Mrs. Titlebaum's was a

> home for wayward souls, foreign spirits, nearly domesticated university students, oddball artists, off-the-wall musicians, raggedy-ribboned writers; small-time has-beens, would-be politicians who claimed now to be nationalists; fellow travelers who sold grave plots by dawn's early light; obese lunatics with thin portfolios. (9)

Among their number were also "several black nationalists awaiting the impending advent of an imperial African messiah, who could and would arrive upon the White House lawn [. . .] in a black, green, and red chariot (to match his cape) at high noon with a staff of angelic officers armed to the grinding of teeth, their rifles ready" (9); three drop-out Muslims who were disenchanted with Elijah Muhammad and who still grieved Malcolm X's death (as if it had just happened); a number of exchange students who purported to have revolutionary agendas to restore independence to their homelands; and, finally, "identity-crackled African Americans, searching in twelve different tormented-air circles for an ideal core soul source" (10).

Joubert is critical of all of these "students/activists/dreamers"—the Nationalists who await the African messiah, a few of whom believed in a Jewish conspiracy; the former Muslims who are somewhat identity-less without their belief in Black Islam and, hence, obsess over Malcolm X; and the "revolutionary" exchange students who vow to overturn their CIA-spawned home governments, though they have not been "home" in seven to ten years. But of all of the different types that populate the house, Joubert is seemingly most critical of the African Americans who claim to be thinkers but who have no real sense of themselves. He describes them as

> intellectual babes of toyland, ever pulling after and pinching for elusive and high-bouncing balloons, which, when punctured, did actually explode an odorless gas, guaranteeing death to the reasoning portion of the brain, as these rhetoricians mongered on, sucking up large gasps of the heavily polluted air of their own creation. (10)

Spun from similar cloth are the three gentlemen Joubert mockingly dubs the Deep Brown Study Eggheads. Spewing rhetoric on anything from race to uplift to Garveyism, the Eggheads are seemingly incapable of counter-arguing. Instead, "they were only a tenth of a degree to the left or to the right of one debating team's stalwart position, which might be best articulated by the simple, trite proverb 'I'd rather be right than be president'"

(104). Yet they argued profusely every day with whomever they encountered. Deeming themselves among the black intelligentsia, both the "intellectual babes of toyland" and the Eggheads were absolutely convinced that their engagement in race arguments would somehow facilitate racial progress. Their absolute unawareness of their futility is what gives Joubert enough comfort to mock an otherwise noble attempt to solve "the Problem." Despite the fact that they engage themselves mentally, they ultimately fail at the art of self-invention because they choose to abandon their old selves rather than reconciling this tension by simply modifying their approaches to life. For them, self-invention moves beyond being a coping mechanism and borders on the realm of psychosis.

These intellectuals are portrayed in stark contrast with Joubert's uneducated grandparents Forester and Gussie. Both respect Joubert for his "book learning," but they are also both clearly aware of the dangers of higher education when it is not accompanied with common sense, a clear idea of the self that is independent of an other, and a propensity for survival. Though he only completed third grade, Forester knows that he is better off than many academics, and he tries to get Joubert to help him convince Gussie that "lots of those high professors in great colleges is stone crazy" (24). Agreeing with his grandfather, Joubert also criticizes the limitations of misplaced intellect. He knows that he is able to avoid going "stone crazy" because his current position as Chair in Creative Writing and Literature

> doesn't intellectually circumscribe [him] into extolling any of the foolish literary theories abounding most contemporary English departments; nor is there any attempt to edge [him] off into embracing the "patty-cake, patty-cake baker's man, roll 'em in the oven just as fast as you can," programmed *theories* of M.F.A. writing program chefs or cooks. (202)

Instead, he can use the African American traditions of language and orality (especially orality's use of memory) as resources of self-invention to shape both his life and his writing. Free to ignore the limitations traditional literary theory create for him as an artist, he is free to articulate in his writing how the "Negro" keeps reshaping himself while singing "One More River to Cross."

This freedom is most pronounced in the fourth novella, "To the Magical Memory of Rain," which adopts myth and style as its form of self-invention. Unlike the other novellas in which characters engage in self-invention (both successfully and unsuccessfully), in "To the Magical

Memory of Rain" it is the narrative, more so than the main character, that enacts the principle of self-invention most aggressively. Appropriating fairy tale and myth, the novella takes place in a magical world that, as Cawelti notes in the editors' appendix, "seems to exist alongside the real world of Forest County, and Desiree steps into it, like Alice in Wonderland, as if she is stepping through a mirror" (266). The novella's opening narration is our first clue that, in this story, Forrest engages the language and style of myth and fairy tale and that this novella will be different from the others.

> There was a young woman by the name of Desiree Dobbs, who was quite strange, very beautiful, and easily enchanted by some things and not so enchanted by others; she had been sheltered by a mother who had read nothing but fairy tales to the girl up to the time Desiree was fourteen. (Forrest, *Meteor*, 133)

With its oral storytelling beginning, the novella adopts the "once upon a time" structure of the fairy tale, the only stories Desiree has heard. And she is described in the tradition of the female fairy-tale heroine—beautiful and easily enchanted. Aesthetically, we, too, as readers, are being programmed for enchantment, having been given Jorge Luis Borges's "Rain" as the novella's epigraph and lofty language throughout its opening pages. But "To the Magical Memory of Rain" invokes elements of fairy tale for more than aesthetic purposes. Its use of myth and fairy tale creates a sense of orality and gives the impression that the narration is speaking directly but objectively to the reader. This feigned objectivity encourages the reader to forget that a fiction is being created, even as the narration clearly edits which aspects of its story and how its story will be told. In essence, the narration engages in self-invention, even as it pretends simply to exist.

By adopting the Cinderella fairy tale and varied myths of trickster figures, the novella continues this act of self-invention as it modifies these tales to accommodate Desiree's story and to place it at the center. On the evening that Desiree whimsically decides to leave home, she and her mother, Felicity, go out to cash Felicity's monthly pension check and to purchase groceries for the month. But when the weather turns bad only minutes into the return trip home, their rain soaked bags deteriorate, and they lose all of their groceries to the street. Reminiscent of Cinderella, Desiree also loses her left slipper and is too disgusted to attempt to retrieve it. Though she is unsure of how she and her mother will survive since they have no money and no food, Desiree simply writes the incident off as "yet another example of the Dobbs's condemned condition" (150) until her doorbell rings, and she sees on the other side of the door Reign, "the most gorgeous guy in the world." Armed with bags filled with the exact items she and her mother have just lost in the rain storm, the most gorgeous guy in the world tells Desiree that he has come to take her away from her dire situation. When he produces from his pocket the slipper she had lost and tells her to abandon everything and to come with him, he suggests that she leave her mother a note and his "champion belt of priceless value," which he claims is a relic of the Ashante royalty in his family (153). Naïvely, she obliges him and embarks on a journey to the unknown world of Reign.

What Desiree eventually realizes is that her lover's unknown world is the world of drug use. She quickly becomes an avid cocaine user and does not attempt to escape Reign's "reins" until her imagination is plagued with visions of serpents. When she finally does decide to leave his world, she encounters Elderberry, who also appears in another novella as a prominent politically connected preacher, but who proves to be something of a trickster himself. He tells Desiree to run for her life, for Reign, according to Elderberry, is one of seven brothers whose heart is absent from his body and who is without a complete soul. Desiree returns to Reign's quarters to retrieve the bag of hearts to give to Elderberry for her freedom, but Reign returns before she is able to escape. He gives her chase down twenty-eight flights of stairs until he lunges for her, misses, trips over the bag of hearts, and falls down the passageway fourteen floors below. Finally making her escape, Desiree gets into a cab Elderberry hails for her, and when she tells the cab driver what a nice man Elderberry is, he tells her that Elderberry is, indeed, a "smooth dude," but is nothing compared to his "seven sons."

Fortunately for Desiree, she escapes from Reign, the drug culture that almost destroys her, and the alternative reality she self-invents. But the fact that she has been tricked yet again, this time by Elderberry, suggests that at least part of the function of the novella's use of fairy tale and myth is to remind the reader of the lesson Joubert's housemates fail to learn in "All Floundering Oratorio of Souls"—that self-invention has its limits, one of which is the failure that ensues when self-invention attempts to replace reality. Rather than finding a coping mechanism to deal with her desperate situation, Desiree abandons her old life and reality by using drugs to create an alternative reality. In this alternative world, she cannot distinguish the real from the unreal or from myth. She is puzzled by Reign's ability to assume the posture of both man and serpent. What she does not realize is that Reign, as trickster, like Elderberry and Ford, whom she encounters at the carnival, has mastered the art of self-invention, and he knows that the old self cannot be abandoned, only modified, if his attempts at self-invention are to succeed. In short, Desiree must find ways to invent herself in reality rather than in fantasy, because even though her reality is plagued with agony and grief, finding ways to cope in this world is far less destructive than abandoning it for a fantasy one.

Joubert's encounter with the female boxer Martha and her trainer CJ in chapter one of the final novella, "By Dawn's Early Light," suggests a discourse of self-invention as a coping mechanism that acknowledges the evolution of black cultural traditions and, subsequently, is representative of the times—rap. Emerging most aggressively in the early 1970s in New York, rap, like most musical forms, was created largely in response to social conditions. Inasmuch as slavery birthed the sorrow songs and the spiritual, the imported African's rhythmic dance practices birthed ragtime, his need to express with hope his agony about being free but still unequal birthed the blues, his tendency to improvise and to stylize classical music to counteract Jim Crow birthed jazz, and the blues man's return to the church after identifying heavily with the secular form birthed gospel music, the disappointment that followed the civil rights and black power movements gave birth to rap and to a culture identified today as hip-hop. Hip-hop culture, much like the blues and jazz, can be accurately characterized as an act of self-invention in the sense that, in addition to critiquing the world that denies African American youth full humanity, it also attempts to speak into being a reality that is desired but inaccessible. Like their musical forbears, early rap artists were concerned about finding ways to validate their experiences and the experiences of those around them. Instead of being enveloped by the destitution of their highly racialized existence, early hip-hop artists used music to assert the value of their voices in a culture that ignored black youth. Rather than look outside of the culture to have their worth assessed, they created a subculture that gave meaning to their existence without denigrating it.

Joubert taps into this art after an engaging ride home from the Greyhound bus station to his campus office. During the short trip, he is highly entertained by CJ and Martha, who, in turn, are entertained by Joubert's sharp wit. Just as he is about to part their company, Joubert, feeling particularly inspired by CJ and Martha's signifying, decides to render a rap for the ladies.

> Just because I'm a so-phis-ti-cate (having known the great and near great), don't get faked out by my balding pate. Don't contemplate; you can't re-pu-di-ate. Or try to up-date, low-rate nor con-tam-i-nate, or even com-pli-cate. This bad-ass-prime-mate's fate. . . . Just

> you get your own soul straight. . . . So turn your cab 'round. Go straight back downtown. Interrogate and turn all around those clowns and clones, heed the 'pealing tones. Who would complicate the fate—Who would slay the estate of this man—Joubert Jones! (195–96)

Joubert's rap is so well received that both women scream with surprise—"as if [they] had just seen and heard General Colin Powell suddenly rise up from his chair before the Joint Chiefs and not give his prepared speech, but rather launch into a rap before this distinguished gathering" (196). But he quickly moves beyond self-amusement to thoughts of his Aunt Eloise (who would have made him wash his mouth out with "a lot of soap and water" if she had heard his rhyme) and of Leonard (who would have, undoubtedly, accused him of once again acting frivolously). Nevertheless, Joubert realizes that his ability to tap into contemporary cultural forms has sustaining powers. Though "rap talk," as Forrest terms it, is one of the newer traditions influenced by the rap culture, the old bases (signifying, playing the dozens, and tall tales) are still there, providing sustenance (Forrest and Byerman, 440). And inasmuch as rap provides relief from a racialized existence by transforming language into personal expressions of worth, rap becomes yet another viable medium through which one can engage self-invention and live within a racially informed culture without being consumed by it.

After CJ and Martha drop him off, Joubert arrives at his office and tackles the stack of mail atop his desk. Before he can get to his graduate students' papers and other students' requests for letters of recommendation, he notices the headline in the *New York Post*, which reads:

DRUGGED OUT POET ROBBED
LEFT FOR DEAD IN THE GUTTER.

The "drugged out poet" is, of course, Leonard Foster, whose body has been discovered "in the rainswept streets of a New York slum, near a drug den, with a packet of cocaine stashed away in his purple beret" (Forrest, *Meteor*, 199). Leonard's life and tragic end vaguely parallel that of Huey Newton, who was also killed in a drug-related shooting.

Thus Leonard can be likened to the many activists who, out of frustration and distress, turned to drugs as a coping mechanism. As ex-Panther David Hilliard suggests in his autobiography, Newton's drug addiction began almost immediately after fellow Panther George Jackson's assassination in Soledad. Traumatized by Jackson's death, Newton was physically isolated from virtually everyone in the party following the killing. And in an attempt to help Newton cope with increased alienation and paranoia, among other things, Hilliard introduced Newton to cocaine. Though Newton's drug use was indeed a personal choice, his choice was not without context. And neither is Leonard's.

As an orphan obsessed with making the world better, Leonard invites defeat because he refuses to find ways to transform his grief internally, insisting instead that the world change to suit his honorable desires. But as Veena Deo notes of Forrest's fatherless characters' conditions more generally, because the African American experience is located in a liminal space, which is neither in Africa nor in America completely, endless problems abound. The orphaned African Americans' existence in this liminal space precludes any

> real freedom to define their lives as they wish even though America has always been a place for many that start their lives over again. Social, cultural, and religious institutions of the dominating culture define the parameters of their lives in ways so that self-definition from this language of domination is almost impossible. (Deo, 190)

This is perhaps why Leonard ultimately abandons his quest for a meaningful connection with all human beings and adopts and modifies the language of religion as a pseudo-act of self-invention instead. But this attempt fails because, rather than using language to resolve his conflict internally, he adopts the technique to exploit people through religion and reinvented African traditions rather than to survive.

Plagued with guilt about Leonard's death, Joubert comforts himself with a shot of Maker's Mark and the concession that "Leonard was so needy (always peddling in the wrong market for a spiritual high and comfort, in order not to deal with the horrors of abandonment) with his own river-deep vulnerabilities and callous insecurities" (Forrest, *Meteor*, 201) that there was really little Joubert could have done for him. Joubert recalls that the last time he had seen Leonard alive was in the middle of Joubert's grandson Xavier's graduation celebration at the Holiday Inn, when he tipped out of the room to go to the bathroom and to peek into other activity rooms. He heard Leonard's voice coming from one of them, "revealing something about Yoruba culture" (205). As he told the congregation about Orunmila, who is "known for his capacity for bringing order out of chaos," and Esu, who is the go-between for Orunmila and humans, Leonard began to dance and told the congregation that they, too, must dance if they are to "reach true divination exploration" (205). Joubert noticed that Leonard's eyes, which he was unable to see completely "because of the mask the goggle-dark shades provided" (206), seemed "otherworldly." But before Joubert could figure out exactly what Leonard is up to, Leonard spotted Joubert, pointed to him, and told his flock: "'*There,* my beloved, is the epitome of that which I have warned you against [. . . .] Behold the One who moves against the Light. I want him out of my sight'" (207). Members of the congregation came charging after Joubert. They gave him chase, and he was able to escape their wrath only by reinventing himself, literally. From the trunk of his car he took an eye patch, a white pompadour hairpiece, and a pair of work pants. He donned them, was transformed into a pimp/hustler, and reentered the hotel from which Leonard's congregation had chased him. In this humorous exchange, we see that both men utilize self-invention to save themselves—Joubert to return to his grandson's celebration unnoticed and Leonard to exist in a world which denies him the desires of his heart. When Leonard's self-inventing act moves beyond being simply a coping mechanism and into the realm of psychosis, it inevitably fails him, and he turns to drugs and its alternative reality which, ultimately, trap and kill him.

What Leonard needed to have done, the narration seems to suggest, was to adopt a tradition that could sustain him but was less destructive. For many of the characters in the Forest County Sagas, including Lucasta Jones in the first novella and Hopkins Golightly in the final one, this tradition is the blues. A reinvention of Meedmoxy Spears (a character whom Forrest created for a short story in the *Chicago Tribune* series on the city's culture) and blues great Lightnin' Hopkins, Golightly, by combining the techniques of self-invention with the reinventive impulse of the blues, is able not only to transcend his agony, but to thrive. The epitome of the hustler, a character Forrest admired tremendously for his ability to recover from bad situations and to start anew, Golightly constantly reinvents himself with success. Joubert marvels at the fact that with "the evolution of the Civil Rights Movement—which rolled right into the Black Power thrust—Hopkins Golightly," who at one point was down on his luck, "was soon observed right in the swarm of things. The late 1960s and early 1970s found Golightly completely bald, so in order to stay current he had to purchase and don a high-arching Afro wig" (238). Constantly regaining his footing, as an assistant director of an Urban Progress Center, Golightly is seen wearing purple and dark blue bellbottoms and high platform shoes. On the weekends, he wears a Nehru wine-colored or blue suit. But at a protest rally to condemn the arrest of two black youth who are accused of killing a white child, he wears his "dungarees, brogans, a farmer's red handkerchief swept about his neck, and a purple and red dashiki bloused about his waist" (239). He changes as situations change. And because he can see the limits of stasis and the benefits of perpetual self-invention, he survives.

Joubert is in awe of Golighty's evolution because Joubert's first encounter with Golightly was when the latter was employed at Riverview Park as a target in the dunking cages. Fired because he refused to "blacken up" (he was the only fair-skinned target among several dark African Americans), Golightly began to play his harmonica to earn money, and Joubert heard him play "The Battle Hymn of the Republic" for the first time. Years later, Joubert sees Golightly again after he has returned to the blues scene, after being a numbers runner, a waiter, an assistant precinct captain whose job was to buy votes during election time, and a street salesman who pushed popular representations of "blackness"—dashikis, African jewelry, sculptures, medallions, and the like. Introduced as a friend of Old Fox Foster who had come "screaming out of the Delta" in a pickup truck up Highway 61, Golightly takes the stage dressed in patched-up overalls and a blue shirt. After Golightly plays a mixed set of Delta songs and Chicago-brand blues, Joubert stands on his chair, with his arms raised, repeatedly requesting that Golightly play "something out of 'The Battle Hymn of the Republic.'" Just as Joubert is about to be thrown out of the club and booed to death by the unknowing (and primarily white) audience, Golightly responds:

> Nowhere you may roam, there is always some fat-meat from your own used-to-be-home. That voice out there—I can't make the face out—knows something out of my past, trying to put some fat-meat on my head and not no wig hat either. Important to me, been running from it, embracing it, and then again denying it. So, yes, I'll respond. Hell yes! I'll wail on down "The Battle Hymn of the Republic." (242)

As Golightly plays, Joubert astutely connects the African Americans' inaccessibility to the song's pronouncements of freedom, truth, and equality as he realizes that Golightly, with tears streaming down his face,

> was not simply turning "The Battle Hymn" upside down and upon its head, Golightly was trying to breathe the breath of jokes, heartaches, agony, duplicity, hustles of all kinds, triumphs, and

failures, and blasting out his life's laboratory into the ruptured, rowdy, no-holds-barred, cruel saga of this country. (242)

Golightly's interpretation of the blues, as Joubert describes it, heralds the power of self-invention and highlights the blues as one of the few mediums capable of expressing the African American's tragic fate of trying to assert his humanity in a republic that cannot reconcile its lived ideology and discrimination with the promise of its creed of equality. Ralph Ellison's frequently quoted definition of the blues bears repeating here. Golighty's engagement of the blues reveals the blues to be "an impulse to keep the painful details and episodes of a brutal experience alive in one's aching consciousness, to finger its jagged grain, and to transcend it [. . .] by squeezing from it a near-tragic, near-comic lyricism" (Ellison, *Shadow and Act*, 78–79). As self-inventive coping mechanism, its impulse to survive without abandoning reality or without ignoring the soul's agony is life sustaining. Even as Golightly's rendering of "The Battle Hymn" recognizes the song's irony, it does so by squeezing from the traditional rendition the near-tragic, near-comic lyricism Ellison writes of. Noting that his request had helped Golightly retrieve if not redeem his invented self, Joubert realizes:

> Lawd today, Golightly had to turn back to the blues and its potential for rifling an unearthing saga about all the lies concerning the self and the state of the Republic. The wonder irreverence of the blues pitched through the silver instrument at his lips helped old Golightly in his attempt to re-create a new consciousness about this tragic, embattled Republic so constantly in need of a wailing-on-down-blues-hymn. (Forrest, *Meteor*, 242)

Again, the transformation is internal. Knowing that the republic was not going to change in meaningful ways any time soon, Golightly adopts the blues impulse to help him live with and to transcend the agony and the grief America repeatedly dumps on him.

Joubert's memory of this incident with Golightly is the last event he narrates coherently after he falls victim to gang violence and moves toward death in the final novella. While in Williemain's barbershop retrieving the glasses he discovers are missing when he is making arrangements for Leonard's funeral at Memphis Raven-Snow's funeral home, Joubert is shot by someone "in a ski mask hanging out of the window" (216). And though his life ends abruptly and he is no longer able to use memory or language to invent himself, he dies having achieved voice in ways that had hitherto sustained him. As Merle Drown observes in his introduction to the novellas, by *Meteor*, Joubert, who is largely an observer in *Divine Days*, becomes a force within himself. He takes on the author's "wit and wisdom" and exerts a full presence. And while countless autobiographical elements are undeniably present in each of Forrest's novels, for the first time, in *Meteor*, the author bestows upon his narrator much of his own wisdom and a boldness to articulate this wisdom, particularly as it relates to finding ways to cope with the African American's racialized identity and his subsequent agony. In this sense, Forrest's authorial voice seems more optimistic than ever that the lost-found African American is, indeed, capable of survival in a world that, with the help of the artist, all too often denies him his humanity and then challenges him to rise above this denial. Ironically, this seems to be so despite the fact that Joubert and his alter ego, Leonard Foster, suffer at death via violent crimes and many of the other characters fail miserably at life and living.

As Forrest's final work of fiction, *Meteor in the Madhouse* brings to an end the almost real sagas of more than three generations of Bloodworths, Witherspoons, and Joneses in the fictional world of Forest County. We know not what ultimately happens to Nathaniel Witherspoon, and Joubert continues to search for "the light" even after he has been shot during a drive-by. Though the novellas soften the aggressive manner in which Forrest had come to treat the importance of spiritual and religious experiences, *Meteor* nevertheless tackles the significance of transcending the spiritual agony created by loss, agony, and grief. As the final novella closes, the narration has given voice to its epiphany regarding the transformation of grief—at the very least, it takes constant self-invention and internal transformation (as the phase of survival just beyond reinvention) to find ways to cope with agony and, ultimately, to experience more permanent transcendence. And this is why, even as Joubert dies, he seeks internal transformation beyond the darkness of unknowing and can graciously cross over into death, chanting "*LET THERE BE LIGHT, Baby, LET THERE BE LIGHT.*"

Epilogue

Leon Forrest's contemporary Toni Cade Bambara once noted that she wrote stories that saved lives. In her fiction, she proclaimed, "[s]alvation is the issue."[1] And although Forrest never made a similar proclamation overtly, he, too—feeling that salvation was a real issue for the contemporary African American, who still struggled to negotiate his racist past to function successfully in the present—wrote stories that saved lives. He recognized that fiction that dealt with the soul's agony and its desire to transcend this agony was what was missing in contemporary African American literature when he began writing seriously (Forrest, *Furious Voice,* 29). In response to this void, he wrote novels that aggressively dealt with the soul's condition and, subsequently, helped to create a tradition in contemporary African American literature I have come to refer to as *healing narratives.*

Around the same time that she was an editor for both Forrest and Bambara, Toni Morrison issued a call for the African American writer to facilitate healing. She wrote:

> For a long time, the art form that was healing for Black people was music. That music is no longer *exclusively* ours [. . .] so another form has to take that place, and it seems to me that the novel is needed by African-Americans now in a way that was not needed before [. . . .] We don't live in places where we can hear those stories anymore; parents don't sit around and tell their children those [. . .] stories that we heard years ago. But the new information has got to get out, and there are several ways to do it. One is in the novel. ("Rootedness," 340)

What Forrest offers in his fiction, I contend, is the novel as an art form that borrows from oral traditions to tell those stories we don't hear anymore and, thus, the novel as an agent of healing.

The healing narrative, as Forrest and a number of his contemporaries present it, is a modern text that engages the historical past, particularly as it relates to racial oppression, in an attempt to show the reader, through the characters, ways to negotiate the legacy of a racist past without being trapped in it. In its acknowledgment of an oppressive past, the healing narrative also acknowledges that the African American created and used cultural traditions to survive this past. Thus, Forrest's narratives investigate the cultural traditions the African American has used in the past and questions their viability as techniques of survival of this legacy of oppression in the contemporary moment.[2]

To a large degree, the effectiveness of Forrest's narratives as agents of healing rests in the author's adaptation of oral and musical traditions within his texts. Storytelling is paramount throughout Forrest's fiction. But in *Two Wings* especially, the act of storytelling as a pathway to healing is particularly pronounced. Both Sweetie Reed and her father, I. V., believe completely that they *must* tell their stories before they die if they are to die peacefully. Their salvation literally depends on their willingness to participate in the act of storytelling, not only for themselves but also to advance the healing of their listeners. Hearing her father's story offers Sweetie an otherwise inaccessible balm, so she feels compelled to share her father's and her own story with her adopted grandson, with the hope that through storytelling he, too, can be healed.

As much as he loved storytelling and sought to translate it into fiction, Leon Forrest loved music. He frequently commented that he "was bred more on music than books" and that he was "weaned on Billie Holliday's music" (Forrest, *Furious Voice*, 344), and his fiction supports this claim. For Forrest, it is black music that served as the "railroad tracks and the wings for [his] imagination and the migrating train of [his] Southern-turned-Yankee sagas" (21). The tendency of music to heal and to mirror the social, political, and religious aspects of culture had incredible appeal for a writer interested not only in realistically depicting culture but in presenting it with the eloquence of orality. From the blues and the spiritual he took agony and hope; from jazz and gospel he took freedom and improvisation.

Throughout the Forest County Sagas, the interplay of music and narrative as storytelling holds both aesthetic and structural value. He uses the jazz-spiritual motif in *There Is a Tree* as metaphor and as form to present the complex layers of Nathaniel's representative journey of the African American experience. In *Two Wings*, he complements one oral form—storytelling—with another—the blues—to chronicle Sweetie's trials and tribulations, which, like the blues song, laments but shows no signs of surrender. Jazz functions as both theme and structure to complicate *The Bloodworth Orphans*, and *Divine Days* is influenced by the blues, jazz, gospel, and the spiritual alike, with Sugar-Groove ultimately emerging as the jazz hero whose story Joubert so desperately seeks to tell. Thus, for Forrest, black music has almost always has a dual function—for him as writer, it provides a path into the complexity of the contemporary moment. Subsequently, for his characters, it offers a path to healing.

In the figurative sense, the novels are way stations of black survival with black cultural traditions offering characters sustenance. Whether it is Nathaniel trying to transform himself from a motherless child to a man in *There Is a Tree,* Sweetie Reed transforming herself from object to subject in *Two Wings,* or Nathaniel and Joubert transforming themselves into myth-makers and culture-keepers in *The Bloodworth Orphans, Divine Days,* and *Meteor,* in Forrest's fiction, salvation is always the issue. Leon Forrest transcribed oral forms into fiction and wrote stories to save lives.

Notes

Notes to Introduction

1. All references to *black cultural traditions*, which I use intermittently as a subset of *black ethnic culture*, refer to variations of language, customs, and social activities that have become traditionally associated with black American life and experiences. These traditions are often rooted in black experiences of shared oppression rather than in any notion of "race" as biological. These traditions also refer to more modern artistic, linguistic, social, and religious activities that are not limited to black Americans. Throughout Forrest's fiction, black cultural traditions may serve as a culturally specific reinterpretation of a nonblack tradition, as they may have likewise transcended the borders of the black community. Examples of black cultural traditions that appear in Forrest's fiction include folk preaching, communal and familial rituals, storytelling, black music, and black religious traditions.

2. Although black authors dealt with the question of identity in the earliest African American literature, slavery and racial oppression greatly restricted the black American's possibilities for self-definition. Consequently, most renderings of black identity in literature by black authors emerged either as a binary construct (blackness defined as the opposite of whiteness) or as an attempt to assert or to prove what black identity was not. I should also note here that part of later, more contemporary black literature's inadequacy in this regard occurs when authors attempt to define blackness as definitive rather than as variable.

3. Ellison later recognizes the possibilities for meaningful connectedness between the individual and the community and offers jazz as a metaphor to show this connection in *Shadow and Act*. He notes that "true jazz is an art of individual assertion within and against the group" (234). Similarly, in Forrest's fiction, the individual and the group are frequently and paradoxically one. I should also note here that Forrest's portrayal of women as a meaningful source of inspiration, wisdom, and guidance departs from Ellison's and most of his male contemporaries' portrayal of women in their fiction.

4. Marianne Duncan Forrest, telephone conversation with the author, November 19, 2002.

5. See Forrest's unpublished lecture notes/personal papers housed in the archives of Northwestern University Library, Evanston, IL.

6. Richard Moreland, for instance, in "Faulkner and Modernism," makes the following observation about the emergence of modernism: "Some have attributed such cultural self-doubts in the early twentieth century in the United States and Western Europe to a widespread disillusionment with the idea of Progress after the world's most 'civilized' nations conducted the apparently meaningless slaughter of World War I; others point to a threatened loss of masculine privilege, colonial power, religious belief, a presumed cultural consensus" (21).

7. These repeated words—*Let there be Light, baby, Let there be light*—are among the closing words of *Meteor in the Madhouse*, Forrest's final work. In fact, during prepublication

stages the novellas were once titled *Let There Be Light!* For me, the phrase has come to represent an ideological impetus for Forrest's fiction—that it searches for and offers light (healing) to the contemporary African American.

Notes to Chapter One

1. Forrest's close friend and fellow author, Merle Drown, who also coedited *Meteor in the Madhouse*, brought this tendency to my attention. I am grateful to Merle for this and so many other conversations we had about Forrest's writing habits and goals for his fiction.

2. While Forrest is also referred to, though less frequently, in the context of African American modernists and postmodernists such as Albert Murray, Clarence Major, Ishmael Reed, Toni Cade Bambara, James Alan McPherson, and John Edgar Wideman, I have chosen to limit my contextualization of Forrest as an African American modernist author to Toomer, Hurston, Ellison, and Morrison, both to be concise yet thorough and to highlight the ways in which Forrest, in a manner similar to these authors, employs modernism's form to achieve his aesthetic goals while simultaneously critiquing it.

3. See Richard Lehan's interpretation of Edmund Wilson, Harry Levin, and Wyndam Lewis's critiques of Joyce, 94–95.

4. Forrest uses myth, folklore, and biblical stories and images throughout his fiction. Of note here especially, however, is the "Vision" section of *Tree,* where he modifies the Osiris myth (a revision I explore in chapter 2) and combines it with the Crucifixion and with lynching imagery. We see Joyce's influence here if only coincidentally, since it is a version of the Osiris myth that structures *Finnegan's Wake. Divine Days*' structure also mirrors the structure of *Ulysses* and takes place over the course of seven days in the life of Joubert Jones, Forrest's archetypal artist/protagonist who, like Joycean characters, attempts to fulfill himself as an artist and as a moral human being.

5. I examine Forrest's use of jazz as a structuring device in *The Bloodworth Orphans* in greater detail in chapter 3.

6. As Lehan intimates, this is perhaps more postmodernist than it is modernist.

7. Recent examinations of Faulkner also cite his postmodern tendencies and argue that he is as or more accurately characterized as a postmodernist.

8. See Kenneth Warren's "Thinking beyond Catastrophe: Leon Forrest's *There Is a Tree More Ancient Than Eden*" for an interesting reading of *Tree* as a cinematic text. I should also note here that both Merle Drown and John Cawelti suggested to me that Forrest's montage principle was more likely to be influenced by jazz than by cinema, as neither of his friends had heard him speak of film as having any influence on his writing.

9. Like Faulkner, who in the 1930s "was rejected because his forbidding style marked him as an author uninterested, if not absolutely opposed to, the [then] current effect to enlist the arts in building an equitable society" (Kodat, "A Postmodern," 195–96), Forrest is ignored by those literary critics who believe that African American literature should embrace a straightforward style that is accessible to all readers and should be as concerned with propaganda as it is with art. He is similarly ignored by those readers who reject his difficult narrative style and, correspondingly, consider it as a rejection of black literary traditions.

10. Toomer often rejected being labeled *Negro.* See Fredrik L. Rusch's *A Jean Toomer Reader: Selected Unpublished Writings,* 107–8, for Toomer's comments about the "new American race." See also Henry L. Gates Jr.'s commentary on Toomer's attempt to "liberate" race in *Figures in Black,* 210.

11. My examination of literary modernism here, as it relates to Forrest's fiction and the modernist authors who influence his work, is twofold. On one level, I note Forrest's use of specific modernist techniques and highlight the influence of a particular author on Forrest's presentation or reinterpretation of these techniques. And on another level, I examine select authors' internal critique of modernism and the critical limits of modernism as revealed in select texts. Summarily stated, my reading of modernism as rendered in select texts which are racially charged is meant to emphasize the way the authors of these texts modify modernism in an attempt to avoid modernism's fatal flaw of reenacting the domination it critiques. Avoiding this tendency is of special importance to African American authors such as Toomer, Hurston, Morrison, and Forrest for obvious reasons—the tragic history of racial oppression being among them. Thus, their modification of modernism to move beyond its critical limit is especially pronounced and, in many ways, more significant than the authors' adoption of modernist techniques and form. Accordingly, my examination of the modernist African American authors who can be likened to Forrest focuses on these authors' modification of modernism rather than the techniques they use.

12. See Henry L. Gates Jr.'s *The Signifyin(g) Monkey.*

13. Hurston is an exception here. As Carr and Cooper note, readers and critics alike tend to focus so heavily on Hurston's use of ethnography and anthropology in her cultural investigations that the literary techniques she employs go unnoticed or unacknowledged more often than they are investigated. Gates's reading of *Their Eyes* in *Signifying Monkey* is, of course, a seminal and significant exception.

14. *Two Wings to Veil My Face* may not be most accurately characterized as a "neo-slave narrative" per se. It does, however, heavily involve storytelling about characters who were slaves, one of whom (Sweetie's father, I. V.) renders his narrative through direct discourse. As such, I have labeled the novel as an interpretation of the neoslave narrative rather than as a neoslave narrative.

Notes to Chapter Two

1. Unpublished personal notes, Northwestern University library, Evanston, IL.

2. John Cawelti, for instance, points out that "the image of a tree 'more ancient than Eden' suggests an archetypal tree which underlies the many different legendary trees of human mythology and religion. For example [. . .] there is the myth of Ygdrasil, the earth tree, from which all things originate. Another implication of the 'more ancient tree' is the idea that there are human civilizations older than Western civilization and its Biblical roots, particularly Africa" ("Leon Forrest: Labyrinth of Luminosity," 30–31).

3. See James Cones's *A Black Theology of Liberation.*

4. See Timothy Freke and Peter Gandy's *The Jesus Mysteries.*

5. For further examination of Forrest's use of the gospel impulse in his novels, see my "Preachin' and Singin'."

Notes to Chapter Three

1. In Greek mythology, Cronus is the youngest son of Uranus (the first ruler of the universe) and Gaia. At his mother's request, Cronus castrates his father and later learns that his own son would depose him one day. Fearful of the curse, Cronus swallows each of his

children, excepting Zeus, whom his mother hides from Cronus until Zeus can fulfill his destiny. Like the unnamed Bloodworth and his wife, Cronus and his wife, Rheia, have three children—Poseidon, Zeus, and Hades—none of whom is destroyed as their father intends. Notably, Regal's metanarrative has mythic implications as well. He has nightmares in which he is denied his inheritance by his father and dreams of becoming a hero who destroys a boar to save his siblings until they, in turn, stab and kill him with the same knives he uses to save them. Similarly, Cronus, after castrating his father, Uranus, for casting his siblings in Tartarus and for fear that he will be denied his inheritance, frees his siblings but later banishes them to Tartarus again. Additionally, P. F.'s slaying of his father on the open road draws from the myth of Oedipus, who also kills his father unknowingly after trying desperately to avoid a curse.

2. Noah's transformation from African griot to Western storyteller creates interesting dialogue with Henry L. Gates Jr.'s rendering of the Signifyin(g) Monkey. In essense, Noah is, at once, both Esu (African) and the Signifying Monkey (American). Like both interpreters, he can read signs and is endowed with the power to convey the message to his listener at will. Notably, he is the only one who has awareness of Ford and who has the ability to escape the fate that has been given to him at birth. Because he is Esu, he knows that, under the right circumstances, he can change his preordained fate and thus escape the Bloodworth curse. The gift of transformation is also in dialogue with improvisation as musical impulse.

3. "Salvation Is the Issue" is the title of an essay by Toni Cade Bambara. In the essay, she suggests that as an African American writer, she is obligated to try to tell stories that "save lives." I would argue that Forrest viewed himself in this tradition as well.

Notes to Chapter Four

1. I am using the term *neoslave narrative* here as it is most commonly used, to refer to contemporary narratives that engage slave history or the legacy of slavery, especially as this history or legacy relates to the pain and the horror which followed slavery. Although the narration of *Two Wings* is not exclusively about slavery—nor is it narrated by a former slave who attains freedom—I am suggesting that it can be read as a neoslave narrative because it specifically engages slave history in an attempt to show the legacy of slavery the descendants of former slaves inherit.

2. I have taken some liberty here with extending Mitchell's definition of the liberatory narrative, as Mitchell uses the term specifically to describe an enslaved protagonist's attainment of freedom and to investigate the nature of freedom for the formerly enslaved (4). Sweetie Reed is born some years after slavery has ended, but, at least to some degree, she is still enslaved. She is in fact kidnapped, along with her mother who is ultimately raped and killed, by patrollers who perpetuated slavery's legacies and its traditions by becoming body snatchers and forcing their captives to work on plantations.

3. Sweetie's insistence that her family's history be told orally is in dialogue with Gayl Jones' *Corregidora,* which also engages slave history and which also finds its matriarch insisting that the story of female exploitation be told to every generation.

Notes to Chapter Five

1. Forrest's intepretation of the "Flying Fool Myth" is a reinvention itself. It is first published in Roger D. Abrams's *Afro-American Folktales* but appears, with variation, in works such as Ellison's "Flying Home," Richard Wright's *Lawd Today,* and Sterling Brown's "Slim in Hell."

2. In the chapter which follows on *Meteor in the Madhouse,* I attempt to make the distinction between *reinvention,* which focuses on the external, i.e., Sugar-Groove's actions, and *self-invention,* which focuses on the internal, i.e., Sugar-Groove's soul. Joubert can be accurately characterized as a writer in both *Divine Days* and *Meteor,* but in *Divine Days,* he struggles to capture even Sugar-Groove's actions (his tendencies toward reinvention) in writing. But by *Meteor,* he is a successful playwright largely because he is finally able to move beyond chronicling Sugar-Groove's actions and dramatize his soul. Thus, *self-invention* becomes the focus in *Meteor.*

Notes to Chapter Six

1. *Self-invention* is the term I have chosen to use here to describe one of many techniques *Meteor*'s characters (and people) use to cope with otherwise exasperating situations. I openly and eagerly acknowledge that variations of this technique permeate human experience. I name it *self-invention* here not in any naive sense of discovery but out of a very basic need to characterize it linguistically as a perceptible form.

2. The responses Forrest's characters make in *Meteor* that I characterize as indicative of self-invention are not always responses that are culturally specific. Lucasta's adoption of ironing as a work of art rather than simply as a domestic chore, for example, is not a specifically black response. Her willingness to transform this chore into an allegory of her creative desires, however, is heavily informed by traditions of African American culture that dictate that oppressed persons find ways to validate their existence and, hence, to survive. In the discussion which follows, I note the similarities and the differences between self-invention and reinvention, both of which I characterize as black cultural traditions of survival. For a more detailed discussion of *reinvention,* see chapter 5.

3. Because its distinction from reinvention is a fine one, I offer the following somewhat lengthy explanation of both reinvention and self-invention with the hope that the contrast of examples I cite better highlights the techniques' differences. The most exemplary example of reinvention occurs in *Divine Days* where Sugar-Groove describes to St. Peter how it is that his distinctive stylized heavenly flights came to be:

> You see when I died, and they cracked this deal to send me up in here, I was issued an old patched-up set of shattered wings thrown in the Catholic Salvage section and over in the Free Will bin where other angelic vestments were tossed away and cast asunder [. . . .] You see Mister Peter, Sir, they (them officials) plucked up the worst of the discarded wings for me [. . . .] Not to ruffle your feathers, Mister Peter, Sir, but you see part of the deal they

> struck to let me in . . . [was] I'd have to fly about Heaven all of my days, with one wing tied with shipyard rope behind my right shoulder, whipped about my belly [. . . .] (Forrest, *Divine Days,* 103–4)

Sugar-Groove's transformation, or his reinvention of the discarded wings into something embossed and useful, is foremost external. Because of his life experiences, he is capable of taking what is left over and transforming it (externally) into something useful and outwardly visible. With self-invention, the transformation is largely, if not exclusively, internal or psychological. The attempt is still to cope or to survive, but the tension that creates or feeds self-invention exists on psychological levels and, thus, is most often resolved internally rather than externally. When there is one, the outward display of this psychological transformation is secondary. The best example of self-invention with a secondary outward display of a psychological transformation involves *Meteor*'s Hopkins Golightly, who, both during and after mentally processing the racial discrimination he faces, externally expresses his resolution of living in a racially charged existence without being consumed by it through song. After being fired for refusing to don blackface, Golightly is forced to process the discrimination he faces mentally or to accept defeat. His choice to reinterpret "The Battle Hymn of the Republic" is especially telling of his need and his attempt to deal with his grief internally, even as he renders an outward manifestation of this internal struggle in the form of his blues rendition in song. Over and over again, Golightly plays the refrain "at the exact place where the lyrics of the song proclaim" the charge of the songwriter to the soldiers to die to make men free. The narration describes Golightly's playing as having "wonderful wildness, wickedness, invention, but without a core center to its being" (*Meteor,* 71). The missing "core center," I contend, is indicative of his internal, mental struggle to come to terms with his inaccessibility to the freedom "The Battle Hymn" alludes to. By the last novella, Golightly has participated successfully both in reinvention (he changes professions and, correspondingly, his outward appearance with frequency throughout the text) and in self-invention, which, because of its psychological nature and Golightly's willingness to deal with it on that level, ultimately affords him the freedom he alludes to in the song he plays.

4. While Lucasta's engagement of the blues as an act of self-invention is meaningful, it pales in comparison to her ironing and to Hopkins Golightly's engagement of the blues. Thus, I have reserved my commentary about the blues as an act of self-invention until my analysis of Golighty's blues activities, which occurs later in the chapter. I also investigate the impact of women's blues experiences (particularly Bessie Smith and Ma Rainey) on one of Forrest's female characters in chapter 3.

5. In *Liberating Voices,* Gayl Jones notes that "freeings of voice" are often linked to the shedding of narrative frames (160–62). To highlight this contention, she examines differences in voice in Zora Neale Hurston's *Their Eyes Were Watching God* and Ernest Gaines's *The Autobiography of Miss Jane Pittman.* Because Miss Jane tells her own story rather than having it framed by someone, as Janie does in Hurston's text, Miss Jane achieves voice in a way that Janie can only imagine.

Notes to Epilogue

1. See Toni Cade Bambara's "Salvation Is the Issue," in *Black Women Writers*.
2. I should note here that even as they are healing narratives, Forrest's texts are not without their limitations. Nathaniel's role as a centralized, historical African American consciousness in the first three novels, for example, presents challenges to the reader that are as alienating as they are innovative; Joubert's less innovative narrative style weakens the texts' ability to conceal the fact that the narratives are indeed constructed and, hence, products of the author's fictional strategy; even in their presentation of varied black cultural traditions as healing, the texts inevitably omit some; similarly, in their critique of black intellectual traditions and ideologies, the texts, at times, fail to offer working alternatives. But even with their limitations, Forrest's fiction reveals, through its characters, the art of transformation—the ability to find ways to make the wretchedness of the past work in positive ways.

Bibliography

Abrams, Roger D. *Afro-American Folktales.* New York: Pantheon, 1985.
Allen, Jeffrey Renard. "Blood Bastards: *The Bloodworth Orphans* and The Psychology of Form." In *Leon Forrest: Introductions and Interpretations,* ed. John G. Cawelti, 166–83. Bowling Green, OH: Popular, 1997.
Awkward, Michael. "'Unruly and Let Loose': Myth, Ideology, and Gender in *Song of Solomon.*" *Callaloo* 13 (Summer 1990): 482–98.
Baker, Houston A. Jr. *Blues, Ideology, and Afro-American Literature: A Vernacular Theory.* Chicago: University of Chicago Press, 1984.
Baldwin, James. *The Fire Next Time.* 1963. Reprint, New York: Vintage, 1993.
———. "Many Thousands Gone." In *The Price of the Ticket: Collected Nonfiction 1948–1985,* 65–78. New York: St. Martin's, 1985.
Bambara, Toni Cade. *The Salt Eaters.* New York: Random House, 1980.
———. "Salvation is the Issue." In *Black Women Writers (1959–1980): A Critical Evaluation,* ed. Mari Evans, 41–47. Garden City, NJ: Anchor-Doubleday, 1984.
Bethel, Kathleen E. "Leon Forrest: A Bibliography." *Callaloo* 16 (Spring 1993): 448–54.
———, and Leigh Anna Mendenhall. "Leon Forrest: A Bibliography." In Cawelti, *Leon Forrest: Introductions and Interpretations,* 269–77.
Bell, Bernard. *The Afro-American Novel and Its Tradition.* Amherst: University of Massachusetts Press, 1987.
———. "Introduction: Clarence Major's Double Consciousness as a Black Postmodernist Artist." *African American Review* 28 (Spring 1994): 5–9.
Birkerts, Sven. "*Invisible Man* by Sven Birkets: *Divine Days* by Leon Forrest." In Cawelti, *Leon Forrest: Introductions and Interpretations,* 255–62.
Byerman, Keith. "The Flesh Made Word: Family Narrative in *Two Wings to Veil My Face.*" In Cawelti, *Leon Forrest: Introductions and Interpretations,* 199–215.
———. "Orphans and Circuses: The Literary Experiments of Leon Forrest and Clarence Major." In *Fingering the Jagged Grain: Tradition and Form in Recent Black Fiction,* 238–74. Athens: University of Georgia Press, 1985.
Carr, Brian, and Tova Cooper. "Zora Neale Hurston and Modernism at the Critical Limit." *Modern Fiction Studies* 48 (Summer 2002): 285–313.
Cawelti, John G. "Earthly Thoughts on *Divine Days.*" *Callaloo* 16 (Spring 1993): 431–47.
———. Introduction. In *The Bloodworth Orphans,* by Leon Forrest, ix–xliii. Chicago: Another Chicago Press, 1987. Originally published 1977.
———. "Leon Forrest: Labyrinth of Luminosity: An Introduction." In *Leon Forrest: Introductions and Interpretations,* 1–73.
———. "Thoughts on *Meteor in the Madhouse.*" In Leon Forrest, *Meteor in the Madhouse,* ed. John G. Cawelti and Merle Drown, xiii–xviii. Evanston, IL: Northwestern University Press, 2001.

Cawelti, John G., ed. *Leon Forrest: Introductions and Interpretations.* Bowling Green: Popular, 1997.
Cone, James. *The Spirituals and the Blues: An Interpretation.* New York: Orbis, 1972.
———. *A Black Theology of Liberation.* Twentieth Anniversary Edition. New York: Orbis, 1990.
———. "Black Theology in American Religion." In *Introduction to Christian Theology,* ed. Roger A. Badham, 197–211. Louisville, KY: Westminster John Knox Press, 1998.
Crouch, Stanley. "Beyond American Tribalism: Leon Forrest's *Divine Days.*" In Cawelti, *Leon Forrest: Introductions and Interpretations,* 263–68.
Davis, Angela Y. *Blues Legacies and Black Feminism: Gertrude "Ma" Rainey, Bessie Smith, and Billie Holiday.* New York: Pantheon, 1998.
Deo, Veena. "Circle of Safety, Circle of Entrapment: Women's Languages of Self-Invention in Toni Morrison's *Beloved* and Leon Forrest's *Bloodworth Orphans.*" In Cawelti, *Leon Forrest: Introductions and Interpretations,* 184–98.
Dixon, Melvin. "The Black Writer's Use of Memory." In *History and Memory in African American Culture,* ed. Robert O'Meally and Genevieve Fabre, 18–27. New York: Oxford University Press, 1994.
Dodge, Susan. "700 at NU honor writer Leon Forrest." *Chicago Sun-Times,* January 31, 1998.
Drown, Merle. "Leon Forrest's Final Journey." In Forrest, *Meteor in the Madhouse,* xix-xxiv.
DuBois, W. E. B. *The Souls of Black Folk.* Chicago: A. C. McClurg, 1903.
Elder, Arlene. "*Sassafras, Cypress & Indigo:* Ntozake Shange's Neo-Slave/Blues Narrative." *African American Review* 26 (Spring 1992): 99–107.
Ellison, Ralph. *Invisible Man.* 1952. Reprint, New York: Vintage, 1990.
———. *Shadow and Act.* New York: Random House, 1953.
Forrest, Leon. *The Bloodworth Orphans.* New York: Random House, 1977.
———. *Divine Days.* Chicago: Another Chicago Press, 1992.
———. *The Furious Voice for Freedom: Essays on Life.* Wakefield, RI: Asphodel, 1994.
———. *Meteor in the Madhouse,* ed. John G. Cawelti and Merle Drown. Evanston, IL: Northwestern University Press, 2001.
———. *There Is a Tree More Ancient Than Eden.* New York: Random House, 1973.
———. *Two Wings to Veil My Face.* New York: Random House, 1984.
———. Unpublished personal notes. Northwestern University, Evanston, IL.
———, and Keith Byerman. "Angularity: An Interview with Leon Forrest." *African American Review* 33 (Fall 1999): 439–50.
———, and John G. Cawelti. "Leon Forrest at the University of Kentucky: Two Interviews." In Cawelti, *Leon Forrest: Introductions and Interpretations,* 287–313.
———, and Madhu Dubey. "The Mythos of Gumbo: Leon Forrest Talks about *Divine Days. Callaloo* 19 (Summer 1996): 588–602.
———, and Molly McQuade. "The Yeast of Chaos: An Interview with Leon Forrest." *Chicago Review* 41 (1995): 43–51.
———, and Maria K. Mootry. "'If He Changed My Name': An Interview with Leon Forrest." *Massachusetts Review* 18 (1977): 631–42. Reprinted in *Chant of Saints: A Gathering of Afro-American Literature, Art, and Scholarship,* ed. Robert Stepto, John Hope Franklin, and Michael Harper, 146–57 (Urbana: University of Illinois Press, 1979).
———, and Charles Rowell. "Beyond the Hard Work and Discipline: An Interview with Leon Forrest." *Callaloo* 20 (Spring 1997): 342–56.
———, and Kenneth Warren. "The Mythic City: An Interview with Leon Forrest."

Callaloo 16 (Spring 1993): 392–408. Reprinted in Cawelti, *Leon Forrest: Introductions and Interpretations,* 75–96.
Fox, Robert Elliot. "Righteous Rites and Royal Ramblings: Leon Forrest's *Divine Days.*" *MELUS* 2 (Winter 1995): 103–11.
Freke, Timothy, and Peter Gandy. *The Jesus Mysteries.* New York: Harmony Books, 2000.
Gates, Henry L. Jr. *Figure in Black.* New York: Oxford University Press, 1987.
———. *The Signifying Monkey.* New York: Oxford University Press, 1988.
———. "The Trope of the New Negro and the Reconstruction of the Image of the Black." *Representations* 24 (Autumn 1988). Special Issue: America Reconstructed, 1840–1940: 129–55.
Gayle, Addison. *The Black Aesthetic.* New York: Doubleday, 1971.
Genette, Gerard. *Narrative Discourse: An Essay in Method.* Ithaca, NY: Cornell University Press, 1980.
Gilroy, Paul. *The Black Atlantic: Modernity and Double Consciousness.* Cambridge, MA: Harvard University Press, 1993.
Goldstein, Philip. "Critical Realism or Black Modernism? The Reception of *Their Eyes Were Watching God.*" *Reader: Essays in Reader-Oriented Theory, Criticism, and Pedagogy* 41 (Spring 1999): 54–79.
Grimes, Joanna L. "Leon Forrest." In *Dictionary of Literary Biography: Afro-American Fiction Writers after 1955,* ed. Thadious Davis and Trudier Harris, 33:77–83. Detroit: Gale, 1984.
Hamilton, Edith. *Mythology.* Boston: Little, Brown, 1942.
Harris, Trudier. "Barbershops in Black Literature." *Black American Literature Forum* 13 (Autumn 1979): 112–18.
Harrison, Elizabeth Jane, and Shirley Peterson. *Unmanning Modernism: Gendered Re-Readings.* Knoxville: University of Tennessee Press, 1997.
Harwood, John. *Eliot to Derrida: The Poverty of Interpretation.* New York: St. Martin's, 1995.
hooks, bell. *Yearning: Race, Gender, and Cultural Politics.* Boston: South End Press, 1990.
Howe, Irving. Introduction. In *The Idea of the Modern in Literature and the Arts,* 11–40. New York: Horizon, 1967.
Hilliard, David. *This Side of Glory: The Autobiography of David Hilliard and the Story of the Black Panther Party.* Boston: Little, Brown, 1993.
Hubbard, Dolan. "Forrest Spirits: Oral Echoes in Leon Forrest's Prose." *Oral Tradition* 9 (October 1994): 315–27.
———. *The Sermon and the African American Literary Imagination.* Columbia: University of Missouri Press, 1994.
Hurston, Zora Neale. "Characteristics of Negro Expression." In *Within the Circle: An Anthology of African American Literary Criticism from the Harlem Renaissance to the Present,* ed. Angelyn Mitchell, 79–94. Durham, NC: Duke University Press, 1994.
Johnson, James Weldon. *God's Trombones.* New York: Viking Penguin, 1927.
Jones, Gayl. *Liberating Voice: Oral Tradition in African American Literature.* Cambridge, MA: Harvard University Press, 1991.
———. "Re-Imagining the African American Novel." *Callaloo* 17 (Spring 1994): 507–18.
Baraka, Amiri [LeRoi Jones]. *Blues People: The Negro Experience in White America and the Music That Developed from It.* New York: Morrow Quill, 1963.
Jordan, Jennifer. "Cultural Nationalism in the Sixties: Politics and Poetry." In *Race,*

Politics, and Culture: Critical Essays on the Radicalism of the 1960s, ed. Adolph Reed, 29–60. Westport, CT: Greenwood, 1986.

Karade, Baba Ifa. *Imoye: A Definition of the Ifa Tradition.* Brooklyn: A. Henrietta Press, 1999.

Karrer, Wolfgang. "Black Modernism? The Early Poetry of Jean Toomer and Claude McKay." In *Jean Toomer and the Harlem Renaissance,* ed. Genevieve Fabre and Michel Feith, 128–41. New Brunswick, NJ: Rutgers University Press, 2001.

Kawin, Bruce. "The Montage Element in Faulkner's Fiction." In *Faulkner, Modernism, and Film: Faulkner and Yoknapatawpha,* ed. Harrington Evans and Ann J. Abadie, 103–26. Jackson: University Press of Mississippi, 1949.

King, Martin Luther Jr. *Strength to Love.* New York: Harper & Row, 1963.

Kodat, Catherine Gunther. "A Postmodern *Absalom, Absalom!,* A Modern *Beloved:* The Dialectic of Form." In *Unflinching Gaze: Morrison and Faulkner Re-Envisioned,* ed. Stephen M. Ross and Judith Bryant Wittenberg, 181–98. Jackson: University Press of Mississippi, 1997.

———. "To 'Flash White Light from Ebony': The Problem of Modernism in Jean Toomer's *Cane.*" *Twentieth Century Literature* 46 (Spring 2000): 1–19.

Lee, A. Robert. "Equilibrium Out of Their Chaos: Ordered Unorder in the Witherspoon-Bloodworth Trilogy of Leon Forrest." In Cawelti, *Leon Forrest: Introductions and Interpretations,* 97–114.

Lehan, Richard. "James Joyce: The Limits of Modernism and the Realms of the Literary Text." *Arizona Quarterly* 50 (Spring 1994): 87–104.

Malcolm X and Alex Haley. *The Autobiography of Malcolm X.* 1965. Reprint, New York: Ballantine, 1992.

Mellard, James M. "Something New and Hard and Bright: Faulkner, Ideology, and the Construction of Modernism." *Mississippi Quarterly* 48 (Fall 1995): 459–78.

Miller, James A. "Leon Forrest." In *African American Writers,* ed. Valerie Smith, 1:233–45. New York: Scribner, 2001.

———. "Leon Forrest." In *Oxford Companion to African American Literature,* ed. William L. Andrews, Frances Smith Foster, and Trudier Harris, 293–94. New York: Oxford University Press, 1997.

Mitchell, Angelyn. *The Freedom to Remember: Narrative, Slavery, and Gender in Contemporary Black Women's Fiction.* New Brunswick, NJ: Rutgers University Press, 2002.

Moreland, Richard C. "Faulkner and Modernism." In *The Cambridge Companion to William Faulkner,* ed. Philip Weinstein, 17–30. New York: Cambridge University Press, 1995.

Morrison, Toni. *The Bluest Eye.* New York: Holt, Rinehart, 1970.

———. "Rootedness: The Ancestor as Foundation." In *Black Women Writers (1959–1980): A Critical Evaluation,* ed. Mari Evans, 339–45. Garden City, NJ: Anchor-Doubleday, 1984.

———. *Song of Solomon.* New York: Knopf, 1977.

Murray, Albert. *Stomping the Blues.* New York: Vintage, 1976.

———. *Train Whistle Guitar.* 1974. Boston: Northeastern University Press, 1989.

North, Michael. *The Dialect of Modernism.* New York: Oxford University Press, 1994.

Oakley, Giles. *The Devil's Music: A History of the Blues.* New York: Harvest, 1976.

O'Donnell, Patrick. "Faulkner and Postmodernism." In *The Cambridge Companion to William Faulkner,* ed. Philip Weinstein, 31–50. New York: Cambridge University Press, 1995.

O'Meally, Robert, and Genevieve Fabre. *History and Memory in African American Culture.* New York: Oxford University Press, 1994.

Ostendorf, Berndt. "Ralph Waldo Ellison: Anthropology, Modernism, and Jazz." In *New Essays on* Invisible Man, ed. Robert O'Meally, 95–121. Cambridge: Cambridge University Press, 1988.

Reed, Adolph. "The Jug and Its Contents." In *Stirrings in the Jug: Black Politics in the Post-Segregation Era.* Minneapolis: University of Minnesota Press, 1999.

Rosenburg, Bruce. "Forrest Spirits: Oral Echoes in Leon Forrest's Prose." *Oral Tradition* 9 (October 1994): 315–27.

———. "Leon Forrest and the African-American Folk Sermon." In Cawelti, *Leon Forrest: Introductions and Interpretations,* 115–26.

Rusch, Fredrik L. *A Jean Toomer Reader: Selected Unpublishing Writings.* New York: Oxford University Press, 1993.

Scott, Bonnie Kime, ed. *The Gender of Modernism.* Bloomington: Indiana University Press, 1990.

Singal, Daniel Joseph. "Towards a Definition of American Modernism." *American Quarterly* 39 (Spring 1987): 7–26.

Sollors, Werner. "Ethnic Modernism, 1910–1950." *American Literary History* 15 (Spring 2003): 70–77.

———. "Jean Toomer's *Cane:* Modernism and Race in Interwar America." In *Jean Toomer and the Harlem Renaissance,* eds. Genevieve Fabre and Michel Feith, 18–37. New Brunswick, NJ: Rutgers University Press, 2001.

Stepto, Robert. *From behind the Veil: A Study of Afro-American Narrative.* Urbana: University of Illinois Press, 1979.

Taylor-Guthrie, Danille. "Sermons, Testifying, and Prayers: Looking beneath the Wings in Leon Forrest's *Two Wings to Veil My Face.*" *Callaloo* 16 (Spring 1993): 419–30. Reprinted in Cawelti, *Leon Forrest: Introductions and Interpretations,* 216–32.

Teish, Luisah. *Jambalaya: The Natural Woman's Book of Personal Charms and Practical Charms.* San Francisco: Harper & Row, 1985.

Traylor, Eleanor W. "Music as Theme: The Jazz Mode in the Works of Toni Cade Bambara." In *Black Women Writers: A Critical Evaluation,* ed. Mari Evans, 58–70. Garden City, NJ: Doubleday, 1984.

Thomas, H. Nigel. *From Folklore to Fiction: A Study of Folk Heroes and Rituals in the Black American Novel.* Westport, CT: Greenwood, 1988.

Toomer, Jean. *Cane.* 1923. Reprint, New York: Liveright, 1975.

Warren, Kenneth. "Thinking beyond Catastrophe: Leon Forrest's *There Is a Tree More Ancient Than Eden.*" *Callaloo* 16 (Spring 1993): 409–418. Reprinted in Cawelti, *Leon Forrest: Introductions and Interpretations,* 152–65.

Washington, Robert E. *The Ideologies of African American Literature: From the Harlem Renaissance to the Nationalist Revolt.* Lanham, MD: Rowman and Littlefield, 2001.

Werner, Craig. "Leon Forrest, the AACM, and the Legacy of the Chicago Renaissance." *Black Scholar* 23 (Summer–Fall 1993): 10–23. Reprinted in Cawelti, *Leon Forrest: Introductions and Interpretations,* 127–51.

———. *Playing the Changes: From Afro-Modernism to the Jazz Impulse.* Urbana: University of Illinois Press, 1994.

White, John Valery. "'Black Is So Terrible It's Terrifying': The Black Aesthetic, Blackness, and the Denigration of Social Policy on Race." Unpublished essay, n.d.

Wideman, John Edgar. "In Memoriam: Leon Forrest, 1937–1997." *Callaloo* 21 (Winter 1998): vii–ix.

Williams, Dana A. "History, Memory, Narrative, and Culture: Figuring Ancestry in Leon Forrest's Bloodworth Trilogy." Ph.D. dissertation. Howard University, 1998.

———. "Leon Forrest." In *Contemporary African American Novelists: A Bio-Bibliographical Sourcebook,* ed. Emmanuel S. Nelson, 158–63. Westport, CT: Greenwood, 1999.

———. "Preachin' and Singin' Just to Make It Over: The Gospel Impulse as Survival Strategy in Leon Forrest's Bloodworth Trilogy." *African American Review* 36 (Fall 2002): 475–85.

Williams, Sherley Anne. "The Black Musician: The Black Hero as Light Bearer." In *Give Birth to Brightness: A Thematic Study in Neo-Black Literature,* 135–66. New York: Dial, 1972.

Index

Absolom, Absolom! (Faulkner), 23
Alinsky, Saul, 4
Allen, Jeffrey Renard, 74
Alvin Ailey Dance Theatre, 95
Anderson, T. J., 5
Armstrong, Louis, 36, 81
Austin, C. J., 1, 17

Baby Suggs, 18
Baker, Houston, 80
Baldwin, James, 58
Bambara, Toni Cade, xiii, 114, 136, 140n. 2, 142n. 3, 145n. 1
Baraka, Amiri, 110
"The Battle Hymn of the Republic," 12, 133–34, 144n. 3
Baylor, Elgin, 70
Beauchamp, Mollie, 118
Bell, Lenora, 2
Bellow, Saul, 5
Beloved (Morrison), 18, 32–33
black aesthetic, xvi, xiii, xvii, 6, 9, 110–11, 115
black arts movement, ix, xii, xiii, 6, 9, 110, 113, 115, 123
Blackbird, 4
Black Muslim, xiv, 7, 66–67, 77, 104
black nationalism movement, 38
blaxploitation, 97
Bloodworth Orphans, The (Forrest), xiv, xv, xvi, 2, 7, 12, 15, 21–23, 56–78, 95, 100, 103–4, 137–38
blues, xi, xv, xvii, 8, 11–12, 31, 52–53, 62–63, 66–68, 71, 78–92, 100, 117, 122–23, 129, 132–34, 137–38, 144nn. 3–4
Bluest Eye, The (Morrison), xiii, 5
Borges, Jorge Luis, 127
Burke, Kenneth, 96
Brown, Sterling, 97, 114, 143n. 1

Byerman, Keith, 7, 84

Campbell, Joseph, 96
Cane (Toomer), 27–28, 112
Carew, Jan, 5
Cawelti, John, viii, 11, 16, 21, 24, 39, 55, 57–58, 76, 95, 119, 127, 140n. 8, 141n. 2
Chestnut, Charles, 19
civil rights movement, ix, x, xiv, 38, 57, 106, 113, 118, 132
Clifton, Tod, 112
Cole, Nat King, 42
Cook County Hospital (Chicago), 1
Cullen, Countee, 3, 112

Davis, Allison, 4
Davis, Angela, 87
Dedalus, Stephen, 35
Diaspora, 47, 55
Divine Days (Forrest), xiv, xvi, xvii, 4, 7–8, 12, 14–15, 17, 24, 26, 29, 40, 56, 93–116, 135, 137–38, 140n. 4, 143nn. 2–3
Doctor J, 70
Dorsey, Thomas, 1, 11
double-consciousness, xvii, 19, 110–11, 114
Douglass, Frederick, 36
Drown, Merle, viii, 135, 140n. 1
Dubey, Madhu, xii, 14–15, 96–97, 102, 105, 110
DuBois, W. E. B., xvii, 3, 19, 48–49, 111, 114
Duncan, Marianne, 5. *See also* Forrest, Marianne Duncan
Durham, Richard, 5–6

El-Hajj Malik El-Shabazz, 111. *See also* Malcolm X

Ellington, Duke, xiii, 69–70
Ellison, Ralph, x, xii, xiii, xv, 3–5, 13–15, 17, 19, 30–31, 38, 56, 77, 81, 105, 112, 134, 139n. 3, 140n. 2, 143n. 1
Englewood Bulletin, 4
eschatology, 50

Fabre, Genevieve, 42, 47
Fard, W. D., 7, 104–5
Faulkner, William, 3, 17, 19, 22–25, 30, 32, 70, 118, 139n. 6, 140nn. 7, 9
Finney, Leon, Jr., 4
folk preacher, xii, xviii, 15–18, 54
Forrest, Adeline Green, 1–2
Forrest, Leon (father), 1
Forrest, Marianne., 139n. 4. *See also* Duncan, Marianne.
408 Liquors, 4
Franklin, C. L., 1, 17
Fuller, Hoyt, 110
Furious Voice for Freedom, The (Forrest), 7, 11, 67

Gates, Henry L., Jr., 28, 140n. 10, 141n. 13, 142n. 2
Gayle, Addison, 110
Gilroy, Paul, 18–19
Go Down, Moses (Faulkner), 23, 118
gospel, xi, xv, 1, 8, 11, 31, 52–53, 63–66, 68, 71, 90, 123, 137–38, 141n. 5
Great Migration, 2–3, 11, 77

Harlem Renaissance, 30
Hansberry, Lorraine, 111–12
Harris, Trudier, 107
Hilliard, David, 130–31
hipster, xviii, 57
Holiday, Billie, 9–10, 26, 37, 122, 137
Hopkins, Lightnin', xiii, 12, 132
Hughes, Langston, 3
Hunt, Richard, 5,
Hurston, Zora Neale, xv, 19, 29, 31, 93, 97, 112, 140n. 2, 141nn. 11, 13, 144n. 5
Hyde Park High School (Chicago), 3

Invisible Man (Ellison), 48–49, 81, 112

Invisible Man, x, xii, 35, 38

Jackson, George, 130–31
Jackson, Mahalia, xiii, 9
Jamison, Judith, 95
jazz, xi, xv, xvii, 8, 10, 12–16, 22, 24, 30–31, 56, 58, 60, 67–72, 74, 93–94, 100, 116, 129, 137–39, 140nn. 5, 8
Jim Crow, x, 38, 106, 118, 129
Johnson, James Weldon, 114
Johnson, Lyndon B., 38, 53
Jones, Gayl, xiii, 58, 142n. 3, 144n. 5
joto, 47
Joyce, James, xv, 8, 19–23, 31, 140n. 4
juneteenth (Ellison), 13

Karenga, Ron, 123
Kennedy, John F., 68
King, Martin Luther, Jr., 38, 48–49, 54–55

Lee, A. Robert, 77
liberatory narrative, xvii, 80–81, 86–87, 92, 142n. 2
Lincoln, Abraham, 36, 40–41, 44–45
Lowrey, Perrin, 3–4, 17
Lukacs, Georg, 29

Major, Clarence, 140n. 2
Malcolm X, xiv, 8, 48–49, 68, 125. *See also* El-Hajj Malik El-Shabazz
McCluskey, John, xiii
McPherson, James Alan, xiii, 110, 140n. 2
Meteor in the Madhouse (Forrest), xiv, xvi, xviii, 3, 12, 24, 116–35, 138, 139n. 7, 140n. 1, 143nn. 2 (ch. 5), 1–2 (ch. 6), 144n. 3
Middle Passage, 25–26, 37, 46–47, 77
Mitchell, Angelyn, viii, xvii, 80, 142n. 2
modernism, xv, 15, 18–34, 77, 139n. 6, 140n. 2, 141n. 11. *See also* modernist
modernist, x, xi, xv, xvi, 18, 20–24, 26–32, 140nn. 2, 6, 141n. 11. *See also* modernism
Monroe, Earl "The Pearl," 70
Morrison, Toni, vii, xiii, xv, 5–6, 18, 23, 32, 39, 107, 110, 114, 136, 140n. 2,

141n. 11
motherlessness, xi, 1, 36, 53, 57–58, 62–63, 66
Muhammad, Elijah, 7–8, 67–68, 125
Muhammad Speaks, 4–7, 67, 104
Murray, Albert, 37, 96, 140
Muslim, 6–7, 58, 60, 67–68, 125

Nation of Islam, 4, 6–7, 67–68
Neal, Larry, 110
Newton, Huey, xv, 130–31
Nixon, Richard, 38
Nkrumah, 112

O'Meally, Robert, 42, 47
Osiris, 51, 140

Parker, Charlie, 9
Pilgrim Baptist Church (Chicago), 1
Plumpp, Sterling, 6
postmodernism, 19, 111, 140nn. 6, 7
Portrait of the Artist as a Young Man, A (Joyce), 21
Powell, Adam Clayton, 54–55
Powell, Colin, 130
Price, Leontyne, xiii
Pryor, Richard, 54–55

Raglan, Lord, 96
Rainey, Ma, xvii, 144n. 4
Re-Creation (Forrest and Anderson), 5
Reed, Ishmael, 140n. 2
reinvention, xvii, 2, 10–11, 48, 53, 62–63, 93–100, 105, 107–8, 112, 114–15, 116–18, 135, 143nn. 2 (ch. 5), 2–3 (ch. 6), 144n. 3
Richardson, Maude, 2
Robeson, Paul, 42
Robinson, Sugar Ray, 42
Roosevelt University (Chicago), 3
Rowell, Charles, 6–7, 13, 17

selido, 47
spirituals, xii, 8, 10–11, 14, 16, 31, 64–66, 71, 123, 129, 137–38
Smith, Bessie, xvii, 122, 144n. 4
Soldier Boy, Soldier (Forrest and Anderson), 5
"Solo Long-Song: For Lady Day," 9

Spears, Meedmoxy, 132
Stepto, Robert, 41, 56
Stevenson, Adlai Ewing, 42
stream-of-consciousness, xi, 20
Sullivan, Leon, 54–55

Theatre of the Soul (Forrest), 5
Their Eyes Were Watching God (Hurston), 29, 97
There Is a Tree More Ancient Than Eden (Forrest), vii, xi, xiv, xx, xvi, 2, 4, 9, 14–15, 21–26, 28–29, 35–58, 63, 73, 76, 94, 116, 137–38, 140nn. 4, 8
Thomas, H. Nigel, 59, 64, 66, 105
Toomer, Jean, xv, 19, 27–28, 30–31, 112, 140n. 2, 141n. 11
Train Whistle Guitar (Murray), 37
Traylor, Eleanor W., vii, viii
trickster, xviii, 7, 29, 60, 67, 74, 96, 103–7, 112, 115, 127–28
Tubman, Harriet, 36, 40
Two Wings to Veil My Face (Forrest), xiv, xv, xvii, 2, 12, 14–15, 25–26, 33, 53, 56, 79–92, 95, 101, 116, 118, 137–38, 141n. 14, 142n. 1

Ulysses (Joyce), 21, 140n. 4
Uncle Remus, 107
Underground Railroad, 37, 40
University of Chicago, xiii, 3–4, 113

vernacular, xi, 10–11, 34, 97

Walker, Alice, 110, 122
Warren, Kenneth, 3, 16, 110, 140n. 8
Washington, Booker T., 48–49, 101
Wendell Phillips Elementary School (Chicago), 3
Werner, Craig, 19
White, Maude, 2
Wideman, John Edgar, 110, 140n. 2
Wilson Junior College (Chicago), 3
Woodlawn Booster, 4
Woodlawn Observer, 4
Woolf, Virginia, 32
Wright, Richard, 2, 143n. 1

Yemoja, 47

www.ingramcontent.com/pod-product-compliance
Lightning Source LLC
Chambersburg PA
CBHW020949230426
43666CB00005B/241